高等学校工程管理专业规划教材

工程管理专业英语

徐勇戈　马继伟
焦英博　贾广社　编
王守清　卢有杰　审

中国建筑工业出版社

图书在版编目（CIP）数据

工程管理专业英语/徐勇戈等编．—北京：中国建筑工业出版社，2006
高等学校工程管理专业规划教材
ISBN 978-7-112-08060-1

Ⅰ．工⋯　Ⅱ．徐⋯　Ⅲ．建筑工程-施工管理-英语-高等学校-教材　Ⅳ．H31

中国版本图书馆 CIP 数据核字（2006）第 035310 号

高等学校工程管理专业规划教材
工程管理专业英语
徐勇戈　马继伟
焦英博　贾广社　编
王守清　卢有杰　审

*

中国建筑工业出版社出版、发行（北京西郊百万庄）
各地新华书店、建筑书店经销
北京红光制版公司制版
北京富生印刷厂印刷

*

开本：787×1092 毫米　1/16　印张：14¾　字数：354 千字
2006 年 7 月第一版　2012 年 8 月第十一次印刷
定价：**24.00** 元
ISBN 978-7-112-08060-1
(20873)

版权所有　翻印必究
如有印装质量问题，可寄本社退换
（邮政编码 100037）

英语是了解国外科技发展动向和进行国际学术交流的重要工具。本书旨在使读者掌握工程管理专业英语术语，培养和提高读者阅读和笔译专业英语文献资料的能力，并通过课堂英语交流，提高学生英语口语能力。

本书素材取自国外最近几年工程管理各个领域的经典教材、专著、论文和计算机网络信息，内容涉及工程管理各领域当前的状况和最新进展。本书主要内容包括：业主视角，项目管理组织，设计与施工过程，劳动力、材料与设备的利用，成本估算，投资项目的经济评价，建设工程项目融资，工程承包价格的确定与合同，施工计划，基本进度计划程序，高级进度计划技术，成本控制、监督与会计，质量控制与施工安全，以及工程项目信息的组织与应用。书后附参考译文。

本书内容新颖、覆盖面广、系统性强、可读性好，是学习工程管理专业英语的实用教材。本书既可供高等院校的工程管理专业和土木工程相关专业师生使用，也可用作工程管理专业人员及其他有兴趣人员的学习参考读物。

* * *

责任编辑：张　晶　戚琳琳
责任设计：崔兰萍
责任校对：张景秋　关　健

前　言

　　编写《工程管理专业英语》的目的在于为土建类高等学校的工程管理专业及土木工程相关专业的本科生及研究生提供一本既能使读者掌握工程项目管理专业英语术语，又能培养和提高读者阅读与笔译专业英语文献的能力，并了解国外工程管理领域最新发展动态和前沿知识的融实用性和前瞻性于一体的教学用书。通过使用本教材不仅能提高读者以英语为工具进行外文文献阅读和翻译能力，还能够开拓其专业视野，并为日后从事相关的工程管理工作和理论研究打下坚实的基础。

　　本书的特色主要在于从业主的视角出发，对工程项目的整个管理流程予以系统整合地介绍，所选取的素材以被北美国家奉为"工程项目管理圣经"的由翰觉克森博士所著的《建设项目管理》一书为主，该书具有极强的系统性和完整的体系，再版了16次，且不断对内容进行补充与更新，同时又从能够反映本学科领域的最新动态和前沿知识的文献及论文选取一部分内容作为补充。这样一来，不仅保证了作为教材所需的系统性与完整性，也保证了知识的新颖性，从而有利于学生积累知识并开拓了他们的视野。

　　书中涵盖了包括项目管理组织、投资项目的经济评价、建设工程项目融资、工程承包价格的确定与合同、高级进度计划技术、成本控制、质量控制以及工程项目信息的组织与应用等诸多内容在内的工程项目管理领域的理论体系和方法论的精粹，并附有几乎所有的工程管理专业术语和专有表达，是对学生有关专业课知识的最好补充。此外还能够使读者对于工程管理的理论体系有一个系统而全面的认识。

　　本书中每一章的第一篇通常都是读者熟悉的内容。对于英语水平较好的读者，可以泛读或跳过该节；而对于初学者，建议精读这一篇。教师可以根据各章标题，在每一章中挑选若干篇文章进行教学。作为练习，可选择若干章节让学生笔译，并进行课堂讨论。

　　鉴于英语口语越来越重要，专业英语课程应提供一种英语环境来提高学生的英语口语能力。我们建议在教学过程中，教师可对每一章选择几个题目，让学生事先准备好用自己的语言来表达相关内容，然后分组进行讨论，再选派代表在课堂上交流。

　　全书分为14章，第7、8、9、11、12、13章由西安建筑科技大学徐勇戈编写，第3、4、5、6章由同济大学马继伟编写，第1、2章由西安唯赢人才培训中心总裁兼美国项目管理学院中国首席代表焦英博女士编写，第10、14章由同济大学贾广社编写，并由徐勇戈进行统稿。全书由清华大学王守清、卢有杰两位教授主审。

　　感谢翰觉克森博士允许我们使用其享誉工程管理界的著作《建设项目管理》中的部分内容作为本书的主要素材。在本书的编写过程中，焦英博女士的助手曾缓，西安建筑科技大学管理学院的硕士研究生韩雪、沈亚婷等为本书的编写给予了支持和帮助，在此我们一并表示感谢。

　　限于作者水平，书中难免存在不妥和错误之处，敬请读者批评指正。

CONTENTS

Chapter 1　The Owners' Perspective 1
　1.1　The Project Life Cycle 1
　1.2　Major Types of Construction 6
　1.3　Selection of Professional Services 11
　1.4　Construction Contractors 16

Chapter 2　Organizing for Project Management 19
　2.1　What is Project Management? 19
　2.2　Professional Construction Management 22
　2.3　Leadership and Motivation for the Project Team 25
　2.4　Perceptions of Owners and Contractors 27

Chapter 3　The Design and Construction Process 30
　3.1　Design and Construction as an Integrated System 30
　3.2　Design Methodology 34
　3.3　Functional Design 37
　3.4　Construction Planning 41

Chapter 4　Labor, Material and Equipment Utilization 44
　4.1　Factors Affecting Job-Site Productivity 44
　4.2　Material Procurement and Delivery 48
　4.3　Construction Equipment 52
　4.4　Queues and Resource Bottlenecks 56

Chapter 5　Cost Estimation 61
　5.1　Approaches to Cost Estimation 61
　5.2　Types of Construction Cost Estimates 63
　5.3　Unit Cost Method of Estimation 69
　5.4　Cost Indices 72

Chapter 6　Economic Evaluation of Facility Investments 75
　6.1　Basic Concepts of Economic Evaluation 75

  6.2 Investment Profit Measures 77
  6.3 Methods of Economic Evaluation 80
  6.4 Public Versus Private Ownership of Facilities 84

Chapter 7 Financing of Constructed Facilities 89
  7.1 The Financing Problem 89
  7.2 Institutional Arrangements for Facility Financing 91
  7.3 Project versus Corporate Finance 95
  7.4 Shifting Financial Burdens 99
  7.5 Construction Financing for Contractors 101

Chapter 8 Construction Pricing and Contracting 105
  8.1 Pricing for Constructed Facilities 105
  8.2 Contract Provisions for Risk Allocation 108
  8.3 Types of Construction Contracts 113
  8.4 Resolution of Contract Disputes 116
  8.5 Negotiation Simulation: An Example 118

Chapter 9 Construction Planning 124
  9.1 Basic Concepts in the Development of Construction Plans 124
  9.2 Choice of Technology and Construction Method 126
  9.3 Defining Work Tasks 130
  9.4 Defining Precedence Relationships Among Activities 134

Chapter 10 Fundamental Scheduling Procedures 138
  10.1 Relevance of Construction Schedules 138
  10.2 The Critical Path Method 140
  10.3 Activity Float and Schedules 143
  10.4 Presenting Project Schedules 146

Chapter 11 Advanced Scheduling Techniques 151
  11.1 Scheduling with Uncertain Durations 151
  11.2 Scheduling in Poorly Structured Problems 154
  11.3 Calculations for Monte Carlo Schedule Simulation 158
  11.4 Improving the Scheduling Process 161

Chapter 12 Cost Control, Monitoring and Accounting 163

12.1	The Cost Control Problem	163
12.2	Forecasting for Activity Cost Control	166
12.3	Schedule and Budget Updates	168
12.4	Relating Cost and Schedule Information	173

Chapter 13 Quality Control and Safety During Construction 177
13.1　Quality and Safety Concerns in Construction 177
13.2　Total Quality Control 181
13.3　Quality Control by Statistical Methods 184
13.4　Safety 186

Chapter 14 Organization and Use of Project Information 192
14.1　Types of Project Information 192
14.2　Computerized Organization and Use of Information 194
14.3　Relational Model of Databases 198
14.4　Information Transfer and Flow 205

Reference
1.2　Major Types of Construction 209
2.1　What is Project Management? 210
3.4　Construction Planning 211
4.2　Material Procurement and Delivery 212
5.1　Approaches to Cost Estimation 214
6.1　Basic Concepts of Economic Evaluation 215
7.1　The Financing Problem 216
8.2　Contract Provisions for Risk Allocation 217
9.2　Choice of Technology and Construction Method 219
10.1　Relevance of Construction Schedules 220
11.2　Scheduling in Poorly Structured Problems 221
12.1　The Cost Control Problem 223
13.2　Total Quality Control 224
14.1　Types of Project Information 225

目 录

第1章 业主视角 ·· 1
 1.1 项目生命周期 ··· 1
 1.2 建设项目的主要类型 ··· 6
 1.3 专业化服务选择 ·· 11
 1.4 建筑承包商 ·· 16

第2章 项目管理组织 ·· 19
 2.1 何为项目管理? ··· 19
 2.2 专业化项目管理 ·· 22
 2.3 项目团队的领导与激励 ··· 25
 2.4 业主与承包商的感悟 ·· 27

第3章 设计与施工过程 ··· 30
 3.1 作为一个整体的设计与施工 ·· 30
 3.2 设计方法论 ·· 34
 3.3 功能设计 ··· 37
 3.4 施工组织设计 ··· 41

第4章 劳动力、材料与设备的利用 ·· 44
 4.1 影响现场劳动生产率的主要因素 ·· 44
 4.2 材料采购与运输 ·· 48
 4.3 施工设备 ··· 52
 4.4 排队与资源瓶颈 ·· 56

第5章 成本估算 ··· 61
 5.1 成本估算的方法 ·· 61
 5.2 建设成本估算的类型 ·· 63
 5.3 单位成本估算的方法 ·· 69
 5.4 成本指数 ··· 72

第6章 投资项目的经济评估 ··· 75
 6.1 经济评估的基本概念 ·· 75

 6.2 投资收益计算方法 ……………………………………………………………… 77
 6.3 经济评估方法 …………………………………………………………………… 80
 6.4 公众与私人的设施所有权对比 ………………………………………………… 84

第7章 建设工程项目融资 …………………………………………………………… 89
 7.1 融资问题 ………………………………………………………………………… 89
 7.2 设施融资的制度安排 …………………………………………………………… 91
 7.3 项目与公司财务 ………………………………………………………………… 95
 7.4 财务负担转移 …………………………………………………………………… 99
 7.5 承包商的建设融资 ……………………………………………………………… 101

第8章 工程承包价格的确定与合同 …………………………………………………… 105
 8.1 工程承包价格 …………………………………………………………………… 105
 8.2 分担风险的合同条款 …………………………………………………………… 108
 8.3 工程承包合同的类型 …………………………………………………………… 113
 8.4 合同争议的解决 ………………………………………………………………… 116
 8.5 谈判模拟：一个案例 …………………………………………………………… 118

第9章 施工计划 ……………………………………………………………………… 124
 9.1 施工计划的基本概念 …………………………………………………………… 124
 9.2 施工技术与方案的选择 ………………………………………………………… 126
 9.3 定义工作任务 …………………………………………………………………… 130
 9.4 定义工作之间的逻辑关系 ……………………………………………………… 134

第10章 基本进度计划程序 ………………………………………………………… 138
 10.1 进度计划的概念 ……………………………………………………………… 138
 10.2 关键线路法 …………………………………………………………………… 140
 10.3 工作时差与进度计划 ………………………………………………………… 143
 10.4 项目进度计划的表示方法 …………………………………………………… 146

第11章 高级进度计划技术 ………………………………………………………… 151
 11.1 作业时间不确定的进度计划 ………………………………………………… 151
 11.2 棘手问题的进度计划 ………………………………………………………… 154
 11.3 蒙特卡罗模拟技术 …………………………………………………………… 158
 11.4 进度计划过程的改进 ………………………………………………………… 161

第12章 成本控制、监督与会计 …………………………………………………… 163

12.1　成本控制问题 …………………………………………………… 163
　　12.2　工作成本预测 …………………………………………………… 166
　　12.3　进度与预算的更新调整 ………………………………………… 168
　　12.4　成本与进度的相关信息 ………………………………………… 173

第 13 章　质量控制与施工安全 …………………………………………… 177
　　13.1　关注施工中的质量与安全 ……………………………………… 177
　　13.2　全面质量控制 …………………………………………………… 181
　　13.3　质量控制的统计方法 …………………………………………… 184
　　13.4　施工安全 ………………………………………………………… 186

第 14 章　工程项目信息的组织与应用 …………………………………… 192
　　14.1　工程项目信息的类型 …………………………………………… 192
　　14.2　信息组织与应用的计算机化 …………………………………… 194
　　14.3　数据库关系模型 ………………………………………………… 198
　　14.4　信息的传递与流通 ……………………………………………… 205

参考译文

1.2　建设项目的主要类型 ……………………………………………… 209
2.1　何为项目管理? ……………………………………………………… 210
3.4　施工组织设计 ……………………………………………………… 211
4.2　材料采购与运输 …………………………………………………… 212
5.1　成本估算的方法 …………………………………………………… 214
6.1　经济评估的基本概念 ……………………………………………… 215
7.1　融资问题 …………………………………………………………… 216
8.2　分担风险的合同条款 ……………………………………………… 217
9.2　施工技术与方案的选择 …………………………………………… 219
10.1　进度计划的概念 …………………………………………………… 220
11.2　棘手问题的进度计划 ……………………………………………… 221
12.1　成本控制问题 ……………………………………………………… 223
13.2　全面质量控制 ……………………………………………………… 224
14.1　工程项目信息的类型 ……………………………………………… 225

Chapter 1 The Owners' Perspective

1.1 The Project Life Cycle

The acquisition of a constructed facility usually represents a major capital investment, whether its owner happens to be an individual, a private corporation or a public agency. Since the commitment of resources for such an investment is motivated by market demands or perceived needs, the facility is expected to satisfy certain objectives within the constraints specified by the owner and relevant regulations[1]. With the exception of the speculative housing market, where the residential units may be sold as built by the real estate developer, most constructed facilities are custom made in consultation with the owners[2]. A real estate developer may be regarded as the sponsor of building projects, as much as a government agency may be the sponsor of a public project and turns it over to another government unit upon its completion. From the viewpoint of project management, the terms "owner" and "sponsor" are synonymous because both have the ultimate authority to make all important decisions[3]. Since an owner is essentially acquiring a facility on a promise in some forms of agreement, it will be wise for any owner to have a clear understanding of the acquisition process in order to maintain firm control of the quality, timeliness and cost of the completed facility[4].

From the perspective of an owner, the project life cycle for a constructed facility may be illustrated schematically in Figure 1-1. Essentially, a project is conceived to meet market demands or needs in a timely fashion. Various possibilities may be considered in the conceptual planning stage, and the technological and economic feasibility of each alternative will be assessed and compared in order to select the best possible project[5]. The financing schemes for the proposed alternatives must also be examined, and the project will be programmed with respect to the timing for its completion and for available cash flows[6]. After the scope of the project is clearly defined, detailed engineering design will provide the blueprint for construction, and the definitive cost estimate will serve as the baseline for cost control[7]. In the procurement and construction stage, the delivery of materials and the erection of the project on site must be carefully planned and controlled. After the construction is completed, there is usually a brief period of start-up or shake-down of the constructed facility when it is first occupied. Finally, the management of the facility is turned over to the owner for full occupancy until the facility lives out its useful life and is

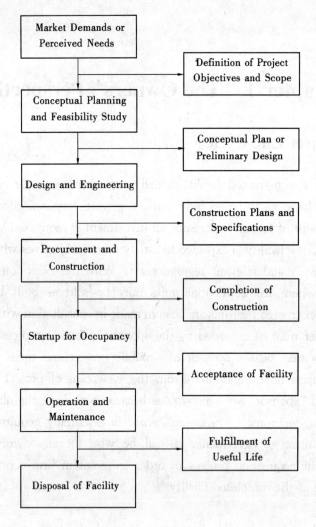

Figure 1-1 The Project Life Cycle of a Constructed Facility

designated for demolition or conversion[8].

Of course, the stages of development in Figure 1-1 may not be strictly sequential. Some of the stages require iteration, and others may be carried out in parallel or with overlapping time frames, depending on the nature, size and urgency of the project[9]. Furthermore, an owner may have in-house capacities to handle the work in every stage of the entire process, or it may seek professional advice and services for the work in all stages[10]. Understandably, most owners choose to handle some of the work in-house and to contract outside professional services for other components of the work as needed. By examining the project life cycle from an owner's perspective, we can focus on the proper roles of various activities and participants in all stages regardless of the contractual arrangements for different types of work[11].

In the United States, for example, the U. S. Army Corps of Engineers has in-house capabilities to deal with planning, budgeting, design, construction and operation of waterway and flood control structures. Other public agencies, such as state transportation departments, are also deeply involved in all phases of a construction project. In the private sector, many large firms such as DuPont, Exxon, and IBM are adequately staffed to carry out most activities for plant expansion. All these owners, both public and private, use outside agents to a greater or lesser degree when it becomes more advantageous to do so[12].

The project life cycle may be viewed as a process through which a project is implemented from cradle to grave[13]. This process is often very complex; however, it can be decomposed into several stages as indicated by the general outline in Figure 1-1. The solutions at various stages are then integrated to obtain the final outcome. Although each stage requires different expertise, it usually includes both technical and managerial activities in the knowledge domain of the specialist. The owner may choose to decompose the entire process into more or less stages based on the size and nature of the project, and thus obtain the most efficient result in implementation[14]. Very often, the owner retains direct control of work in the planning and programming stages, but increasingly outside planners and financial experts are used as consultants because of the complexities of projects[15]. Since operation and maintenance of a facility will go on long after the completion and acceptance of a project, it is usually treated as a separate problem except in the consideration of the life cycle cost of a facility. All stages from conceptual planning and feasibility studies to the acceptance of a facility for occupancy may be broadly lumped together and referred to as the design/construct process, while the procurement and construction alone are traditionally regarded as the province of the construction industry[16].

Owners must recognize that there is no single best approach in organizing project management throughout a project's life cycle. All organizational approaches have advantages and disadvantages, depending on the knowledge of the owner in construction management as well as the type, size and location of the project[17]. It is important for the owner to be aware of the approach which is most appropriate and beneficial for a particular project. In making choices, owners should be concerned with the life cycle costs of constructed facilities rather than simply the initial construction costs. Saving small amounts of money during construction may not be worthwhile if the result is much larger operating costs or not meeting the functional requirements for the new facility satisfactorily[18]. Thus, owners must be very concerned with the quality of the finished product as well as the cost of construction itself. Since facility operation and maintenance is a part of the project life cycle, the owners' expectation to satisfy investment objectives during the project life cycle will require consideration of the cost of operation and maintenance[19]. Therefore, the facility's operating management should also be considered as early as possible, just as the construction process should be kept in mind at the early stages of planning and programming.

Words

represent　代表，表示
commitment　承诺，义务
regard　看作，认为
ultimate　最终的
feasibility　可行性
erection　树立，建立
iteration　重复
facility　设施
owner　业主
the real estate developer　房地产开发商
perspective　视角，角度
feasibility　可行性
blueprint　蓝图
procurement　采购
sequential　顺序的
transportation　运输
outline　轮廓
contract　合约/合同，订合约/订合同
private sector　私营机构
decompose　分解，拆分
maintenance　维护

design/construct process　设计/施工过程
corporation　企业（尤指股份制企业）
residential　居住的
viewpoint　观点
fashion　方式
conceptual　概念的
demolition　拆毁
overlap　搭接，交叠
public agency　公共机构
speculative housing market　投机性住宅市场
project management　项目管理
the project cycle life　项目全寿命期
the scope of the project　项目范围
baseline　基线
construction　施工
in-house　内部的
integrate　整合
professional services　专业服务
from cradle to grave　从头到尾
the knowledge domain　知识领域
objective　目标

Notes

[1] specified by… 是过去分词短语，修饰前面的 constraints。全句可译为：由于该投资的资源投入受市场需求的驱动，所以建筑设施应在其业主和相关规范规定的约束条件内满足特定的目标。

[2] in consultation with 意为"与……协商"。全句可译为：除了投机性住宅市场，在那里住宅单元由负责建造的房地产开发商销售之外，大多数的建筑设施都是在与业主协商一致的基础上定制的。

[3] synonymous 意为"同义的，同义词的"。全句可译为：从项目管理的角度而言，"业主"和"发起人"这两个术语是同义词，这是因为他们都有做所有重大决策的最终权力。

[4] 全句可译为：由于业主实质上是以某种形式的合约为保证来获得一项建筑产品的，那么为了保证对完工产品的质量、工期和成本的有力控制，对于任何业主而言，他

们应当对项目的全过程有一个清晰和完整的理解。

[5] conceptual planning stage 意为："概念规划阶段"。alternative 指"备选方案"。全句可译为：在项目的概念规划阶段，很多不同的可能方案都可能被考虑，同时每一个备选方案的技术和经济可行性都经过评估和比较，以选出最优方案。

[6] 全句可译为：我们还需检验备选方案的财务计划，同时按照项目完工期限和现金流量来安排项目的进度计划。

[7] the scope of project 意为"项目的范围"。detailed engineering design 是指"详细的工程设计"。全句可译为：一旦项目的范围被明确确定，详细的工程设计就能为施工提供蓝图，最终的成本预算作为成本控制的基准。

[8] is turned over to … 意为"被移交给……"。conversion 在这里指"转作他用"。全句可译为：最后，设施的管理将移交给业主全权使用和管理，直至其使用期结束，或者拆除，或者转作他用。

[9] 全句可译为：某些阶段可以重复，同时也可以和其他阶段平行或搭接进行，这一切取决于项目的特点、规模和紧迫性。

[10] in-house 指"内部的"。全句可译为：而且，业主可能自己有能力处理项目全过程中各阶段的工作，也可能就各阶段的所有工作寻求专业化的建议和服务。

[11] 全句可译为：从业主的角度审视项目的全寿命期，我们得以把注意力集中在所有阶段中不同活动和参与方的适当角色上，而不用去考虑不同工作类型合约的安排。

[12] outside agents 指"外部的代理机构"。to a greater or lesser degree 意为"或多或少地"。全句可译为：而所有的这些业主，无论是公是私，当其觉得合适时，他们也会或多或少地将项目的某些工作分包给公司以外的机构去做。

[13] be viewed as 意为"被看作是"。Through which…是定语从句，修饰 a process。from cradle to grave 意为"从头到尾"。

[14] 全句可译为：业主可以根据项目的规模和特点有选择地把项目的全过程分解成或多或少的不同阶段，从而获得最高效的实施结果。

[15] 全句可译为：业主通常保留规划和计划阶段的直接控制工作，而随着项目复杂程度的不断增加，会将其他工作委托给外部的咨询单位。

[16] 全句可译为：尽管只有采购和施工阶段被认为是建筑业的传统领域，但是从项目概念规划和可行性研究直至设施的接受占用都被广义地认为属于设计和建造过程。

[17] depending on…是现在分词短语作状语，修饰前面的主句，可译为"取决于业主在项目管理上的知识以及项目的类型、规模和地点"。

[18] 全句可译为：如果建筑设施的运营成本很高或者不能满足设施在功能上的需求，在施工阶段省一点钱就显得不那么值得。

[19] facility operation and maintenance 意为"设施的运营与维护"。全句可译为：由于设施的运营和维护是项目全寿命期的一部分，业主为了满足其项目寿命期内投资目标的期望就需要考虑运营和维护成本。

1.2 Major Types of Construction

Since most owners are generally interested in acquiring only a specific type of constructed facility, they should be aware of the common industrial practices for the type of construction pertinent to them[1]. Likewise, the *construction industry* is a conglomeration of quite diverse segments and products. Some owners may procure a constructed facility only once in a long while and tend to look for short term advantages. However, many owners require periodic acquisition of new facilities and/or rehabilitation of existing facilities. It is to their advantage to keep the construction industry healthy and productive. Collectively, the owners have more power to influence the construction industry than they realize because, by their individual actions, they can provide incentives or disincentives for innovation, efficiency and quality in construction[2]. It is to the interest of all parties that the owners take an active interest in the construction and exercise beneficial influence on the performance of the industry.

In planning for various types of construction, the methods of procuring professional services, awarding construction contracts, and financing the constructed facility can be quite different. For the purpose of discussion, the broad spectrum of constructed facilities may be classified into four major categories, each with its own characteristics.

Residential Housing Construction

Residential housing construction includes single-family houses, multi-family dwellings, and high-rise apartments[3]. During the development and construction of such projects, the developers or sponsors who are familiar with the construction industry usually serve as surrogate owners and take charge, making necessary contractual agreements for design and construction, and arranging the financing and sale of the completed structures[4]. Residential housing designs are usually performed by architects and engineers, and the construction executed by builders who hire subcontractors for the structural, mechanical, electrical and other specialty work. An exception to this pattern is for single-family houses as is shown in Figure 1-2, which may be designed by the builders as well.

The residential housing market is heavily affected by general economic conditions, tax laws, and the monetary and fiscal policies of the government. Often, a slight increase in total demand will cause a substantial investment in construction, since many housing projects can be started at different locations by different individuals and developers at the same time[5]. Because of the relative ease of entry, at least at the lower end of the market, many new builders are attracted to the residential housing construction. Hence, this market is highly competitive, with potentially high risks as well as high rewards.

Figure 1-2 Residential Housing Construction (courtesy of Caterpillar, Inc.)

Institutional and Commercial Building Construction

Institutional and commercial building construction encomprasses a great variety of project types and sizes, such as schools and universities, medical clinics and hospitals, recreational facilities and sports stadiums, retail chain stores and large shopping centers, warehouses and light manufacturing plants, and skyscrapers for offices and hotels, as is shown in Figure 1-3[6]. The owners of such buildings may or may not be familiar with construction industry practices, but they usually are able to select competent professional consultants and arrange the financing of the constructed facilities themselves. Specialty architects and engineers are often engaged for designing a specific type of building, while the builders or general contractors undertaking such projects may also be specialized in only that type of building.

Because of the higher costs and greater sophistication of institutional and commercial buildings in comparison with residential housing, this market segment is shared by fewer competitors[7]. Since the construction of some of these buildings is a long process which once started will take some time to proceed until completion, the demand is less sensitive to general economic conditions than that for speculative housing. Consequently, the owners may confront an oligopoly of general contractors who compete in the same market. In an oligopoly situation, only a limited number of competitors exist, and a firm's price for services may be based in part on its competitive strategies in the local market.

Specialized Industrial Construction

Specialized industrial construction usually involves very large scale projects with a high degree of technological complexity, such as oil refineries, steel mills, chemical processing plants and coal-fired or nuclear power plants, as is shown in Figure 1-4[8]. The owners usually are deeply involved in the development of a project, and prefer to work with

Figure 1-3 Construction of the PPG Building in Pittsburgh,
Pennsylvania (courtesy of PPG Industries, Inc.)

designers-builders such that the total time for the completion of the project can be shortened. They also want to pick a team of designers and builders with whom the owner

Figure 1-4 Construction of a Benzene Plant in Lima, Ohio
(courtesy of Manitowoc Company, Inc.)

has developed good working relations over the years.

Although the initiation of such projects is also affected by the state of the economy, long range demand forecasting is the most important factor since such projects are capital intensive and require considerable amount of planning and construction time[9]. Governmental regulation such as the rulings of the Environmental Protection Agency and the Nuclear Regulatory Commission in the United States can also profoundly influence decisions on these projects.

Infrastructure and Heavy Construction

Infrastructure and heavy construction includes projects such as highways, mass transit systems, tunnels, bridges, pipelines, drainage systems and sewage treatment plants, as is shown in Figure 1-5. Most of these projects are publicly owned and therefore financed either through bonds or taxes. This category of construction is characterized by a high degree of mechanization, which has gradually replaced some labor intensive operations.

The engineers and builders engaged in infrastructure construction are usually highly specialized since each segment of the market requires different types of skills[10]. However, demands for different segments of infrastructure and heavy construction may shift with saturation in some segments. For example, as the available highway construction projects are declining, some heavy construction contractors quickly move their work force and equipment into the field of mining where jobs are available.

Figure 1-5   Construction of the Dame Point Bridge in Jacksonville, Florida
(courtesy of Mary Lou Maher)

Words

conglomeration 混合物，聚集
rehabilitation 修复
disincentive 抑制，抑制因素
spectrum 波谱，光谱，范围
surrogate 代理，替代
architect 建筑师
fiscal 财政的
entry 进入，编入
clinic 诊所
stadium 露天大型体育场
skyscraper 摩天大楼
sophistication 复杂
construction industry 建筑业
high-rise apartments 高层公寓
institution and commercial building construction 办公和商业用房建设
oligopoly 垄断，求过于供
confront 面对
infrastructure 基础设施
pipeline 管道
sewage 污水，下水道
specialized industrial construction 专业化工业项目建设

infrastructure and heavy construction 重大基础项目建设
procure 获得
incentive 动机
innovation 创新
residential housing construction 住宅类房屋建设
take charge 负责
execute 执行
substantial 实质的、重大的
encompass 包围，包括
recreational 娱乐的
retail 零售
proceed 开展，进行
segment 部分，份额
single-family house 独户住宅
professional consultant 专业咨询人士
general contractor 总承包商
initiation 启动
strategy 策略
tunnel 隧道
drainage 排水系统
saturation 饱和

Notes

[1] 全句可译为：由于大多数业主通常只对获得某种特定类型的建筑物感兴趣，因而他们应当对适合于他们的建设类型的实务有着一定的了解。

[2] 全句可译为：这些业主有着他们自己也没有意识到的影响建筑业的能力，因为通过其个人行为，他们可以对建筑业的创新、效率以及质量施加积极的或消极的影响。

[3] multi-family dwellings 指"多居户楼房"。

[4] 全句可译为：在开发建设这类项目的过程中，了解建筑业的开发商或发起人通常以代理的身份出现，负责制定设计和施工的合同条款，同时负责融资和完工房屋的销售。

[5] 全句可译为：由于许多住宅项目可以在不同的地点由不同的开发商同时开工，因此往往市场总需求的一点微小增加就可能引起此类建筑投资的急剧增加。

[6] recreational facilities 意为"娱乐设施"。

[7]　　in comparison with 是"与……相比"。全句可译为：与住宅类房屋建设相比，此类房屋建设成本高且功能复杂，所以市场份额由较少的竞争者来瓜分。

[8]　　a high degree of 意为："高等级的"。

[9]　　the state of economy 意为"经济状况"。capital intensive 意为"资金密集的"。全句可译为：尽管这类项目的启动受经济状况的影响，由于这类项目属于资金密集型，且需要相当长时间的规划和建设，故长期的需求预测是最重要的因素。

[10]　　全句可译为：由于不同项目需要不同的专门技术，参与基础设施项目建设的设计方和建造方都具有相当程度的专业化水平。

1.3　Selection of Professional Services

When an owner decides to seek professional services for the design and construction of a facility, he is confronted with a broad variety of choices. The type of services selected depends to a large degree on the type of construction and the experience of the owner in dealing with various professionals in the previous projects undertaken by the firm[1]. Generally, several common types of professional services may be engaged either separately or in some combination by the owners.

Financial Planning Consultants

At the early stage of strategic planning for a capital project, an owner often seeks the services of financial planning consultants such as certified public accounting (CPA) firms to evaluate the economic and financial feasibility of the constructed facility, particularly with respect to various provisions of federal, state and local tax laws which may affect the investment decision[2]. Investment banks may also be consulted on various options for financing the facility in order to analyze their long-term effects on the financial health of the owner organization.

Architectural and Engineering Firms

Traditionally, the owner engages an architectural and engineering (A/E) firm or consortium as technical consultant in developing a preliminary design[3]. After the engineering design and financing arrangements for the project are completed, the owner will enter into a construction contract with a general contractor either through competitive bidding or negotiation[4]. The general contractor will act as a constructor and/or a coordinator of a large number of subcontractors who perform various specialties for the completion of the project. The A/E firm completes the design and may also provide on site quality inspection during construction. Thus, the A/E firm acts as the prime professional on behalf of the owner and supervises the construction to insure satisfactory results. This practice is most common in building construction.

In the past two decades, this traditional approach has become less popular for a number of reasons, particularly for large scale projects. The A/E firms, which are engaged by the owner as the prime professionals for design and inspection, have become more isolated from the construction process[5]. This has occurred because of pressures to reduce fees to A/E firms, the threat of litigation regarding construction defects, and lack of knowledge of new construction techniques on the part of architect and engineering professionals[6]. Instead of preparing a construction plan along with the design, many A/E firms are no longer responsible for the details of construction nor do they provide periodic field inspection in many cases. As a matter of fact, such firms will place a prominent disclaimer of responsibilities on any shop drawings they may check, and they will often regard their representatives in the field as observers instead of inspectors. Thus, the A/E firm and the general contractor on a project often become antagonists who are looking after their own competing interests. As a result, even the constructibility of some engineering designs may become an issue of contention. To carry this protective attitude to the extreme, the specifications prepared by an A/E firm for the general contractor often protects the interest of the A/E firm at the expense of the interests of the owner and the contractor.

In order to reduce the cost of construction, some owners introduce *value engineering*, which seeks to reduce the cost of construction by soliciting a second design that might cost less than the original design produced by the A/E firm[7]. In practice, the second design is submitted by the contractor after receiving a construction contract at a stipulated sum, and the saving in cost resulting from the redesign is shared by the contractor and the owner. The contractor is able to absorb the cost of redesign from the profit in construction or to reduce the construction cost as a result of the re-design. If the owner had been willing to pay a higher fee to the A/E firm or to better direct the design process, the A/E firm might have produced an improved design which would cost less in the first place. Regardless of the merit of value engineering, this practice has undermined the role of the A/E firm as the prime professional acting on behalf of the owner to supervise the contractor[8].

Design/Construct Firms

A common trend in industrial construction, particularly for large projects, is to engage the services of a design/construct firm[9]. By integrating design and construction management in a single organization, many of the conflicts between designers and constructors might be avoided[10]. In particular, designs will be closely scrutinized for their constructibility. However, an owner engaging a design/construct firm must insure that the quality of the constructed facility is not sacrificed by the desire to reduce the time or the cost for completing the project. Also, it is difficult to make use of competitive bidding in this type of design/construct process. As a result, owners must be relatively sophisticated in negotiating realistic and cost-effective construction contracts.

One of the most obvious advantages of the integrated design/construct process is the use of *phased construction* for a large project. In this process, the project is divided up into several phases, each of which can be designed and constructed in a staggered manner. After the completion of the design of the first phase, construction can begin without waiting for the completion of the design of the second phase, etc. If proper coordination is exercised, the total project duration can be greatly reduced. Another advantage is to exploit the possibility of using the *turnkey* approach whereby an owner can delegate all responsibility to the design/construct firm which will deliver to the owner a completed facility that meets the performance specifications at the specified price[11].

Professional Construction Managers

In recent years, a new breed of construction managers (CM) offers professional services from the inception to the completion of a construction project[12]. These construction managers mostly come from the ranks of A/E firms or general contractors who may or may not retain dual roles in the service of the owners. In any case, the owner can rely on the service of a single prime professional to manage the entire process of a construction project. However, like the A/E firms of several decades ago, the construction managers are appreciated by some owners but not by others. Before long, some owners find that the construction managers too may try to protect their own interest instead of that of the owners when the stakes are high. It should be obvious to all involved in the construction process that the party which is required to take higher risk demands larger rewards. If an owner wants to engage an A/E firm on the basis of low fees instead of established qualifications, it often gets what it deserves; or if the owner wants the general contractor to bear the cost of uncertainties in construction such as foundation conditions, the contract price will be higher even if competitive bidding is used in reaching a contractual agreement[13]. Without mutual respect and trust, an owner cannot expect that construction managers can produce better results than other professionals. Hence, an owner must understand its own responsibility and the risk it wishes to assign to itself and to other participants in the process[14].

Operation and Maintenance Managers

Although many owners keep a permanent staff for the operation and maintenance of constructed facilities, others may prefer to contract such tasks to professional managers. Understandably, it is common to find in-house staff for operation and maintenance in specialized industrial plants and infrastructure facilities, and the use of outside managers under contracts for the operation and maintenance of rental properties such as apartments and office buildings[15]. However, there are exceptions to these common practices. For example, maintenance of public roadways can be contracted to private firms. In any case, managers can provide a spectrum of operation and maintenance services for a specified time period in accordance to the terms of contractual agreements. Thus, the owners can be spared the provision of in-house expertise to operate and maintain the facilities.

Facilities Management

As a logical extension for obtaining the best services throughout the project life cycle of a constructed facility, some owners and developers are receptive to adding strategic planning at the beginning and facility maintenance as a follow-up to reduce space-related costs in their real estate holdings[16]. Consequently, some architectural/engineering firms and construction management firms with computer-based expertise, together with interior design firms, are offering such front-end and follow-up services in addition to the more traditional services in design and construction. This spectrum of services is described in *"Engineering News-Record"* (ENR) as follows:

Facilities management is the discipline of planning, designing, constructing and managing space——in every type of structure from office buildings to process plants. It involves developing corporate facilities policy, long-range forecasts, real estate, space inventories, projects (through design, construction and renovation), building operation and maintenance plans and furniture and equipment inventories[17].

A common denominator of all firms entering into these new services is that they all have strong computer capabilities and heavy computer investments. In addition to the use of computers for aiding design and monitoring construction, the service includes the compilation of a computer record of building plans that can be turned over at the end of construction to the facilities management group of the owner[18]. A computer data base of facilities information makes it possible for planners in the owner's organization to obtain overview information for long range space forecasts, while the line managers can use as-built information such as lease/tenant records, utility costs, etc. for day-to-day operations.

Words

undertake 承担
long-term 长期的
competitive bidding 竞争性招/投标
inspection 视察
disclaim 放弃，拒负责任
solicit 恳求

supervise 监督
re-design 重新设计
architectural and engineering (A/E) film
建筑和工程设计公司
constructibility 可建造性
turnkey 交钥匙

scrutinize 审查
duration 持续时间
Operation and Maintenance Managers 运行与维护经理
expertise 专门技术
inventory 财产目录（清单）
monitor 监督
lease （土地、房产等的）租约，契约
day-to-day 日常的
evalutate 评价
preliminary 初始的
subcontractors 分包商
prominent 显著的

antagonist 对手
stipulate 规定
value engineering 价值工程
Design/Construct Firms 设计/施工公司
coordination 协调
contract price 合同价格
stagger 摇晃，蹒跚
peformence 绩效，执行情况
deserve 应得
extension 延伸
renovation 翻修
facilities management 设施管理
tenant 承租人，租户，佃户，房客

Notes

[1] undertaken by the firm 为过去分词短语，修饰前面的 the previous projects。全句可译为：业主所选择的服务在很大程度上取决于项目的类型，以及业主与以前项目中承担专业服务的专业人员打交道的经验。

[2] certified public accounting（CPA）指"特许公共会计师"。全句可译为：在一个资本项目战略规划的前期，业主通常会向会计公司寻求财务规划咨询服务，用来评估建设项目经济和财务上的可行性，尤其是当项目涉及影响投资决策的各联邦、州或地方法律条款的时候。

[3] 全句可译为：传统上，业主会聘请建筑和工程设计（A/E）公司做前期设计的技术咨询。

[4] 全句可译为：当项目的工程设计和融资安排完成后，业主便会通过竞争性招标或谈判的方式与一家总承包商签订建设合同。

[5] which are engaged by… 为定语从句，修饰前面的 the A/E firms，可译为"受雇于业主，作为设计和监理的主要专业人员"。

[6] 全句可译为：之所以发生这种事情是由于迫于减少给 A/E 公司付费的压力，关于建筑缺陷所导致的诉讼威胁，以及建筑师和工程师缺乏对建筑新技术方面的知识等原因所致。

[7] which seeks to … 为定语从句，修饰前面的 value engineering。全句可译为：有些业主引入了价值工程技术，以降低成本为目的，寻找比 A/E 公司原设计更省钱的第二个设计方案。

[8] 全句可译为：不考虑价值工程的优点，这种做法实际上削弱了 A/E 公司代表业主作为首要技术咨询人员来监督承包商的作用。

[9] a common trend 意为"一个常见的趋势"。engage 在这里是"雇佣"的意思。全句可译为：对于工业建设项目，尤其是大型工业项目，目前有一个雇佣设计/施工公

司为业主服务的趋势。

[10] 全句可译为：在一个项目中，把设计和施工管理同时交给一个机构，就可以避免原先存在于设计和施工者之间的许多矛盾。

[11] turnkey approach 意为"交钥匙方式"。全句可译为：此方式的另一个优点是可拓展成为交钥匙方式，在这种方式中，业主将所有责任委派给设计/施工公司一并承担，而该公司以商定的价格为业主提交满足功能要求的完整设施。

[12] a new breed of 意为"一个新的系列"。construction managers（CM）是指"职业化的建设项目经理"。全句可译为：近年来，出现了为项目从启动到完工提供全过程服务的职业化的建设项目经理（CM）系列。

[13] 全句可译为：如果业主在雇佣 A/E 公司时，考虑的只是较低的取费而不是资质能否胜任，那么业主将为此付出代价；或者业主想让总承包商承担像地基施工中的条件不确定性所发生的成本，那么即使在达成的合同协议中使用竞争性的投标方式，合同价格也会比较高。

[14] it wishes to…是省略了 that 的定语从句，修饰前面的 the risk。全句可译为：因此，业主必须懂得项目当中属于其自身的风险和义务须由其自己来承担。

[15] 全句可译为：容易理解，对于像专业化工业项目和基础设施项目，可以由其内部的人员来从事有关的运营和维护工作；而对于像公寓和办公楼这样的项目，这些工作则通常外包给专业经理做。

[16] 全句可译为：作为建筑设施项目管理全寿命周期可获得最佳服务的逻辑延伸，一些房地产项目的业主和开发商乐于接受在项目启动阶段追加战略规划服务，而在项目维护阶段追加设施管理服务。

[17] 全句可译为：设施管理的具体工作包括公司设施政策、长期预测、固定资产、楼宇的运营和维护以及家具设施清单等的管理。

[18] 全句可译为：除了用计算机进行辅助设计和监控施工之外，这些企业还能提供把施工信息进行编辑反馈的计算机文档化服务，而这为管理者利用计算机进行设施管理提供了方便。

1.4 Construction Contractors

Builders who supervise the execution of construction projects are traditionally referred to as *contractors*, or more appropriately called *constructors*[1]. The *general contractor* coordinates various tasks for a project while the *specialty contractors* such as mechanical or electrical contractors perform the work in their specialties[2]. Material and equipment suppliers often act as *installation contractors*; they play a significant role in a construction project since the conditions of delivery of materials and equipment affect the quality, cost, and timely completion of the project. It is essential to understand the operation of these contractors in order to deal with them effectively.

General Contractors

The function of a general contractor is to coordinate all tasks in a construction project.

Unless the owner performs this function or engages a professional construction manager to do so, a good general contractor who has worked with a team of superintendents, specialty contractors or subcontractors together for a number of projects in the past can be most effective in inspiring loyalty and cooperation[3]. The general contractor is also knowledgeable about the labor force employed in construction. The labor force may or may not be unionized depending on the size and location of the projects. In some projects, no member of the work force belongs to a labor union; in other cases, both union and non-union craftsmen work together in what is called an open shop, or all craftsmen must be affiliated with labor unions in a closed shop[4]. Since labor unions provide hiring halls staffed with skilled journeyman who have gone through apprentice programs for the projects as well as serving as collective bargain units, an experienced general contractor will make good use of the benefits and avoid the pitfalls in dealing with organized labor[5].

Specialty Contractors

Specialty contractors include mechanical, electrical, foundation, excavation, and demolition contractors among others. They usually serve as subcontractors to the general contractor of a project. In some cases, legal statutes may require an owner to deal with various specialty contractors directly. In the State of New York, for example, specialty contractors, such as mechanical and electrical contractors, are not subjected to the supervision of the general contractor of a construction project and must be given separate prime contracts on public works[6]. With the exception of such special cases, an owner will hold the general contractor responsible for negotiating and fulfilling the contractual agreements with the subcontractors.

Material and Equipment Suppliers

Major material suppliers include specialty contractors in structural steel fabrication and erection, sheet metal, ready mixed concrete delivery, reinforcing steel bar detailers, roofing, glazing etc. Major equipment suppliers for industrial construction include manufacturers of generators, boilers and piping and other equipment. Many suppliers handle on-site installation to insure that the requirements and contractual specifications are met[7]. As more and larger structural units are prefabricated off-site, the distribution between specialty contractors and material suppliers becomes even less obvious.

Words

coordinate 协调
inspire 鼓励，激发
affiliate 参加，加入
contractor 承包商

specialty contractor 专业承包商
statute 法规
craftsman 工匠，技术工人
superintendent 监督，指挥

employ	雇佣，使用	installation contractors	安装承包商
pitfall	陷阱	on-site installation	现场安装
constructors	建造商		

Notes

[1] supervise 意为"监督"。全句可译为：负责建设项目监督与实施的建造者传统上被称为承包商，或更确切地称作建造商。

[2] 全句可译为：总包商协调项目任务的分工协作，而专业承包商如设备和电气承包商则负责完成其专业任务。

[3] 全句可译为：除非业主自己发挥这项职能或聘请职业化的 CM 做这件事情，一个经验丰富的总承包商是能够协同专业承包商和分包商尽职尽责地完成任务的。

[4] an open shop 意为"开放的工作环境"。a closed shop 意为"有组织的工作环境"。全句可译为：在有些项目中，工人可以不隶属于任何一个工会组织；而在另外一些情况下，非工会组织的工人和工会组织的工人可以在一个开放的工作环境下共同工作，也可以是所有的工人都加入一个工会组织从而在一个有组织的工作环境下工作。

[5] 全句可译为：由于工会组织起着劳动力中介的作用，即不仅作为集体协议单位而存在，同时还提供已经经历了专为项目而设的学徒工培训计划的技术工人，所以有经验的总承包商会充分利用这些好处并试图避免在与有组织的劳工打交道时处于不利境地。

[6] are not subjected to…可译为"不直接受建设项目总承包商的监督管理，并且在公共项目中必须授予其独立的主合同"。

[7] 全句可译为：许多供应商还负责现场安装以满足合同的规定和要求。

Exercise

Translate the text of lesson 1.4 into Chinese.

Chapter 2　Organizing for Project Management

2.1　What is Project Management?

The management of construction projects requires knowledge of modern management as well as an understanding of the design and construction process. Construction projects have a specific set of objectives and constraints such as a required time frame for completion. While the relevant technology, institutional arrangements or processes will differ, the management of such projects has much in common with the management of similar types of projects in other specialty or technology domains such as aerospace, pharmaceutical and energy developments[1].

Generally, project management is distinguished from the general management of corporations by the mission-oriented nature of a project[2]. A project organization will generally be terminated when the mission is accomplished. According to the Project Management Institute, the discipline of project management can be defined as follows[3]:

Project management is the art of directing and coordinating human and material resources throughout the life of a project by using modern management techniques to achieve predetermined objectives of scope, cost, time, quality and participation satisfaction.

By contrast, the general management of business and industrial corporations assumes a broader outlook with greater continuity of operations[4]. Nevertheless, there are sufficient similarities as well as differences between the two so that modern management techniques developed for general management may be adapted for project management.

The basic ingredients for a project management framework may be represented schematically in Figure 2-1. A working knowledge of general management and familiarity with the special knowledge domain related to the project are indispensable. Supporting disciplines such as computer science and decision science may also play an important role. In fact, modern management practices and various special knowledge domains have absorbed various techniques or tools which were once identified only with the supporting disciplines[5]. For example, computer-based information systems and decision support systems are now common-place tools for general management. Similarly, many operations research techniques such as linear programming and network analysis are now widely used in many knowledge or application domains[6]. Hence, the representation in Figure 2-1 reflects only the sources from which the project management framework evolves.

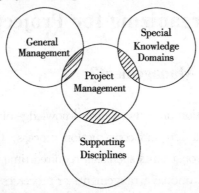

Figure 2-1   Basic Ingredients in Project Management

Specifically, project management in construction encompasses a set of objectives which may be accomplished by implementing a series of operations subject to resource constraints[7]. There are potential conflicts between the stated objectives with regard to scope, cost, time and quality, and the constraints imposed on human, material and financial resources. These conflicts should be resolved at the onset of a project by making the necessary tradeoffs or creating new alternatives. Subsequently, the functions of project management for construction generally include the following:

1. Specification of project objectives and plans including delineation of scope, budgeting, scheduling, setting performance requirements, and selecting project participants.
2. Maximization of efficient resource utilization through procurement of labor, materials and equipment according to the prescribed schedule and plan[8].
3. Implementation of various operations through proper coordination and control of planning, design, estimating, contracting and construction in the entire process[9].
4. Development of effective communications and mechanisms for resolving conflicts among the various participants.

The Project Management Institute focuses on nine distinct areas requiring project manager knowledge and attention:

1. Project integration management to ensure that the various project elements are effectively coordinated.
2. Project scope management to ensure that all the work required (and only the

required work) is included.
3. Project time management to provide an effective project schedule.
4. Project cost management to identify needed resources and maintain budget control.
5. Project quality management to ensure functional requirements are met.
6. Project human resource management to development and effectively employ project personnel.
7. Project communications management to ensure effective internal and external communications.
8. Project risk management to analyze and mitigate potential risks.
9. Project procurement management to obtain necessary resources from external sources.

These nine areas form the basis of the Project Management Institute's certification program for project managers in any industry.

Words

domain 领域	aerospace 航天
pharmaceutical 医药的	distinguish 区别，区分
mission-oriented 以目标(任务)为导向的	predetermined 预定的
continuity 连续性	ingredient 组成部分，成分
indispensable 不可或缺的	framework 框架，构架
discipline 纪律	scope 范围
common-place 常见的	linear programming 线性规划
onset 开始	trade off 均衡，权衡
schedule 进度	delineation 叙述，说明
maximization 最大化	utilization 使用
communication 沟通	integration 综合，整合
certification 认证	

Notes

[1] in common with 指"有共同之处"。in other specialty or technology domains 意为"在其他的专业或技术领域"。全句可译为：尽管相关的技术、组织机构或流程会有所不同，但建设项目同其他一些如航天、医药和能源等专业领域的项目在管理上仍然有共同之处。

[2] 全句可译为：一般而言，项目的以目标为导向特征是项目管理与一般的企业管理的主要不同。

[3] the Project Management Institute (PMI) 指"美国项目管理协会"。

[4] by contrast 指"与此形成对照"。全句可译为：与此形成对照，一般的工商企业管理更广泛地着眼于业务的更佳连贯性和连续性。

[5] special knowledge domains 意为"专业知识领域"。
[6] linear programming 指"线性规划"。network analysis 指"网络分析"。
[7] which may be…为定语从句，修饰前面的 objectives，可译为"通过实施给定资源约束下的一系列运作才能实现的"。
[8] 全句可译为：根据规定的进度和规划，通过对劳动力、材料和设备的采购使资源的有效利用最大化。
[9] 全句可译为：在项目全过程中，通过对计划、设计、估算、合同和施工的适当协调控制来实施各项运作。

2.2 Professional Construction Management

Professional construction management refers to a project management team consisting of a professional construction manager and other participants who will carry out the tasks of project planning, design and construction in an integrated manner[1]. Contractual relationships among members of the team are intended to minimize adversarial relationships and contribute to greater response within the management group[2]. A professional construction manager is a firm specialized in the practice of professional construction management which includes:

- Work with owner and the A/E firms from the beginning and make recommendations on design improvements, construction technology, schedules and construction economy[3].
- Propose design and construction alternatives if appropriate, and analyze the effects of the alternatives on the project cost and schedule.
- Monitor subsequent development of the project in order that these targets are not exceeded without the knowledge of the owner.
- Coordinate procurement of material and equipment and the work of all construction contractors, and monthly payments to contractors, changes, claims and inspection for conforming design requirements[4].
- Perform other project related services as required by owners.

Professional construction management is usually used when a project is very large or complex. The organizational features that are characteristics of mega-projects can be summarized as follows:

- The overall organizational approach for the project will change as the project advances. The "functional" organization may change to a "matrix" which maychange to a "project" organization (not necessarily in this order)[5].
- Within the overall organization, there will probably be functional, project, and

matrix suborganizations all at the same time. This feature greatly complicates the theory and the practice of management, yet is essential for overall cost effectiveness.

- Successful giant, complex organizations usually have a strong matrix-type suborganization at the level where basic cost and schedule control responsibility is assigned[6]. This suborganization is referred to as a "cost center" or as a "project" and is headed by a project manager. The cost center matrix may have participants assigned from many different functional groups. In turn, these functional groups may have technical reporting responsibilities to several different and higher tiers in the organization. The key to a cost effective effort is the development of this project suborganization into a single team under the leadership of a strong project manager.
- The extent to which decision-making will be centralized or decentralized is crucial to the organization of the mega-project[7].

Consequently, it is important to recognize the changing nature of the organizational structure as a project is carried out in various stages.

Example 2-1: Managing of the Alaska Pipeline Project

The Alaska Pipeline Project was the largest, most expensive private construction project in the 1970's, which encompassed 800 miles, thousands of employees, and 10 billion dollars.

At the planning stage, the owner (a consortium) employed a Construction Management Contractor (CMC) to direct the pipeline portion, but retained centralized decision making to assure single direction and to integrate the effort of the CMC with the pump stations and the terminals performed by another contractor[8]. The CMC also centralized its decision making in directing over 400 subcontractors and thousands of vendors. Because there were 19 different construction camps and hundreds of different construction sites, this centralization caused delays in decision making.

At about 15% point of physical completion, the owner decided to reorganize the decision making process and change the role of the CMC. The new organization was a combination of owner and CMC personnel assigned within an integrated organization[9]. The objective was to develop a single project team responsible for controlling all subcontractors. Instead of having nine tiers of organization from the General Manager of the CMC to the subcontractors, the new organization had only four tiers from the Senior Project Manager of the owner to subcontractors. Besides unified direction and coordination, this reduction in tiers of organization greatly improved communications and the ability to make and implement decisions[10]. The new organization also allowed decentralization of decision making by treating five sections of the pipeline at different geographic locations as separate projects, with a section manager responsible for all functions of the section as a profit center.

At about 98% point of physical completion, all remaining activities were to be consolidated to identify single bottom-line responsibility, to reduce duplication in management staff, and to unify coordination of remaining work. Thus, the project was first handled by separate organizations but later was run by an integrated organization with decentralized profit centers[11]. Finally, the organization in effect became small and was ready to be phased out of operation.

Example 2-2: Managing the Channel Tunnel Construction from Britain to France
The underground railroad tunnel from Britain to France is commonly called the Channel Tunnel or Chunnel. It was built by tunneling from each side. Starting in 1987, the tunnels had a breakthrough in 1990.

Management turmoil dogged the project from the start. In 1989, seven of the eight top people in the construction organization left. There was a built in conflict between the contractors and government overseers: "The fundamentally wrong thing is that the constructors own less than 6% of Eurotunnel. Their interest is to build and sell the project at a profit. (Eurotunnel's) interest is for it to operate economically, safely and reliably for the next 50 years."

Words

minimize　使最小化
adversarial　对手的，对抗的
subsequent　随后的，后继的
claim　索赔
matrix　矩阵
suborganization　次级组织
characteristic　特征
decentralize　使分散化，分权
terminal　终端
geogrphic　地理的
tier　层级
turmoil　混乱
staff（全体）职员

firm　公司
recommendation　推荐，建议
exceed　超过，超出
"functional" organization　"职能式"组织
"project" organization　"项目式"组织
assign　分配，分派
centralize　使中心化，使集权
pump　泵
vendor　商贩
duplication　复制
consolidate　整合，合并
overseer　监督者

Notes

[1] consisting of …是现在分词短语作定语，修饰前面的 a project management team。句中 who will carry out…是定语从句，也修饰前面的 a project management team。全句可译为：职业化建设项目管理是指由职业建设项目经理和其他各方组成的项目管理队伍，以集成的方式负责完成项目的规划、设计和施工等任务。

[2] 全句可译为：团队成员之间的合约关系在试图将项目组织间的对立情绪降低到最低程度的同时，还能有助于各管理队伍间的协调。

[3] make recommendations 指"提供建议"。全句可译为：在项目前期，同业主和 A/E 公司一道工作，对改进设计、施工技术、进度计划和建筑经济等提供建议。

[4] monthly payments 指"月付款额"。changes 在这里指"变更"。claims 指"索赔"。全句可译为：协调处理材料和设备的采购、承包商的施工活动、承包商月进度款的支付、设计变更、索赔和监督设计要求的落实。

[5] 全句可译为：随着项目的进展，项目总体的组织方式将发生变化，即由"职能式"组织变化成"矩阵式"组织，再变到"项目式"组织（不一定严格按照这个顺序）。

[6] matrix-type suborganization 是指"矩阵式次级组织"。全句可译为：成功的巨型复杂组织通常都有强矩阵式次级组织，负责承担基本的成本和进度控制责任。

[7] mage-project 意为"巨型或特大型项目"。全句可译为：决策的集权或分权程度对特大型项目组织而言至关重要。

[8] Construction Management Contractor（CMC）指"建设项目管理承包商"。the pump stations 意为"泵站"。全句可译为：在项目规划阶段，业主（一家财团）聘请了一家 CMC 来管理管道部分，但业主为了确保集中指挥，它整合了 CMC 和另一家负责泵站与终端建设的承包商的工作。

[9] assigned within…是过去分词短语作定语修饰前面的 CMC personnel。全句可译为：新的组织是由业主和 CMC 人员共同组成的综合体。

[10] unified direction and coordination 意为"统一的指挥和协作"。全句可译为：除了统一的指挥和协作，这种组织层次的减少还极大地改善了沟通和决策与实施的能力。

[11] decentralized 意为"分权的"。全句可译为：这样，项目从开始的不同组织的管理变成后来的含不同利益机构的综合性组织的管理。

2.3 Leadership and Motivation for the Project Team

The project manager, in the broadest sense of the term, is the most important person for the success or failure of a project. The project manager is responsible for planning, organizing and controlling the project. In turn, the project manager receives authority from the management of the organization to mobilize the necessary resources to complete a project[1].

The project manager must be able to exert interpersonal influence in order to lead the project team. The project manager often gains the support of his/her team through a combination of the following:

- Formal authority resulting from an official capacity which is empowered to issue orders[2].
- Reward and/or penalty power resulting from his/her capacity to dispense directly or indirectly valued organization rewards or penalties[3].
- Expert power when the project manager is perceived as possessing special knowledge or expertise for the job.
- Attractive power because the project manager has a personality or other characteristics to convince others.

In a matrix organization, the members of the functional departments may be accustomed to a single reporting line in a hierarchical structure, but the project manager coordinates the activities of the team members drawn from functional departments[4]. The functional structure within the matrix organization is responsible for priorities, coordination, administration and final decisions pertaining to project implementation. Thus, there are potential conflicts between functional divisions and project teams. The project manager must be given the responsibility and authority to resolve various conflicts such that the established project policy and quality standards will not be jeopardized[5]. When contending issues of a more fundamental nature are developed, they must be brought to the attention of a high level in the management and be resolved expeditiously.

In general, the project manager's authority must be clearly documented as well as defined, particularly in a matrix organization where the functional division managers often retain certain authority over the personnel temporarily assigned to a project[6]. The following principles should be observed:

- The interface between the project manager and the functional division managers should be kept as simple as possible.
- The project manager must gain control over those elements of the project which may overlap with functional division managers[7].
- The project manager should encourage problem solving rather than role playing of team members drawn from various functional divisions[8].

Words

term 术语	exert 施加
motivation 激励	authority 权利，授权
mobilize 动员，调配	interpersonal 人际的
empower 给予权利	issue 发布
dispense 分配，分发	possess 拥有
hierarchical 等级的	priority 优先权
administration （行政、事务性）管理	implementation 执行、实施
pertain to 属于，从属于	jeopardize 损害，危害
interface 界面	overlap 重叠

Notes

[1] 全句可译为：反过来，项目经理拥有组织管理层授予的调动所有资源完成项目的权力。

[2] resulting from…为现在分词短语作定语。which is…为定语从句，修饰前面的authority。全句可译为：通过正式授权而得到的发布指令的权力。

[3] 全句可译为：组织授予的根据个人表现对其实施直接或间接奖励或惩罚的权利。

[4] be accustomed to 意为"习惯于"。drawn from…为过分词短语作定语，修饰前面的the team members。全句可译为：在矩阵式组织当中，来自各职能部门的项目成员仍习惯于等级式结构里单线的汇报制度，这时项目经理应当协调这些选自不同职能部门的人员之间的活动。

[5] 全句可译为：为了使既定的项目方针和质量标准不受损害，项目经理应当被授予解决冲突的责任和权力。

[6] where…为定语从句，修饰 a matrix organization。全句可译为：一般而言，项目经理的权责不仅应当明确定义，还应当予以确认，尤其是在矩阵式组织，因为职能部门的经理们，通常对部门中暂时被分派到项目上的人员还保持一定的影响力。

[7] which may…为定语从句，修饰前面的 those elements。全句可译为：当项目要素和职能部门发生重叠时，项目经理必须拥有对这些要素的控制权。

[8] 全句可译为：面对问题，项目经理必须采取积极解决的态度，而不是和从不同职能部门抽调的成员一起消极观望。

2.4 Perceptions of Owners and Contractors

Although owners and contractors may have different perceptions on project management for construction, they have a common interest in creating an environment leading to successful projects in which performance quality, completion time and final costs are within prescribed limits and tolerances[1]. It is interesting therefore to note the opinions of some leading contractors and owners who were interviewed in 1984.

From the responses of six contractors, the key factors cited for successful projects are:

- well defined scope.
- extensive early planning.
- good leadership, management and first line supervision[2].
- positive client relationship with client involvement.
- proper project team chemistry[3].
- quick response to changes.
- engineering managers concerned with the total project, not just the engineering elements.

Conversely, the key factors cited for unsuccessful projects are:

- ill-defined scope[4].
- poor management.
- poor planning.
- breakdown in communication between engineering and construction.
- unrealistic scope, schedules and budgets.
- many changes at various stages of progress.
- lack of good project control.

The responses of eight owners indicated that they did not always understand the concerns of the contractors although they generally agreed with some of the key factors for successful and unsuccessful projects cited by the contractors[5]. The significant findings of the interviews with owners are summarized as follows:

- All owners have the same perception of their own role, but they differ significantly in assuming that role in practice[6].
- The owners also differ dramatically in the amount of early planning and in providing information in bid packages.
- There is a trend toward breaking a project into several smaller projects as the projects become larger and more complex.
- Most owners recognize the importance of schedule, but they adopt different requirements in controlling the schedule.
- All agree that people are the key to project success.

From the results of these interviews, it is obvious that owners must be more aware and involved in the process in order to generate favorable conditions for successful projects. Design professionals and construction contractors must provide better communication with each other and with the owner in project implementation[7].

Words

perception	理解，感知，认知	tolerance	容忍
prescribe	规定	extensive	广泛的
budget	预算	concern	关注，关心
summarize	总结	assume	承担
client	客户，顾客	ill-defined	定义不清的，错误定义的
budget	预算	indicate	表明，显示
interview	接待，受访	trend	趋势

Notes

[1] in which…为定语从句，修饰前面的 projects。全句可译为：尽管业主和承包商对于建设项目管理有着不同的理解，但他们共同关心营造项目的成功环境，以保证项目的质量、工期和最终成本在预定限度和误差内。

[2] first line supervision 意为"基层监督"。

[3] proper project team chemistry 意为"和谐的项目团队氛围"。

[4] ill-defined scope 意为"定义不清的范围"。

[5] 全句可译为：从八个受访业主的反映来看，尽管他们同意承包商所引述的成功项目和失败项目的一些关键因素，但他们也表示出对承包商忧虑的不解。

[6] 全句可译为：所有的业主对其角色有着相同的认知，但当他们具体承担这个角色时却存在着很大的差别。

[7] 全句可译为：专业设计人员和承包商在项目的进展中，必须保持与业主相互间的良好沟通。

Exercise

Translate the text of lesson 2.4 into Chinese.

Chapter 3　The Design and Construction Process

3.1　Design and Construction as an Integrated System

In the planning of facilities, it is important to recognize the close relationship between design and construction. These processes can best be viewed as an integrated system. Broadly speaking, design is a process of creating the description of a new facility, usually represented by detailed plans and specifications; construction planning is a process of identifying activities and resources required to make the design a physical reality[1]. Hence, construction is the implementation of a design envisioned by architects and engineers. In both design and construction, numerous operational tasks must be performed with a variety of precedence and other relationships among the different tasks.

Several characteristics are unique to the planning of constructed facilities and should be kept in mind even at the very early stage of the project life cycle. These include the following:

- Nearly every facility is custom designed and constructed, and often requires a long time to complete.
- Both the design and construction of a facility must satisfy the conditions peculiar to a specific site.
- Because each project is site specific, its execution is influenced by natural, social and other locational conditions such as weather, labor supply, local building codes, etc[2].
- Since the service life of a facility is long, the anticipation of future requirements is inherently difficult.
- Because of technological complexity and market demands, changes of design plans during construction are not uncommon.

In an integrated system, the planning for both design and construction can proceed almost simultaneously, examining various alternatives which are desirable from both viewpoints and thus eliminating the necessity of extensive revisions under the guise of value engineering[3]. Furthermore, the review of designs with regard to their constructability can be carried out as the project progresses from planning to design. For example, if the sequence of assembly of a structure and the critical loadings on the partially assembled structure during construction are carefully considered as a part of the overall structural design, the impacts of the design on construction false work and on assembly details can be anticipated. However, if the design professionals are expected to assume such responsibilities, they must be rewarded for sharing the risks as well as for undertaking these additional tasks. Similarly, when construction contractors are expected to take over the responsibilities of engineers, such as devising a very elaborate scheme to erect an unconventional structure, they too must be rewarded accordingly. As long as the owner does not assume the responsibility for resolving this risk-reward dilemma, the concept of a truly integrated system for design and construction cannot be realized[4].

Example 3-1: Responsibility for Shop Drawings
The willingness to assume responsibilities does not come easily from any party in the current litigious climate of the construction industry in the United States[5]. On the other hand, if owner, architect, engineer, contractor and other groups that represent parts of the industry do not jointly fix the responsibilities of various tasks to appropriate parties, the standards of practice will eventually be set by court decisions. In an attempt to provide a guide to the entire spectrum of participants in a construction project, the American Society of Civil Engineers issued a Manual of Professional Practice entitled *Quality in the Constructed Project* in 1990. This manual is intended to help bring a turn around of the fragmentation of activities in the design and construction process.

Shop drawings represent the assembly details for erecting a structure which should reflect the intent and rationale of the original structural design[6]. They are prepared by the construction contractor and reviewed by the design professional. However, since the responsibility for preparing shop drawings was traditionally assigned to construction contractors, design professionals took the view that the review process was advisory and assumed no responsibility for their accuracy. This justification was ruled unacceptable by a court in connection with the walkway failure at the Hyatt Hotel in Kansas City in 1985. In preparing the ASCE Manual of Professional Practice for Quality in the Constructed Project, the responsibilities for preparation of shop drawings proved to be the most difficult to develop. The reason for this situation is not difficult to fathom since the responsibilities for the task are diffused, and all parties must agree to the new responsibilities assigned to each in the recommended risk-reward relations shown in Table 3-1.

Traditionally, the owner is not involved in the preparation and review of shop drawings, and perhaps is even unaware of any potential problems. In the recommended practice, the owner is required to take responsibility for providing adequate time and funding, including approval of scheduling, in order to allow the design professionals and construction contractors to perform satisfactorily[7].

Table 3-1 Recommended Responsibility for Shop Drawings

Task	Responsible Party		
	Owner	Design Professional	Construction Contractor
Provide adequate time and funding for shop drawing preparation and review	Prime		
Arrange for structural design	Prime		
Provide structural design		Prime	
Establish overall responsibility for connection design		Prime	
Accomplish connection design (by design professional)		Prime	
Alternatively, provide loading requirement and other information necessary for shop drawing preparation		Prime	
Alternatively, accomplish some or all of connection design (by constructor with a licensed P.E.)			Prime
Specify shop drawing requirements and procedures	Review	Prime	
Approve proper scheduling	Prime	Assisting	Assisting
Provide shop drawing and submit the drawing on schedule			Prime
Make timely reviews and approvals		Prime	
Provide erection procedures, construction bracing, shoring, means, methods and techniques of construction, and construction safety			Prime

Example 3-2: Model Metro Project in Milan, Italy

Under Italian law, unforeseen subsurface conditions are the owner's responsibility, not the contractor's. This is a striking difference from U.S. construction practice where changed conditions clauses and claims and the adequacy of prebid site investigations are points of contention. In effect, the Italian law means that the owner assumes those risks. But under the same law, a contractor may elect to assume the risks in order to lower the bid price and thereby beat the competition.

According to the Technical Director of Rodio, the Milan-based contractor which is heavily involved in the grouting job for tunneling in the Model Metro project in Milan, Italy, there are two typical contractual arrangements for specialized subcontractor firms such as theirs. One is to work on a unit price basis with no responsibility for the design. The other is what he calls the "nominated subcontractor" or turnkey method: prequalified subcontractors offer their own designs and guarantee the price, quality, quantities, and, if they wish, the risks of unforeseen conditions.

At the beginning of the Milan metro project, the Rodio contract ratio was 50/50 unit price and turnkey. The firm convinced the metro owners that they would save money with the turnkey approach, and the ratio became 80% turnkey. What's more, in the work packages where Rodio worked with other grouting specialists, those subcontractors paid Rodio a fee to assume all risks for unforeseen conditions.

Words

envisioned 想像，预想，展望	erection 安装
shop drawings 施工图，安装图	dilemma 困境
fathom 看透，推想	risk-reward 风险和回报
assembly 安装	review 检查，审核
simultaneously 同时地	scheme 计划
scheduling 进度计划	structural design 结构设计
prebid site 投标前现场	specialized subcontractor 专业分包商
nominated subcontractor 指定分包商	work package 工作包
prequalified 预审合格	grouting specialists 专业灌浆公司
stratigraphy 地层地形图	ratio 比率
an manual of professional practice 专业人员从业手册	clause 条款

Notes

[1] Broadly speaking 意为"广义而言"。全句可译为：广义而言，设计是一个创造对新设施的描述过程，通常用详细的图纸和设计说明来表示；施工规划是确定将设计变为现实所需工作和资源的过程。

[2] site specific 意为"特定的现场"。全句可译为：因为每个项目都与特定的现场相关，它的实施都要受到自然的、社会的和其他当地条件的影响，如天气、劳动力供应、当地建筑规范等。

[3] value engineering 意为"价值工程"。全句可译为：从双方的共同需求出发审视不同的方案，而不需再以价值工程的名义进行任何大的变更。

[4] risk-reward dilemma 意为"风险-回报难题"。全句可译为：只要业主不愿意承担解决这种风险-回报难题的责任，一个完全集成的设计/施工体系是不可能实现的。

[5] in the current litigious climate 意为"在当前的法律氛围下"。

[6] represent 意为"显示"。assembly details 意为"安装细节"。"a structure which should reflect the intent and rationale of the original structural design"为 which 引到的定语从句，a structure 为先行词，rationale 意为"基本原理"。全句可译为：施工详图显示了结构施工中的安装细节，并应反映原始结构设计的意图和原理。

[7] take responsibility for 意为"承担责任"。approval of 意为"批准"。全句可译为：在实践中要求业主承担提供合适的时间和资金方面的责任，包括批准施工计划等，从而使专业设计人员和承包商能满意地工作。

3.2 Design Methodology

While the conceptual design process may be formal or informal, it can be characterized by a series of actions: formulation, analysis, search, decision, specification, and modification[1]. However, at the early stage in the development of a new project, these actions are highly interactive as illustrated in Figure 3-1. Many iterations of redesign are expected to refine the functional requirements, design concepts and financial constraints, even though the analytic tools applied to the solution of the problem at this stage may be very crude.

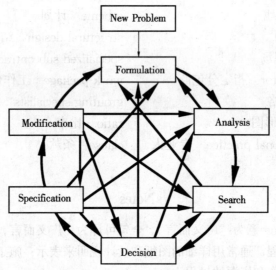

Figure 3-1 Conceptual Design Process
(Adapted with permission from R.W. Jensen and C.C. Tonies,
Prentice Hall, Englewood Cliffs, NJ, 1979, p.22)

The series of actions taken in the conceptual design process may be described as follows:

- Formulation refers to the definition or description of a design problem in broad terms through the synthesis of ideas describing alternative facilities.
- Analysis refines the problem definition or description by separating important from peripheral information and by pulling together the essential detail. Interpretation and prediction are usually required as part of the analysis[2].
- Search involves gathering a set of potential solutions for performing the specified functions and satisfying the user requirements.

As the project moves from conceptual planning to detailed design, the design process becomes more formal. In general, the actions of formulation, analysis, search, decision, specification and modification still hold, but they represent specific steps with less random interactions in detailed design. The design methodology thus formalized can be applied to a variety of design problems[3]. For example, the analogy of the schematic diagrams of the structural design process and of the computer program development process is shown in Figure 3-2.

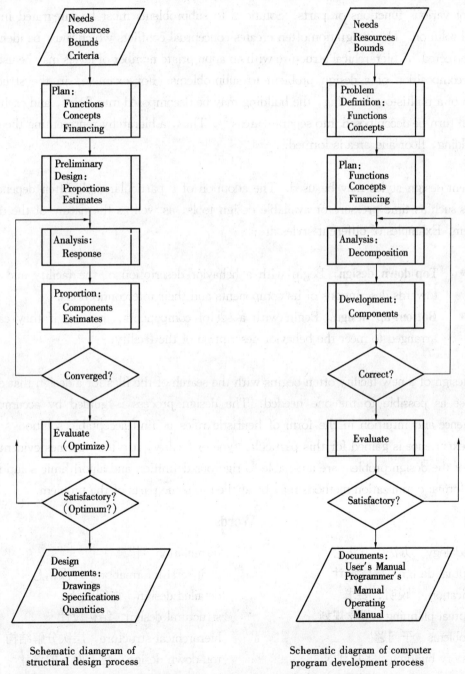

Figure 3-2 An Analogy Between Structural Design and Computer Program Development Process (Reprinted with permission from E. H. Gaylord and C. N. Gaylord, eds., *Structural Engineering Handbook*, 2nd Ed., McGraw-Hill Book Company, New York, 1979.)

The basic approach to design relies on decomposition and integration[4]. Since design problems are large and complex, they have to be decomposed to yield subproblems that are small enough to solve. There are numerous alternative ways to decompose design problems, such as decomposition by functions of the facility, by spatial locations of its parts, or by links of various functions or parts. Solutions to subproblems must be integrated into an overall solution. The integration often creates conceptual conflicts which must be identified and corrected. A hierarchical structure with an appropriate number of levels may be used for the decomposition of a design problem to subproblems. For example, in the structural design of a multistory building, the building may be decomposed into floors, and each floor may in turn be decomposed into separate areas[5]. Thus, a hierarchy representing the levels of building, floor and area is formed.

Different design styles may be used. The adoption of a particular style often depends on factors such as time pressure or available design tools, as well as the nature of the design problem. Examples of different styles are:

- **Top-down design.** Begin with a behavior description of the facility and work towards descriptions of its components and their interconnections.
- **Bottom-up design.** Begin with a set of components, and see if they can be arranged to meet the behavior description of the facility.

The design of a new facility often begins with the search of the files for a design that comes as close as possible to the one needed. The design process is guided by accumulated experience and intuition in the form of heuristic rules to find acceptable solutions[6]. As more experience is gained for this particular type of facility, it often becomes evident that parts of the design problem are amenable to rigorous definition and algorithmic solution[7]. Even formal optimization methods may be applied to some parts of the problem.

Words

methodology 方法，方法论
conceptual design 概念设计
specification 说明，要求
conceptual planning 概念规划
subproblems 子问题
multistory building 多层建筑
bottom-up design 自下而上的设计
interconnection 相互关联
amenable 顺从的，可引导的

formulation 构思
peripheral information 外围信息
detailed design 详细设计
structural design 结构设计
hierarchical structure 层次分解结构
top-down design 自上而下的设计
intuition 直觉
adoption 采纳
algorithmic 算法的

Notes

[1] be characterized by 意为"由…构成"。全句可译为：概念设计可能是正式的或非正式的，它由一系列的典型工作构成：构思、分析、查找、决策、说明和修改。

[2] separate 意为"分离"。pull together 意为"汇集"。全句可译为：通过分离外围信息中重要信息，并汇集基本细节的分析工作，明确问题的定义和描述；解释和预测通常是分析工作中的一部分。

[3] be applied to 意为"被应用于"。a variety of 意为"大量的，不同的"。全句可译为：由此形成的设计方法可应用于不同的设计工作。

[4] approach 意为"方法，途径"，经常与介词 to 使用。rely on 意为"取决于，依靠"。

[5] be decomposed into 意为"被分解成…"。全句可译为：例如，在一个多层建筑的结构设计中，建筑物可以分解为楼层，则每一层又可分解为不同的区域。

[6] is guided by… 意为"被…指导"。全句可译为：设计过程是受所积累的经验和以启发式规则为形式的直觉的指导下寻求可接受的解决方案的过程。

[7] rigorous definition 意为"明确的定义"。algorithmic solution 意为"规则系统的解决方案"。全句可译为：当对某一类设施的经验越丰富，对设计中的某些问题，常常更容易找到界定规则系统的解决方案。

3.3 Functional Design

The objective of functional design for a proposed facility is to treat the facility as a complex system of interrelated spaces which are organized systematically according to the functions to be performed in these spaces in order to serve a collection of needs[1]. The arrangement of physical spaces can be viewed as an iterative design process to find a suitable floor plan to facilitate the movement of people and goods associated with the operations intended.

A designer often relies on a heuristic approach, i.e., applying selected rules or strategies serving to stimulate the investigation in search for a solution. The heuristic approach used in arranging spatial layouts for facilities is based generally on the following considerations:

1. identification of the goals and constraints for specified tasks.
2. determination of the current state of each task in the iterative design process.
3. evaluation of the differences between the current state and the goals.
4. means of directing the efforts of search towards the goals on the basis of past experience.

Hence, the procedure for seeking the goals can be recycled iteratively in order to make tradeoffs and thus improve the solution of spatial layouts[2].

Consider, for example, an integrated functional design for a proposed hospital. Since the responsibilities for satisfying various needs in a hospital are divided among different groups of personnel within the hospital administrative structure, a hierarchy of functions corresponding to different levels of responsibilities is proposed in the systematic organization of hospital functions. In this model, the functions of a hospital system are decomposed into a hierarchy of several levels:

1. Hospital —— conglomerate of all hospital services resulting from top policy decisions.

2. Division —— broadly related activities assigned to the same general area by administrative decisions.

3. Department —— combination of services delivered by a service or treatment group.

4. Suite —— specific style of common services or treatments performed in the same suite of rooms.

5. Room —— all activities that can be carried out in the same internal environment surrounded by physical barriers[3].

6. Zone —— several closely related activities that are undertaken by individuals.

7. Object —— a single activity associated with an individual.

In the integrated functional design of hospitals, the connection between physical spaces and functions is most easily made at the lowest level of the hierarchy, and then extended upward to the next higher level[4]. For example, a bed is a physical object immediately related to the activity of a patient. A set of furniture consisting of a bed, a night table and an armchair arranged comfortably in a zone indicates the sphere of private activities for a patient in a room with multiple occupancy. Thus, the spatial representation of a hospital can be organized in stages starting from the lowest level and moving to the top. In each step of the organization process, an element (space or function) under consideration can be related directly to the elements at the levels above it, to those at the levels below it, and to those within the same level.

Since the primary factor relating spaces is the movement of people and supplies, the objective of arranging spaces is the minimization of movement within the hospital. On the other hand, the internal environmental factors such as atmospheric conditions (pressure, temperature, relative humidity, odor and particle pollution), sound, light and fire protection produce constraining effects on the arrangement of spaces since certain spaces cannot be placed adjacent to other spaces because of different requirements in environmental conditions. The consideration of logistics is important at all levels of the hospital system. For example, the travel patterns between objects in a zone or those between zones in a room are frequently equally important for devising an effective design. On the other hand, the adjacency desirability matrix based upon environmental conditions will not be important for organization of functional elements below the room level since a room is the lowest level that can provide a physical barrier to contain desirable environmental conditions. Hence, the organization of functions for a new hospital can be carried out through an interactive process, starting from the functional elements at the lowest level that is regarded as stable by the designer, and moving step by step up to the top level of the hierarchy[5]. Due to the strong correlation between functions and the physical spaces in which they are performed, the arrangement of physical spaces for accommodating the functions will also follow the same iterative process. Once a satisfactory spatial arrangement is achieved, the hospital design is completed by the selection of suitable building components which complement the spatial arrangement.

Example 3-3: Top-down design style
In the functional design of a hospital, the designer may begin with a "reference model", i.e. the spatial layouts of existing hospitals of similar size and service requirements[6]. On the basis of past experience, spaces are allocated to various divisions as shown schematically in Figure 3-3[7]. The space in each division is then divided further for various departments in the division, and all the way down the line of the hierarchy. In every step along the way, the pertinent information of the elements immediately below the level under consideration will be assessed in order to provide input for making necessary adjustments at the current level if necessary. The major drawback of the top-down design style is that the connection between physical spaces and functions at lower levels cannot be easily anticipated. Consequently, the new design is essentially based on the intuition and experience of the designer rather than an objective analysis of the functions and space needs of the facility. Its greatest attraction is its simplicity which keeps the time and cost of design relatively low.

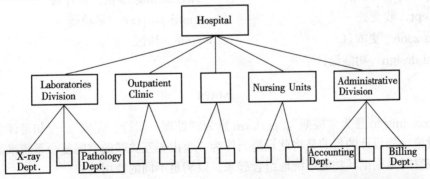

Figure 3-3 A Model for Top-Down Design of a Hospital

Example 3-4: Bottom-up design style
A multi-purpose examination suite in a hospital is used as an illustration of bottom-up design style. In Figure 3-4, the most basic elements (furniture) are first organized into zones

which make up the room[8]. Thus the size of the room is determined by spatial layout required to perform the desired services. Finally, the suite is defined by the rooms which are parts of the multi-purpose examination suite[9].

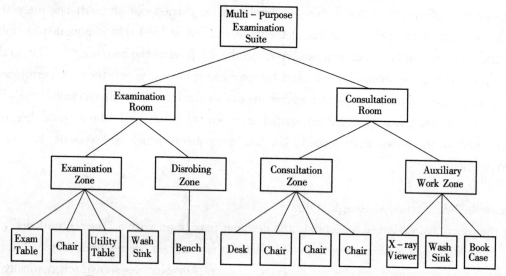

Figure 3-4　A Model for Bottom-up design of an Examination Suite

Words

physical spaces　物理空间
responsibility　职责
atmospheric conditions　空气状况
hospital design　医院设计
Outpatient Clinic　门诊部
Administration Division　行政管理部门
Pathology Dept.　病理科
Billing Dept.　收费处
Disrobing zone　更衣区
functional design　功能设计

administrative structure　管理结构
adjacency desirability matrix　相邻需求矩阵
logistics　物流
Nursing Units　护理部门
X-ray Dept.　放射科
Accounting Dept.　会计科
multi-purpose　多功能
suite　诊区

Notes

[1] according to 意为"根据"。perform 意为"处理,实行,完成"。全句可译为:拟建设施功能设计的目的是将此设施当作一个由相互关联的空间复合系统来处理,这些空间是根据其功能系统地组合起来,以满足不同的使用需要。

[2] make tradeoffs 意为"权衡,决策"。improve the solution of spatial layouts 意为"优化空间布局解决方案"。全句可译为:因此,这种寻求目标的过程可以循环反复,权衡利弊从而优化空间布局解决方案。

[3] carry out 意为"完成、实施、执行"。全句可译为:物理内部空间内可完成所有的活动。

[4]　at the lowest level of the hierarchy 意为"在结构的最底层"。全句可译为：在医院的集成功能设计中，最底层的物理空间和功能之间的联系是最容易确定的，然后向上一个层次扩展。

[5]　is regarded as 意为"被认为"。step by step 意为"一步一步地"。全句可译为：所以，一所新医院的功能组织可以通过交互过程来实现，即从设计人员所认为的最稳定的最底层的功能要素开始，然后一步一步地向最顶层发展。

[6]　reference model 意为"参考模型"。spatial layouts 意为"空间布置"。全句可译为：在医院的功能设计中，设计人员可以从一个"参考模型"开始，如现有的具有同等规模和服务内容医院的空间布置。

[7]　are allocated to 意为"被分配"。全句可译为：在以往经验的基础上，将空间分配给不同的分院，如图3-3所示。

[8]　are organized into 意为"被划分"。make up 意为"安排，布置"。

[9]　multi-purpose examination suite 意为"多功能诊室"。全句可译为：最终，由构成多功能诊区各个部分的多个诊室共同组成。

3.4　Construction Planning

The development of a construction plan is very much analogous to the development of a good facility design[1]. The planner must weigh the costs and reliability of different options while at the same time insuring technical feasibility. Construction planning is more difficult in some ways since the building process is dynamic as the site and the physical facility change over time as construction proceeds[2]. On the other hand, construction operations tend to be fairly standard from one project to another, whereas structural or foundation details might differ considerably from one facility to another.

Forming a good construction plan is an exceptionally challenging problem. There are numerous possible plans available for any given project. While past experience is a good guide to construction planning, each project is likely to have special problems or opportunities that may require considerable ingenuity and creativity to overcome or exploit. Unfortunately, it is quite difficult to provide direct guidance concerning general procedures or strategies to form good plans in all circumstances.

There are some recommendations or issues that can be addressed to describe the *characteristics* of good plans, but this does not necessarily tell a planner how to discover a good plan. However, as in the design process, strategies of decomposition in which planning is divided into subproblems and hierarchical planning in which general activities are repeatable subdivided into more specific tasks can be readily adopted in many cases.

From the standpoint of *construction contractors* or the construction divisions of large firms, the planning process for construction projects consists of three stages that take place between the moment in which a planner starts the plan for the construction of a facility to the moment in which the evaluation of the final output of the construction process is finished[3].

The *estimate* stage involves the development of a cost and duration estimate for the construction of a facility as part of the proposal of a contractor to an owner[4]. It is the stage in which assumptions of resource commitment to the necessary activities to build the facility are made by a planner. A careful and thorough analysis of different conditions imposed by the construction project design and by site characteristics are taken into consideration to determine the best estimate[5]. The success of a contractor depends upon this estimate, not only to obtain a job but also to construct the facility with the highest profit. The planner has to look for the time-cost combination that will allow the contractor to be successful in his commitment[6]. The result of a high estimate would be to lose the job, and the result of a low estimate could be to win the job, but to lose money in the construction process. When changes are done, they should improve the estimate, taking into account not only present effects, but also future outcomes of succeeding activities. It is very seldom the case in which the output of the construction process exactly echoes the estimate offered to the owner.

In the *monitoring and control stage* of the construction process, the construction manager has to keep constant track of both activities' durations and ongoing costs. It is misleading to think that if the construction of the facility is on schedule or ahead of schedule, the cost will also be on the estimate or below the estimate, especially if several changes are made[7]. Constant evaluation is necessary until the construction of the facility is complete. When work is finished in the construction process, and information about it is provided to the planner, the third stage of the planning process can begin.

The *evaluation* stage is the one in which results of the construction process are matched against the estimate. A planner deals with this uncertainty during the estimate stage. Only when the outcome of the construction process is known is he/she able to evaluate the validity of the estimate. It is in this last stage of the planning process that he or she determines if the assumptions were correct. If they were not or if new constraints emerge, he/she should introduce corresponding adjustments in future planning.

Words

construction planning 施工计划
technical feasibility 技术可行性
construction operations 施工作业
structural or foundation details 结构或基础的具体情况
ingenuity and creativity 灵活性和创造性
construction contractors 施工承包商
monitoring and control 监督和控制
facility design 设施设计
challenging 有挑战性的
characteristics 特性
estimate stage 估算阶段
evaluation stage 评估阶段

Notes

[1] is analogous to 意为"和……一样"。全句可译为：施工计划的制定过程与好的设计过程一样。

[2] dynamic 意为"动态的"。be difficult in… 意为"在……有困难"。the physical facility 意为"建成设施"。全句可译为：施工规划更为困难，这是因为施工过程是动态的，因为现场和建成设施会随着工程的进展而有所变化。

[3] consists of 意为"由……组成，包括"。此句包括三个定语从句，第一个定语从句的先行词是 three stages，第二、三个定语从句的先行词是 the moment。全句可译为：从施工承包商或大公司的施工部的角度来看，从计划人员开始制订设施的施工计划，到完成施工产品的评估为止，施工规划包括三个阶段。

[4] cost and duration estimate 意为"费用和工期估算"。全句可译为：估算阶段包括估算设施建设的费用和工期，作为承包商提交给业主的建议的一部分。

[5] take into consideration 意为"考虑"。全句可译为：必须仔细和全面分析项目设计和工地特点的不同情况，以做出最好的估算。

[6] time-cost combination 意为"工期和费用组合"。全句可译为：计划者必须综合考虑工期和费用的各种组合，以便使承包商能成功地完成任务。

[7] on schedule or ahead of schedule 意为"按期或提前"。changes 意为"变更"。全句可译为：那种认为只要建设能按期或提前完成，那么费用也必然不会超出预算的想法是不正确的，尤其是发生了很多变更时。

Exercise

Translate the text of lesson 3.3 into Chinese.

Chapter 4 Labor, Material and Equipment Utilization

4.1 Factors Affecting Job-Site Productivity

Job-site productivity is influenced by many factors which can be characterized dither as labor characteristics, project work conditions or as non-productive activities. The labor characteristics include:
- age, skill and experience of workforce.
- leadership and motivation of workforce.

The project work conditions include among other factors:
- Job size and complexity.
- Job site accessibility.
- Labor availability.
- Equipment utilization.
- Contractual agreements.
- Local climate.
- Local cultural characteristics, particularly in foreign operations.

The non-productive activities associated with a project may or may not be paid by the owner, but they nevertheless take up potential labor resources which can otherwise be directed to the project[1]. The non-productive activities include among other factors:
- Indirect labor required to maintain the progress of the project.
- Rework for correcting unsatisfactory work.
- Temporary work stoppage due to inclement weather or material shortage.
- Time off for union activities.
- Absentee time, including late start and early quits.
- Non-working holidays.
- Strikes.

Each category of factors affects the productive labor available to a project as well as the on-site labor efficiency.

Labor Characteristics

Performance analysis is a common tool for assessing worker quality and contribution. Factors that might be evaluated include:

- Quality of Work-caliber of work produced or accomplished.
- Quantity of Work-volume of acceptable work.
- Job Knowledge-demonstrated knowledge of requirements, methods, techniques and skills involved in doing the job and in applying these to increase productivity.
- Related Work Knowledge-knowledge of effects of work upon other areas and knowledge of related areas which have influence on assigned work.
- Judgment-soundness of conclusions, decisions and actions.
- Initiative-ability to take effective action without being told.
- Resource Utilization-ability to delineate project needs and locate, plan and effectively use all resources available.

These different factors could each be assessed on a three point scale: (1) recognized strength; (2) meets expectations; (3) area needing improvement. Examples of work performance in these areas might also be provided.

Project Work Conditions

Job-site labor productivity can be estimated either for each craft (carpenter, bricklayer, etc.) or each type of construction (residential housing, processing plant, etc.) under a specific set of work conditions. A *base labor productivity may* be defined for a set of work conditions specified by the owner or contractor who wishes to observe and measure the labor performance over a period of time under such conditions. A *labor productivity index* may then be defined as the ratio of the job-site labor productivity under a different set of work conditions to the base labor productivity, and is a measure of the relative labor efficiency of a project under this new set of work conditions[2].

The effects of various factors related to work conditions on a new project can be estimated in advance, some more accurately than others. For example, for very large construction projects, the labor productivity index tends to decrease as the project size and/or complexity increase because of logistic problems and the "learning" that the work force must undergo before adjusting to the new environment[3]. Job-site accessibility often may reduce the labor productivity index if the workers must perform their jobs in round about ways, such as avoiding traffic in repaving the highway surface or maintaining the operation of a plant during renovation. Labor availability in the local market is another factor. Shortage of local labor will force the contractor to bring in non-local labor or schedule overtime work or both. In either case, the labor efficiency will be reduced in addition to incurring additional expenses. The degree of equipment utilization and mechanization of a construction project clearly will have direct bearing on job-site labor productivity[4]. The contractual agreements play an important role in the utilization of union or non-union labor, the use of subcontractors and the degree of field supervision, all of which will impact job-site labor productivity. Since on-site construction essentially involves outdoor activities, the local climate will influence the efficiency of workers directly. In foreign operations, the cultural characteristics of the host country should be observed in assessing the labor efficiency.

Non-Productive Activities

The non-productive activities associated with a project should also be examined in order to examine the *productive labor yield*, which is defined as the ratio of direct labor hours devoted to the completion of a project to the potential labor hours[5]. The direct labor hours are estimated on the basis of the best possible conditions at a job site by excluding all factors which may reduce the productive labor yield. For example, in the repaving of highway surface, the flagmen required to divert traffic represent indirect labor which does not contribute to the labor efficiency of the paving crew if the highway is closed to the traffic[6]. Similarly, for large projects in remote areas, indirect labor may be used to provide housing and infrastructure for the workers hired to supply the direct labor for a project. The labor hours spent on rework to correct unsatisfactory original work represent extra time taken away from potential labor hours. The labor hours related to such activities must be deducted from the potential labor hours in order to obtain the actual productive labor yield[7].

Example 4-1: Effects of job size on productivity

A contractor has established that under a set of "standard" work conditions for building construction, a job requiring 500,000 labor hours is considered standard in determining the base labor productivity. All other factors being the same, the labor productivity index will increase to 1.1 or 110% for a job requiring only 400,000 labor-hours. Assuming that a linear relation exists for the range between jobs requiring 300,000 to 700,000 labor hours as shown in Figure 4-1, determine the labor productivity index for a new job requiring 650,000 labor hours under otherwise the same set of work conditions[8].

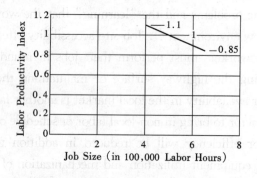

Figure 4-1 Illustrative Relationship between Productivity Index and Job Size

Words

job-site productivity	工地生产率	non-productive activities	非生产性活动
contractual agreements	合同	on-site	现场
strike	罢工	labor characteristics	劳动力的特征
caliber	品质	security sensitivity	安全敏感性
safety consciousness	安全意识	recognized strength	公认的实力
labor productivity	劳动生产率	carpenter	木匠
bricklayer	泥瓦匠	processing plant	加工厂
foreign operations	国外施工	logistic problems	后勤问题
labor efficiency	劳动效率	drilling platform	钻井平台
infrastructure	基础设施	building construction	建筑施工
linear interpolation	线性内插	off-shore	近海,临海
labor jurisdictions	劳动仲裁		

Notes

[1] take up potential labor resources 意为"占据可能的劳动力资源"。associated with…意为"与……相关,与……联系"。全句可译为:与项目有关的非生产性工作业主可以支付,也可以不支付,但他们占据潜在的劳动力资源,这些资源原本可以投入到项目中的。

[2] labor productivity index 意为"劳动生产率指数"。全句可译为:劳动生产率指数可以定义为不同工作条件下现场的劳动生产率和基准劳动生产率的比率,它是对新工作条件下的项目中劳动力相对效率的计量。

[3] the project size and/or complexity 意为"工程规模和/或复杂性"。logistic problems 意为"后勤问题"。全句可译为:例如,对大型的建设项目,因为后勤问题和劳动力在适应新环境前必须经过的"学习"过程,随着项目规模和(或)复杂性的增长,劳动生产力指数趋于下降。

[4] equipment utilization and mechanization 意为"设备利用率和机械化"。union or non-union 意为"工会或非工会"。全句可译为:建筑项目的设备利用率和机械化程度对现场的劳动生产率有直接的影响,在使用工会或非工会劳动力时,合同起着重要的作用。

[5] productive labor yield 意为"有效劳动产出"。potential labor hours 意为"可能工时"。全句可译为:还应该检查与项目有关的非生产性活动,以考察有效劳动产出,即为完成项目的直接工时与可能工时的比率。

[6] the flagmen 意为"信号旗手"。contribute to 意为"贡献"。全句可译为:在重铺高速公路路面时,假如高速公路关闭,疏导指挥交通的信号旗手就是对铺路小组劳动生产率没有贡献的间接劳动力。

[7] be deducted from…意为"从……被减去"。labor hours 意为"工时"。全句可译为:

为了计算实际的有效劳动收益，与这些活动有关的工时必须从可能工时中扣除。

[8] linear relation 意为"线性关系"。全句可译为：假如所需 300000～700000 工时之间存在线性关系，如图 4-1 所示，在完全相同的工作条件下，确定某项需要 650000 工时工作的劳动生产率指数。

4.2 Material Procurement and Delivery

The main sources of information for feedback and control of material procurement are requisitions, bids and quotations, purchase orders and subcontracts, shipping and receiving documents, and invoices. For projects involving the large scale use of critical resources, the owner may initiate the procurement procedure even before the selection of a constructor in order to avoid shortages and delays. Under ordinary circumstances, the constructor will handle the procurement to shop for materials with the best price/performance characteristics specified by the designer[1]. Some overlapping and rehandling in the procurement process is unavoidable, but it should be minimized to insure timely delivery of the materials in good condition.

The materials for delivery to and from a construction site may be broadly classified as: (1) bulk materials; (2) standard off-the-shelf materials; and (3) fabricated members or units. The process of delivery, including transportation, field storage and installation will be different for these classes of materials. The equipment needed to handle and haul these classes of materials will also be different.

Bulk materials refer to materials in their natural or semi-processed state, such as earthwork to be excavated, wet concrete mix, etc. which are usually encountered in large quantities in construction. Some bulk materials such as earthwork or gravels may be measured in bank (solid in site) volume. Obviously, the quantities of materials for delivery may be substantially different when expressed in different measures of volume, depending on the characteristics of such materials.

Standard piping and valves are typical examples of standard off-the-shelf materials which are used extensively in the chemical processing industry. Since standard off-the-shelf materials can easily be stockpiled, the delivery process is relatively simple.

Fabricated members such as steel beams and columns for buildings are pre-processed in a shop to simplify the field erection procedures. Welded or bolted connections are attached partially to the members which are cut to precise dimensions for adequate fit. Similarly, steel tanks and pressure vessels are often partly or fully fabricated before shipping to the field. In general, if the work can be done in the shop where working conditions can better be controlled, it is advisable to do so, provided that the fabricated members or units can be shipped to the construction site in a satisfactory manner at a reasonable cost[2].

As a further step to simplify field assembly, an entire wall panel including plumbing and wiring or even an entire room may be prefabricated and shipped to the site[3]. While the field labor is greatly reduced in such cases, "materials" for delivery are in fact manufactured products with value added by another type of labor. With modern means of transporting construction materials and fabricated units, the percentages of costs on direct labor and materials for a project may change if more prefabricated units are introduced in the construction process.

In the construction industry, materials used by a specific craft are generally handled by craftsmen, not by general labor. Thus, electricians handle electrical materials, pipe-fitters handle pipe materials, etc. This multiple handling diverts scarce skilled craftsmen and contractor supervision into activities which do not directly contribute to construction[4]. Since contractors are not normally in the freight business, they do not perform the tasks of freight delivery efficiently. All these factors tend to exacerbate the problems of freight delivery for very large projects.

Example 4-2: Freight delivery for the Alaska Pipeline Project
The freight delivery system for the Alaska pipeline project was set up to handle 600,000 tons of materials and supplies. This tonnage did not include the pipes which comprised another 500,000 tons and were shipped through a different routing system. The complexity of this delivery system is illustrated in Figure 4-2. The rectangular boxes denote geographical locations. The points of origin represent plants and factories throughout the US and elsewhere. Some of the materials went to a primary staging point in Seattle and some went directly to Alaska. There were five ports of entry: Valdez, Anchorage, Whittier, Seward and Prudhoe Bay[5]. There was a secondary staging area in Fairbanks and the pipeline itself was divided into six sections. Beyond the Yukon River, there was nothing available but a dirt road for hauling. The amounts of freight in thousands of tons shipped to and from various locations are indicated by the numbers near the network branches (with arrows showing the directions of material flows) and the modes of transportation are noted above the branches. In each of the locations, the contractor had supervision and construction labor to identify materials, unload from transport, determine where the material was going, repackage if required to split shipments, and then re-load material on outgoing transport[6].

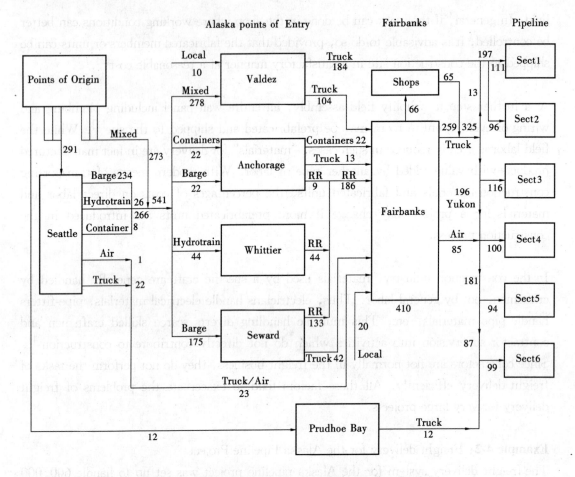

Figure 4-2 Freight Delivery for the Alaska Pipeline Project

Example 4-3: Process plant equipment procurement

The procurement and delivery of bulk materials items such as piping electrical and structural elements involves a series of activities if such items are not standard and/or in stock. The times required for various activities in the procurement of such items might be estimated to be as follows:

Activities	Duration (days)	Cumulative Duration
Requisition ready by designer	0	0
Owner approval	5	5
Inquiry issued to vendors	3	8
Vendor quotations received	15	23
Complete bid evaluation by designer	7	30
Owner approval	5	35
Place purchase order	5	40
Receive preliminary shop drawings	10	50
Receive final design drawings	10	60
Fabrication and delivery	60~200	120~260

As a result, this type of equipment procurement will typically require four to nine months. Slippage or contraction in this standard schedule is also possible, based on such factors as the extent to which a fabricator is busy[7].

Words

material procurement and delivery 材料采购和运输
bulk materials 大宗材料
overlapping and rehandling 搭接和再处理
semi-processed 半加工的, 半成品的
concrete mix 混凝土拌和物
steel beams and columns 钢梁和柱
electricians 电工
the Alaska Pipeline Project 阿拉斯加管道工程
barge 驳船
container 集装箱
vendor 供货商
bids and quotations 投标和报价
off-the-shelf material 现货材料
earthwork to be excavated 土方开挖
stockpile 储存
welded 焊接
pipe-fitters 管工
freight delivery 货物运输
rectangular boxes 矩形箱
hydro train 船队
slippage or contraction 延误或提前

Notes

[1] under…circumstances 意为"在……情况下"。shop for…意为"购买……"。全句可译为：在通常情况下，施工方将根据设计者确定的最优价格/性能特征购买材料。

[2] in general 意为"一般说来"，if 引导的条件状语从句，provided that 意为"如果……"。全句可译为：一般说来，如果工作可以在更可控工作条件的工场内完成，则提倡在工场内完成，条件是可以以满意的方法、合理的成本将所预制的构件运到施工现场。

[3] 全句可译为：进一步简化现场装配的方法是，整个一面墙包括管道和配线，甚至整个房间都可以预制，并且运送到现场。

[4] this multiple handling 意为"多工种操作"。skilled craftsmen and contractor 意为"技术工人和承包商"。全句可译为：这种多工种操作把稀缺的技术工人和承包商的监督转变为对施工没有直接贡献的工作。

[5] 全句可译为：有五个港口可进入：瓦儿迪兹、安克雷奇、惠帝尔、苏华德、普拉德霍湾。

[6] in each of the locations 意为"在各地"。re-load material 意为"再装运"。全句可译为：在各地，承包商监督和派人确认材料、卸货、确定材料运往什么地方，假如要求分开运输时则再打包，然后再装运送出。

[7] 全句可译为：根据安装方忙碌的程度等因素，对这个标准进度安排进行延误或压缩调整同样是可能的。

4.3 Construction Equipment

The selection of the appropriate type and size of construction equipment often affects the required amount of time and effort and thus the job-site productivity of a project. It is therefore important for site managers and construction planners to be familiar with the characteristics of the major types of equipment most commonly used in construction.

Excavation and Loading

One family of construction machines used for excavation is broadly classified as a *crane-shovel* as indicated by the variety of machines in Figure 4-3. The crane-shovel consists of three major components:

- a carrier or mounting which provides mobility and stability for the machine.
- a revolving deck or turntable which contains the power and control units.
- a front end attachment which serves the special functions in an operation.

The type of mounting for all machines in Figure 4-3 is referred to as *crawler mounting*, which is particularly suitable for crawling over relatively rugged surfaces at a job site[1]. Other types of mounting include *truck mounting* and *wheel mounting* which provide

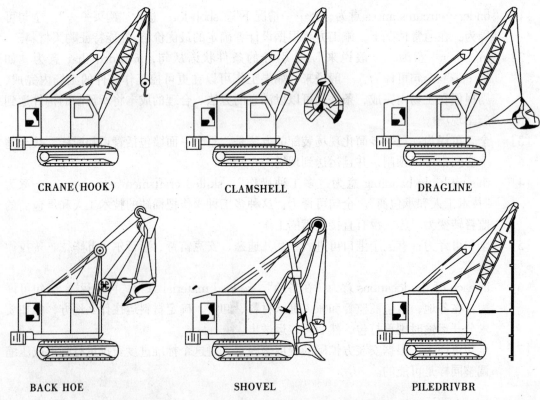

Figure 4-3 Typical Machines in the Crane-Shovel Family

greater mobility between job sites, but require better surfaces for their operation. The revolving deck includes a cab to house the person operating the mounting and/or the revolving deck. The types of front end attachments in Figure 4-3 might include a crane with hook, claim shell, dragline, backhoe, shovel and pile driver.

A tractor consists of a crawler mounting and a non-revolving cab. When an earth moving blade is attached to the front end of a tractor, the assembly is called a bulldozer. When a bucket is attached to its front end, the assembly is known as a loader or bucket loader. There are different types of loaders designed to handle most efficiently materials of different weights and moisture contents.

Scrapers are multiple-units of tractor-truck and blade-bucket assemblies with various combinations to facilitate the loading and hauling of earthwork. Major types of scrapers include single engine two-axle or three axle scrapers, twin-engine all-wheel-drive scrapers, elevating scrapers, and push-pull scrapers[2]. Each type has different characteristics of rolling resistance, maneuverability stability, and speed in operation.

Compaction and Grading

The function of compaction equipment is to produce higher density in soil mechanically. The basic forces used in compaction are static weight, kneading, impact and vibration. The degree of compaction that may be achieved depends on the properties of soil, its moisture content, the thickness of the soil layer for compaction and the method of compaction.

The function of grading equipment is to bring the earthwork to the desired shape and elevation. Major types of grading equipment include motor graders and grade trimmers. The former is an all-purpose machine for grading and surface finishing, while the latter is used for heavy construction because of its higher operating speed.

Drilling and Blasting

Rock excavation is an audacious task requiring special equipment and methods. The degree of difficulty depends on physical characteristics of the rock type to be excavated, such as grain size, planes of weakness, weathering, brittleness and hardness[3]. The task of rock excavation includes loosening, loading, hauling and compacting. The loosening operation is specialized for rock excavation and is performed by drilling, blasting or ripping.

Major types of drilling equipment are percussion drills, rotary drills, and rotary-percussion drills. A percussion drill penetrates and cuts rock by impact while it rotates without cutting on the upstroke. Common types of percussion drills include a jackhammer which is handheld and others which are mounted on a fixed frame or on a wagon or crawl for mobility[4]. A rotary drill cuts by turning a bit against the rock surface. A rotary-percussion drill combines the two cutting movements to provide a faster penetration in rock.

Lifting and Erecting

Derricks are commonly used to lift equipment of materials in industrial or building construction. A derrick consists of a vertical mast and an inclined boom sprouting from the foot of the mast. The mast is held in position by guys or stiff legs connected to a base while a topping lift links the top of the mast and the top of the inclined boom. A hook in the road line hanging from the top of the inclined boom is used to lift loads. Guy derricks may easily be moved from one floor to the next in a building under construction while stiff leg derricks may be mounted on tracks for movement within a work area[5].

Tower cranes are used to lift loads to great heights and to facilitate the erection of steel building frames. Horizon boom type tower cranes are most common in high-rise building construction. Inclined boom type tower cranes are also used for erecting steel structures.

Mixing and Paving

Basic types of equipment for paving include machines for dispensing concrete and bituminous materials for pavement surfaces. Concrete mixers may also be used to mix Portland cement, sand, gravel and water in batches for other types of construction other than paving[6].

A truck mixer refers to a concrete mixer mounted on a truck which is capable of transporting ready mixed concrete from a central batch plant to construction sites. A paving mixer is a self-propelled concrete mixer equipped with a boom and a bucket to place concrete at any desired point within a roadway. It can be used as a stationary mixer or used to supply slip form pavers that are capable of spreading, consolidating and finishing a concrete slab without the use of forms[7].

Automation of Equipment

The introduction of new mechanized equipment in construction has had a profound effect on the cost and productivity of construction as well as the methods used for construction itself. An exciting example of innovation in this regard is the introduction of computer microprocessors on tools and equipment. As a result, the performance and activity of equipment can be continually monitored and adjusted for improvement. In many cases, automation of at least part of the construction process is possible and desirable. For example, wrenches that automatically monitor the elongation of bolts and the applied torque can be programmed to achieve the best bolt tightness[8].

Words

construction equipment	施工设备	site managers	现场经理
construction planners	施工计划者	excavation and loading	开挖和装运
crawler mounting	履带式底盘	a crane with hook	带吊钩的起重机
claim shell	抓铲挖土机	dragline	拉铲挖土机
backhoe	反铲挖土机	shovel	正铲挖土机
piled river	打桩机	the crane-shovel family	起重式挖掘机家族
bulldozer	推土机		
compaction and grading	压实和平整场地	maneuverability stability	机动稳定性
rotary-percussion drills	旋转冲击钻	drilling and blasting	钻孔和爆破
lifting and erecting	提升和安装	dynamite	炸药
bituminous	沥青	derricks	起重机
tunneling equipment	开挖隧道的设备,盾构设备	self-propelled	自牵引式
		earth-pressure-balance	土压平衡法

Notes

[1] is referred to as… 意为"被看作为……"。"crawler mounting, which…"是非限制性定语从句,先行词 crawler mounting 作主语。全句可译为:图 4-3 中所示机器的底盘形式都是履带式底盘,尤其适用于在地面比较崎岖的施工现场爬行。

[2] 全句可译为:铲运机的主要型号包括单引擎双轴或三轴铲运机、双引擎全驱动轮的铲运机、升运式铲运机、推拉式铲运机。

[3] depend on…意为"依赖于……"。excavate 意为"开挖"。全句可译为:(这项任务的)难易程度取决于开挖的岩石类型的物理特性,如粒径大小、软弱位面、风化度、脆度和硬度。

[4] jackhammer 意为"冲击钻"。hand-held 意为"手提式的"。全句可译为:普通形式的冲击钻包括一个手提钻和为了便于移动而安装在固定框架或货车或爬行器的其他部分。

[5] guy derricks 意为"牵索人字起重机"。be moved from…to…意为"从……移动到……"。stiff leg derricks 意为"刚性柱起重机"。全句可译为:牵索人字起重机可以方便地从正在施工的建筑中一个楼层转移到另一个楼层,而刚性柱起重机可安装在轨道上在作业区内移动。

[6] concrete mixers 意为"混凝土搅拌机"。Portland cement 意为"波特兰(普通)水泥"。全句可译为:除了铺路,混凝土搅拌机同样可搅拌波特兰普通水泥、砂子、石子和水而用于其他类型的工程。

[7] be used as…意为"被用作为……"。stationary 意为"固定的"。slip form pavers 意为"滑模铺料机"。全句可译为:它可以作为一个固定的搅拌机,也可以作为滑模铺料机,后者不使用模板就能够进行布料、振捣和抹平混凝土路面。

[8] 全句可译为：例如，可以通过编程让扳手自动监控螺栓的延长度和所施加的扭矩，以达到螺栓的最佳松紧程度。

4.4 Queues and Resource Bottlenecks

A project manager needs to insure that resources required for and/or shared by numerous activities are adequate. Problems in this area can be indicated in part by the existence of queues of resource demands during construction operations. A *queue can be a waiting line* for service. One can imagine a queue as an orderly line of customers waiting for a stationary server such as a ticket seller. However, the demands for service might not be so neatly arranged. For example, we can speak of the *queue* of welds on a building site waiting for inspection. In this case, demands do not come to the server, but a roving inspector travels among the waiting service points. Waiting for resources such as a particular piece of equipment or a particular individual is an endemic problem on construction sites[1]. If workers spend appreciable portions of time waiting for particular tools, materials or an inspector, costs increase and productivity declines. Insuring adequate resources to serve expected demands is an important problem during construction planning and field management.

In general, there is a trade-off between waiting times and utilization of resources. Utilization is the proportion of time a particular resource is in productive use. Higher amounts of resource utilization will be beneficial as long as it does not impose undue costs on the entire operation. For example, a welding inspector might have one hundred percent utilization, but workers throughout the jobsite might be wasting inordinate time waiting for inspections. Providing additional inspectors may be cost effective, even if they are not utilized at all times.

Single-Server with Deterministic Arrivals and Services

Suppose that the cumulative number of demands for service or "customers" at any time t is known and equal to the value of the function A(t) which is shown in Figure 4-4. These "customers" might be crane loads, weld inspections, or any other defined group of items to be serviced. Suppose further that a single server is available to handle these demands, such as a single crane or a single inspector. For this model of queuing, we assume that the server can handle customers at some constant, maximum rate denoted as x "customers" per unit of time. This is a maximum rate since the server may be idle for periods of time if no customers are waiting. This system is *deterministic* in the sense that both the arrival function and the service process are assumed to have no random or unknown component.

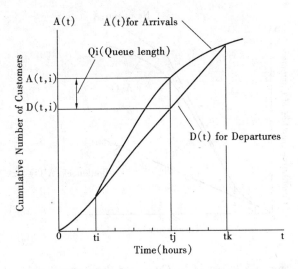

Figure 4-4 Cumulative Arrivals and Departures in a Deterministic Queue

A cumulative arrival function of customers, A(t), is shown in Figure 4-5 in which the vertical axis represents the cumulative number of customers, while the horizontal axis represents the passage of time[2].

ls to the queue exceeds the maximum service rate, then a queue begins to form and the cumulative departures will occur at the maximum service rate. The cumulative departures from the queue will proceed at the maximum service rate of x "customers" per unit of time, so that the slope of D(t) is x during this period. The cumulative departure function D(t) can be readily constructed graphically by running a ruler with a slope of x along the cumulative arrival function A(t). As soon as the function A(t) climbs above the ruler, a queue begins to form. The maximum service rate will continue until the queue disappears, which is represented by the convergence of the cumulative arrival and departure functions A(t) and D(t)[3].

This simple, deterministic model has a number of implications for operations planning. First, an increase in the maximum service rate will result in reductions in waiting time and the maximum queue length. Such increases might be obtained by speeding up the service rate such as introducing shorter inspection procedures or installing faster cranes on a site. Second, altering the pattern of cumulative arrivals can result in changes in total waiting time and in the maximum queue length. In particular, if the maximum arrival rate never exceeds the maximum service rate, no queue will form, or if the arrival rate always exceeds the maximum service rate, the bottleneck cannot be dispersed[4]. Both cases are shown in Figure 4-5.

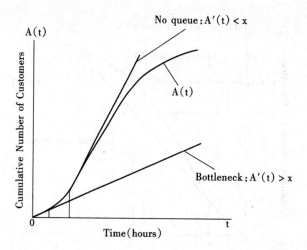

Figure 4-5 Cases of No Queue and Permanent Bottleneck

A practical means to alter the arrival function and obtain these benefits is to inaugurate a reservation system for customers. Even without drawing a graph such as Figure 4-6, good operations planners should consider the effects of different operation or service rates on the flow of work. Clearly, service rates less than the expected arrival rate of work will result in resource bottlenecks on a job.

Multiple Servers

Both of the simple models of service performance described above are limited to single servers. In operations planning, it is commonly the case that numerous operators are available and numerous stages of operations exist. In these circumstances, a planner typically attempts to match the service rates occurring at different stages in the process. For example, construction of a high rise building involves a series of operations on each floor, including erection of structural elements, pouring or assembling a floor, construction of walls, installation of HVAC (Heating, ventilating and air conditioning) equipment, installation of plumbing and electric wiring, etc. A smooth construction process would have each of these various activities occurring at different floors at the same time without large time gaps between activities on any particular floor. Thus, floors would be installed soon after erection of structural elements, walls would follow subsequently, and so on. From the standpoint of a queuing system, the planning problem is to insure that the productivity or service rate per floor of these different activities are approximately equal, so that one crew is not continually waiting on the completion of a preceding activity or interfering with a following activity[5]. In the realm of manufacturing systems, creating this balance among operations is called *assembly line* balancing.

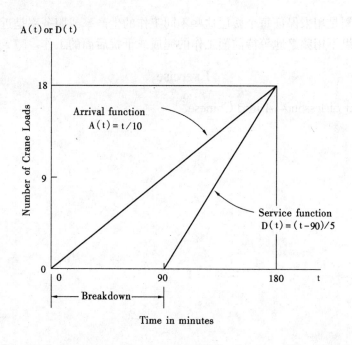

Figure 4-6 Arrivals and Services of Crane Loads with a Crane Breakdown

Words

queue 排队	bottleneck 瓶颈
endemic 地方性的	appreciable 可感觉到的
function 函数	pattern 模式、方式
resource 资源	field management 现场管理
slope 斜率	convergence 收敛
inaugurate 开辟,启用	multiple servers 多服务台
ventilating 通风	air conditioning 空调
backlog 积压	algebraically 代数上地

Notes

[1] an endemic problem on construction sites 意为"施工现场的通病"。全句可译为：等待资源（例如一台特定的设备或某个特定的个人）是施工现场的通病。

[2] the vertical axis 意为"纵轴"。the horizontal axis 意为"横轴"。全句可译为：顾客累计到达函数 A (t)，如图 4-5 表示，纵轴表示累计的顾客数量，横轴表示过去的时间。

[3] 全句可译为：累计到达函数 A (t) 和离开函数 D (t) 的收敛度所表示的最大化服务率将会保持下去，直到排队消除。

[4] 全句可译为：尤其是，如果最大到达率从不超过最大服务率，那么排队将不会形成，或者如果到达率总是超过最大服务率，那么瓶颈将不会消失。

[5] From the standpoint of…意为"从……角度看"。全句可译为：从排队系统的角度

来看，计划是用来保证每个楼层这些不同工作的生产率或服务率是近似相等的，这样每个班组不用频繁地等待前面工作的完成或干扰后面的工作。

Exercise

Translate the text of lesson 4.4 into Chinese.

Chapter 5 Cost Estimation

5.1 Approaches to Cost Estimation

Cost estimating is one of the most important steps in project management. A cost estimate establishes the base line of the project cost at different stages of development of the project. A cost estimate at a given stage of project development represents a prediction provided by the cost engineer or estimator on the basis of available data[1]. According to the American Association of Cost Engineers, cost engineering is defined as that area of engineering practice where engineering judgment and experience are utilized in the application of scientific principles and techniques to the problem of cost estimation, cost control and profitability[2].

Virtually all cost estimation is performed according to one or some combination of the following basic approaches:

Production function In microeconomics, the relationship between the output of a process and the necessary resources is referred to as the production function. In construction, the production function may be expressed by the relationship between the volume of construction and a factor of production such as labor or capital. A production function relates the amount or volume of output to the various inputs of labor, material and equipment. For example, the amount of output Q may be derived as a function of various input factors x_1, x_2,..., x_n by means of mathematical and/or statistical methods[3]. Thus, for a specified level of output, we may attempt to find a set of values for the input factors so as to minimize the production cost. The relationship between the sizes of a building project (expressed in square feet) to the input labor (expressed in labor hours per square foot) is an example of a production function for construction.

Empirical cost inference Empirical estimation of cost functions requires statistical techniques which relate the cost of constructing or operating a facility to a few important characteristics or attributes of the system[4]. The role of statistical inference is to estimate the best parameter values or constants in an assumed cost function. Usually, this is accomplished by means of regression analysis techniques.

Unit costs for bill of quantities   A unit cost is assigned to each of the facility components or tasks as represented by the bill of quantities. The total cost is the summation of the products of the quantities multiplied by the corresponding unit costs. The unit cost method is straightforward in principle but quite laborious in application. The initial step is to break down or disaggregate a process into a number of tasks. Collectively, these tasks must be completed for the construction of a facility. Once these tasks are defined and quantities representing these tasks are assessed, a unit cost is assigned to each and then the total cost is determined by summing the costs incurred in each task[5]. The level of detail in decomposing into tasks will vary considerably from one estimate to another[6].

Allocation of joint costs   Allocations of cost from existing accounts may be used to develop a cost function of an operation. The basic idea in this method is that each expenditure item can be assigned to particular characteristics of the operation. Ideally, the allocation of joint costs should be causally related to the category of basic costs in an allocation process. In many instances, however, a causal relationship between the allocation factor and the cost item cannot be identified or may not exist. For example, in construction projects, the accounts for basic costs may be classified according to (1) labor; (2) material; (3) construction equipment; (4) construction supervision; and (5) general office overhead. These basic costs may then be allocated proportionally to various tasks which are subdivisions of a project[7].

Words

cost estimation   成本估算
cost engineering   工程估价
profitability   赢利
production function   生产函数
statistical inference   统计推断
construction equipment   施工机具
general office overhead   总部管理费

the cost engineer or estimator   估算师
cost control   成本控制
empirical cost inference   经验成本推论法
allocation of joint costs   综合成本的分摊
bill of quantities   工程量清单
construction supervision   施工监督

Notes

[1]   全句可译为：在项目开发过程中的某一特定阶段的成本估算就是造价工程师在现有数据基础上对未来成本的预测。

[2]   According to 意为"根据，按照"。the American Association of Cost Engineers 句中是指"美国估算师协会"。全句可译为：根据美国估算师协会的定义，工程成本是运用理性判断和经验，运用科学原理和技术，解决成本估算、成本控制和盈利能力等问题的实用技术领域。

[3]   be derived as…意为"表示成……"。mathematical and/or statistical methods 意为

"数学和/或统计方法"。全句可译为：例如，代表产出的 Q 可以用由代表各种投入的不同参数 x_1, x_2, $\cdots$, x_n 等通过数学和/或统计方法表达。

[4] Empirical estimation of cost functions 意为"成本函数的近似表达式"。attributes 意为"属性"。全句可译为：根据经验确定成本函数近似表达式需要利用一些统计方法，将建造或使用某一设施的成本与上述各种投入产出变量的几个重要特征或属性联系起来。

[5] 全句可译为：一旦这些任务确定下来，并有了工作量的估算，用单价与每项任务的工作量相乘就可以得到每项任务的成本。

[6] decomposing into 意为"分解"。全句可译为：当然，不同的估算中对每项工作分解的详细程度可能会有很大的差别。

[7] be allocated to 意为"被分摊到"。…which…是限制性定语从句，先行词"various tasks"作主语。subdivisions of a project 意为"工程子项"。全句可译为：这几个基本成本有可能会按比例被分配到工程子项的不同任务当中去。

5.2 Types of Construction Cost Estimates

Construction cost constitutes only a fraction, though a substantial fraction, of the total project cost. However, it is the part of the cost under the control of the construction project manager. The required levels of accuracy of construction cost estimates vary at different stages of project development, ranging from ball park figures in the early stage to fairly reliable figures for budget control prior to construction. Since design decisions made at the beginning stage of a project life cycle are more tentative than those made at a later stage, the cost estimates made at the earlier stage are expected to be less accurate. Generally, the accuracy of a cost estimate will reflect the information available at the time of estimation.

Construction cost estimates may be viewed from different perspectives because of different institutional requirements. In spite of the many types of cost estimates used at different stages of a project, cost estimates can best be classified into three major categories according to their functions. A construction cost estimate serves one of the three basic functions: design, bid and control. For establishing the financing of a project, either a design estimate or a bid estimate is used.

1. **Design Estimates.** For the owner or its designated design professionals, the types of cost estimates encountered run parallel with the planning and design as follows:
    ○ Screening estimates (or order of magnitude estimates)
    ○ Preliminary estimates (or conceptual estimates)
    ○ Detailed estimates (or definitive estimates)
    ○ Engineer's estimates based on plans and specifications

For each of these different estimates, the amount of design information available typically increases.

2. **Bid Estimates.** For the contractor, a bid estimate submitted to the owner either for competitive bidding or negotiation consists of direct construction cost including field supervision, plus a markup to cover general overhead and profits[1]. The direct cost of construction for bid estimates is usually derived from a combination of the following approaches.
    ○ Subcontractor quotations
    ○ Quantity takeoffs
    ○ Construction procedures

3. **Control Estimates.** For monitoring the project during construction, a control estimate is derived from available information to establish:
    ○ Budget estimate for financing
    ○ Budgeted cost after contracting but prior to construction
    ○ Estimated cost to completion during the progress of construction

Design Estimates

In the planning and design stages of a project, various design estimates reflect the progress of the design. At the very early stage, the *screening estimate* or *order of magnitude estimate* is usually made before the facility is designed, and must therefore rely on the cost data of similar facilities built in the past[2]. A *preliminary estimate* or *conceptual estimate* is based on the conceptual design of the facility at the state when the basic technologies for the design are known. The *detailed estimate* or *definitive estimate* is made when the scope of work is clearly defined and the detailed design is in progress so that the essential features of the facility are identifiable. The *engineer's estimate* is based on the completed plans and specifications when they are ready for the owner to solicit bids from construction contractors. In preparing these estimates, the design professional will include expected amounts for contractors' overhead and profits.

The costs associated with a facility may be decomposed into a hierarchy of levels that are appropriate for the purpose of cost estimation. The level of detail in decomposing the facility into tasks depends on the type of cost estimate to be prepared. For conceptual estimates, for example, the level of detail in defining tasks is quite coarse; for detailed estimates, the level of detail can be quite fine.

As an example, consider the cost estimates for a proposed bridge across a river. A screening estimate is made for each of the potential alternatives, such as a tied arch bridge or a cantilever truss bridge. As the bridge type is selected, e.g. the technology is chosen to be a tied arch bridge instead of some new bridge form, a preliminary estimate is made on the basis of the layout of the selected bridge form on the basis of the preliminary or conceptual design. When the detailed design has progressed to a point when the essential details are known, a detailed estimate is made on the basis of the well defined scope of the project[3]. When the detailed plans and specifications are completed, an engineer's estimate can be made on the basis of items and quantities of work.

Bid Estimates

The contractor's bid estimates often reflect the desire of the contractor to secure the job as well as the estimating tools at its disposal. Some contractors have well established cost estimating procedures while others do not. Since only the lowest bidder will be the winner of the contract in most bidding contests, any effort devoted to cost estimating is a loss to the contractor who is not a successful bidder. Consequently, the contractor may put in the least amount of possible effort for making a cost estimate if it believes that its chance of success is not high.

If a general contractor intends to use subcontractors in the construction of a facility, it may solicit price quotations for various tasks to be subcontracted to specialty subcontractors. Thus, the general subcontractor will shift the burden of cost estimating to subcontractors. If all or part of the construction is to be undertaken by the general contractor, a bid estimate may be prepared on the basis of the quantity takeoffs from the plans provided by the owner or on the basis of the construction procedures devised by the contractor for implementing the project[4]. For example, the cost of a footing of a certain type and size may be found in commercial publications on cost data which can be used to facilitate cost estimates from quantity takeoffs. However, the contractor may want to assess the actual cost of construction by considering the actual construction procedures to be used and the associated costs if the project is deemed to be different from typical designs. Hence, items such as labor, material and equipment needed to perform various tasks may be used as parameters for the cost estimates.

Control Estimates

Both the owner and the contractor must adopt some base line for cost control during the construction. For the owner, a *budget estimate* must be adopted early enough for planning long term financing of the facility. Consequently, the detailed estimate is often used as the budget estimate since it is sufficient definitive to reflect the project scope and is available long before the engineer's estimate. As the work progresses, the budgeted cost must be revised periodically to reflect the estimated cost to completion. A revised estimated cost is necessary either because of change orders initiated by the owner or due to unexpected cost overruns or savings.

For the contractor, the bid estimate is usually regarded as the budget estimate, which will be used for control purposes as well as for planning construction financing[5]. The budgeted cost should also be updated periodically to reflect the estimated cost to completion as well as to insure adequate cash flows for the completion of the project.

Example 5-1: Screening estimate of a grouting seal beneath a landfill

One of the methods of isolating a landfill from groundwater is to create a bowl-shaped bottom seal beneath the site as shown in Figure 5-1. The seal is constructed by pumping or pressure-injecting grout under the existing landfill. Holes are bored at regular intervals throughout the landfill for this purpose and the grout tubes are extended from the surface to the bottom of the landfill. A layer of soil at a minimum of 5 ft. thick is left between the grouted material and the landfill contents to allow for irregularities in the bottom of the landfill. The grout liner can be between 4 and 6 feet thick. A typical material would be Portland cement grout pumped under pressure through tubes to fill voids in the soil. This grout would then harden into a permanent, impermeable liner.

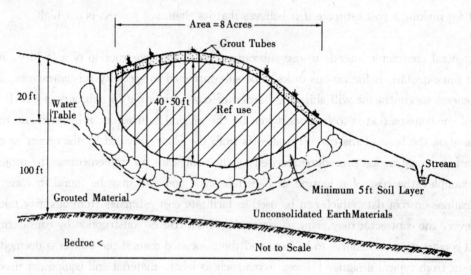

Figure 5-1 Grout Bottom Seal Liner at a Landfill

The work items in this project include (1) drilling exploratory bore holes at 50 ft intervals for grout tubes; and (2) pumping grout into the voids of a soil layer between 4 and 6 ft thick. The quantities for these two items are estimated on the basis of the landfill area:

$$8 \text{ acres} = (8)(43,560 \text{ ft}^2/\text{acre}) = 348,480 \text{ ft}^2$$

(As an approximation, use 360,000 ft² to account for the bowl shape)

The number of bore holes in a 50 ft by 50 ft grid pattern covering 360,000 ft² is given by:

$$\frac{3600,000 \text{ft}^2}{(50\text{ft})(50\text{ft})} = 144$$

The average depth of the bore holes is estimated to be 20 ft. Hence, the total amount of drilling is $(144)(20) = 2,880$ ft.

The volume of the soil layer for grouting is estimated to be:

$$\text{for a 4 ft layer, volume} = (4 \text{ ft})(360,000 \text{ ft}^2) = 1,440,000 \text{ ft}^3$$
$$\text{for a 6 ft layer, volume} = (6 \text{ ft})(360,000 \text{ ft}^2) = 2,160,000 \text{ ft}^3$$

It is estimated from soil tests that the voids in the soil layer are between 20% and 30% of the total volume. Thus, for a 4 ft soil layer:

$$\text{grouting in 20\% voids} = (20\%)(1,440,000) = 288,000 \text{ ft}^3$$
$$\text{grouting in 30\% voids} = (30\%)(1,440,000) = 432,000 \text{ ft}^3$$

and for a 6 ft soil layer:

$$\text{grouting in 20\% voids} = (20\%)(2,160,000) = 432,000 \text{ ft}^3$$
$$\text{grouting in 30\% voids} = (30\%)(2,160,000) = 648,000 \text{ ft}^3$$

The unit cost for drilling exploratory bore holes is estimated to be between $ 3 and $ 10 per foot (in 1978 dollars) including all expenses. Thus, the total cost of boring will be between $(2,880)(3) = \$ 8,640$ and $(2,880)(10) = \$ 28,800$. The unit cost of Portland cement grout pumped into place is between $ 4 and $ 10 per cubic foot including overhead and profit. In addition to the variation in the unit cost, the total cost of the bottom seal will depend upon the thickness of the soil layer grouted and the proportion of voids in the soil. That is:

for a 4 ft layer with 20% voids, grouting cost = $ 1,152,000 to $ 2,880,000
for a 4 ft layer with 30% voids, grouting cost = $ 1,728,000 to $ 4,320,000
for a 6 ft layer with 20% voids, grouting cost = $ 1,728,000 to $ 4,320,000
for a 6 ft layer with 30% voids, grouting cost = $ 2,592,000 to $ 6,480,000

The total cost of drilling bore holes is so small in comparison with the cost of grouting that the former can be omitted in the screening estimate. Furthermore, the range of unit cost varies greatly with soil characteristics, and the engineer must exercise judgment in narrowing the range of the total cost. Alternatively, additional soil tests can be used to better estimate the unit cost of pumping grout and the proportion of voids in the soil. Suppose that, in addition to ignoring the cost of bore holes, an average value of a 5 ft soil layer with 25% voids is used together with a unit cost of $ 7 per cubic foot of Portland cement grouting[6]. In this case, the total project cost is estimated to be:

$$(5 \text{ ft})(360{,}000 \text{ ft}^2)(25\%)(\$7/\text{ft}^3) = \$3{,}150{,}000$$

An important point to note is that this screening estimate is based to a large degree on engineering judgment of the soil characteristics, and the range of the actual cost may vary from \$1,152,000 to \$6,480,000 even though the probabilities of having actual costs at the extremes are not very high[7].

Example 5-2: Example of engineer's estimate and contractors' bids
The engineer's estimate for a project involving 14 miles of Interstate 70 roadway in Utah was \$20,950,859. Bids were submitted on March 10, 1987, for completing the project within 320 working days. The three low bidders were:

1. Ball, Ball & Brosame, Inc., Danville, CA   \$14,129,798
2. National Projects, Inc., Phoenix, AR   \$15,381,789
3. Kiewit Western Co., Murray, Utah   \$18,146,714

It was astounding that the winning bid was 32% below the engineer's estimate. Even the third lowest bidder was 13% below the engineer's estimate for this project. The disparity in pricing can be attributed either to the very conservative estimate of the engineer in the Utah Department of Transportation or to area contractors who are hungrier than usual to win jobs[8].

Words

construction cost 建造成本	prestressed concrete member 预应力混凝土构件
design estimates 设计估算书	
bid estimate 投标估价	construction project manager 项目经理
control estimate 控制估算	tentative 试验性的,尝试的,不确定的
engineer's estimate 工程师估算,标底	screening estimates 匡算
budget estimates 预算估价	conceptual estimate 概念设计估算
grouting seal beneath a landfill 垃圾掩埋厂封底工程	parameter 参数
	pressure-injecting grout 压力注浆法
voids 空隙率	interstate roadway 州际公路
department of Transportation 交通管理局	subgrade 路基
delineators 路边线轮廓标	polyethylene pipe 聚乙烯管

Notes

[1] submitted to…意为"提交给……"。competitive bidding 意为"公开招标"。direct construction cost 意为"工程直接费"。including field supervision 意为"现场监督"。

[2] At the very early stage 意为"在最初阶段"。order of magnitude estimate 意为"量级估算"。rely on 意为"依靠,依赖"。全句可译为:在最初阶段,编制量级估算时,通常是设施的设计还未进行,因此必须依靠过去类似设施的数据。

[3] progressed to a point 意为"进行到一定阶段"。全句可译为:当详细设计进行到一定程度时,重要的细节已经明确,就可以根据很明确的项目范围进行详细估算。

[4] 全句可译为:如果整个或部分工程由总承包商施工,投标估算就要根据业主提供的图纸和工程量或由承包商编制的施工组织计划编制。

[5] planning construction financing 意为"施工资金规划"。全句可译为:对于承包商来说,一般以投标估算作为预算,既可以用于成本控制,也可以用于施工资金使用规划。

[6] Suppose that 意为"假定"。全句可译为:除了忽略钻孔费用,还假定注浆土层平均厚5ft,土层空隙率25%,每立方英尺普通硅酸盐水泥的注浆成本为7美元。

[7] 全句可译为:值得注意的是,这一量级估算在很大程度上是依靠估算师对土的特点的判断,其真实成本的范围可能介于1152000美元和6480000美元之间,尽管真实成本为估价区间两端的概率并不一定大。

[8] The disparity 意为"差别,不同"。conservative 意为"保守"。全句可译为:估算的结果相差如此悬殊,一种可能是犹他州交通管理当局的估算师太保守,另一种可能是当地承包商获得工程的愿望要比平常强烈。

5.3 Unit Cost Method of Estimation

If the design technology for a facility has been specified, the project can be decomposed into elements at various levels of detail for the purpose of cost estimation[1]. The unit cost for each element in the bill of quantities must be assessed in order to compute the total construction cost. This concept is applicable to both design estimates and bid estimates, although different elements may be selected in the decomposition.

For design estimates, the unit cost method is commonly used when the project is decomposed into elements at various levels of a hierarchy as follows:

1. Preliminary Estimates. The project is decomposed into major structural systems or production equipment items, e.g. the entire floor of a building or a cooling system for a processing plant.

2. Detailed Estimates. The project is decomposed into components of various major systems, i.e., a single floor panel for a building or a heat exchanger for a cooling system.

3. Engineer's Estimates. The project is decomposed into detailed items of various components as warranted by the available cost data. Examples of detailed items are slabs and beams in a floor panel, or the piping and connections for a heat exchanger.

For bid estimates, the unit cost method can also be applied even though the contractor may choose to decompose the project into different levels in a hierarchy as follows:

1. Subcontractor Quotations. The decomposition of a project into subcontractor items for quotation involves a minimum amount of work for the general contractor. However, the accuracy of the resulting estimate depends on the reliability of the subcontractors since the general contractor selects one among several contractor quotations submitted for each item of subcontracted work[2].

2. Quantity Takeoffs. The decomposition of a project into items of quantities that are measured (or *taken off*) from the engineer's plan will result in a procedure similar to that adopted for a detailed estimate or an engineer's estimate by the design professional. The levels of detail may vary according to the desire of the general contractor and the availability of cost data.

3. Construction Procedures. If the construction procedure of a proposed project is used as the basis of a cost estimate, the project may be decomposed into items such as labor, material and equipment needed to perform various tasks in the projects[3].

Simple Unit Cost Formula

Suppose that a project is decomposed into n elements for cost estimation. Let Q_i be the quantity of the ith element and u_i be the corresponding unit cost. Then, the total cost of the project is given by:

$$y = \sum_{i=1}^{n} u_i Q_i \qquad (5.1)$$

where n is the number of units. Based on characteristics of the construction site, the technology employed, or the management of the construction process, the estimated unit cost, u_i for each element may be adjusted[4].

Factored Estimate Formula

A special application of the unit cost method is the "factored estimate" commonly used in process industries. Usually, an industrial process requires several major equipment components such as furnaces, towers, drums and pumps in a chemical processing plant, plus ancillary items such as piping, valves and electrical elements. The total cost of a project is dominated by the costs of purchasing and installing the major equipment components and their ancillary items. Let C_i be the purchase cost of a major equipment component i and f_i be a factor accounting for the cost of ancillary items needed for the installation of this equipment component i. Then, the total cost of a project is estimated by:

$$y = \sum_{i=1}^{n} C_i + \sum_{i=1}^{n} f_i C_i = \sum_{i=1}^{n} C_i(1 + f_i) \tag{5.2}$$

where n is the number of major equipment components included in the project. The factored method is essentially based on the principle of computing the cost of ancillary items such as piping and valves as a fraction or a multiple of the costs of the major equipment items[5]. The value of C_i may be obtained by applying the exponential rule so the use of Eq. 5.2 may involve a combination of cost estimation methods.

Formula Based on Labor, Material and Equipment

Consider the simple case for which costs of labor, material and equipment are assigned to all tasks. Suppose that a project is decomposed into n tasks. Let Q_i be the quantity of work for task i, M_i be the unit material cost of task i, E_i be the unit equipment rate for task i, L_i be the units of labor required per unit of Q_i, and W_i be the wage rate associated with L_i. In this case, the total cost y is:

$$y = \sum_{i=1}^{n} y_i = \sum_{i=1}^{n} Q_i(M_i + E_i + W_i L_i) \tag{5.3}$$

Note that $W_i L_i$ yields the labor cost per unit of Q_i, or the labor unit cost of task i. Consequently, the units for all terms in Eq. 5.3 are consistent.

Words

Unit Cost Method of Estimation 单位估价法	Detailed Estimates 详细估算
cooling system 冷却系统	Preliminary Estimates 初步估算
heat exchanger 热交换器	Subcontractor Quotations 分包商报价
slabs and beams 楼板和梁	Construction Procedures 施工方法
furnaces 锅炉	Factored Estimate Formula 系数估算公式
plus ancillary items 辅助设备	reinforcing bars 钢筋
formwork 模板	building foundation 建筑物基础

Notes

[1] technology 在这里意为"待建设施使用的技术"。the design technology 意为"设计者选定的技术"。be decomposed into 意为"分解"。全句可译为：如果设计中已经确定使用何种技术，就可以根据成本估算的用途而将项目分解成为分项工程。

[2] 全句可译为：然而，估算结果的精确程度取决于各分包商的估算是否可靠，因为对每一个分包的分项工程，总承包商总是从几个分包商提交的报价中选择。

[3] 全句可译为：如果以项目的施工方法为基础进行成本估算，则可以分解为各项工作的组成分项，如为完成各项工作所需的劳动力、原材料和机械设备。

[4] 全句可译为：根据施工现场的特点，所采用的施工技术或者管理方法，每个组成元

素的成本单价 u_i 可能要进行调整。

[5]   factored method 意为"系数法"。is based on 意为"以……为基数"。piping and valves 意为"管道和阀门"。全句可译为：系数估算法实际上就是以主要设备的成本为基数，再乘上一个分数或倍数，以此来计算辅助设备和配件（如管道和阀门）的费用。

5.4 Cost Indices

Since historical cost data are often used in making cost estimates, it is important to note the price level changes over time. Trends in price changes can also serve as a basis for forecasting future costs. The input price indices of labor and/or material reflect the price level changes of such input components of construction; the output price indices, where available, reflect the price level changes of the completed facilities, thus to some degree also measuring the productivity of construction.

A price index is a weighted aggregate measure of constant quantities of goods and services selected for the package. The price index at a subsequent year represents a proportionate change in the same weighted aggregate measure because of changes in prices. Let I_t be the price index in year t, and I_{t+1} be the price index in the following year $t+1$. Then, the percent change in price index for year $t+1$ is:

$$j_{t+1} = \frac{I_{t+1} - I_t}{I_t}(100\%) \tag{5.4}$$

or

$$I_{t+1} = I_t(1 + j_{t+1}) \tag{5.5}$$

If the price index at the base year $t=0$ is set at a value of 100, then the price indices I_1, $I_2 \cdots I_n$ for the subsequent years $t=1,2\cdots n$ can be computed successively from changes in the total price charged for the package of goods measured in the index.

The best-known indicators of general price changes are the Gross Domestic Product (GDP) deflators compiled periodically by the U.S. Department of Commerce, and the consumer price index (CPI) compiled periodically by the U.S. Department of Labor[1]. They are widely used as broad gauges of the changes in production costs and in consumer prices for essential goods and services. Special price indices related to construction are also collected by industry sources since some input factors for construction and the outputs from construction may disproportionately outpace or fall behind the general price indices. Examples of special price indices for construction input factors are the wholesale Building Material Price and Building Trades Union Wages, both compiled by the U.S. Department of Labor[2]. In addition, the construction cost index and the building cost index are reported periodically in the *Engineering News-Record* (*ENR*). Both *ENR* cost indices measure the effects of wage rate and material price trends, but they are not adjusted for productivity, efficiency, competitive conditions, or technology changes. Consequently, all these indices measure only the price changes of respective construction *input factors* as represented by constant quantities of material and/or labor. On the other hand, the price indices of various types of completed facilities reflect the price changes of construction output including all pertinent factors in the construction process. The building construction output indices compiled by Turner Construction Company and Handy-Whitman Utilities are compiled in the U. S. *Statistical Abstracts* published each year.

Figure 5-2 and Table 5-1 show a variety of United States indices, including the Gross National Product (GNP) price deflator, the *ENR* building index, the Handy Whitman Utilities Buildings, and the Turner Construction Company Building Cost Index from 1970 to 1998, using 1992 as the base year with an index of 100.

Table 5-1 Summary of Input and Output Price Indices, 1970~1998

Year	1970	1975	1980	1985	1990	1993	1994	1995	1996	1997	1998
Turner Construction-Buildings	28	44	61	83	98	102	105	109	112	117	122
ENR-Buildings	28	44	68.5	85.7	95.4	105.7	109.8	109.8	113	118.7	119.7
US Census-Composite	28	44	68.6	82.9	98.5	103.7	108	112.5	115	118.7	122
Handy-Whitman Public Utility	31	54	78	90	101	105	112	115	118	122	123
GNP Deflator	35	49	70	92	94	103	105	108	110	113	114

Note: Index = 100 in base year of 1992.

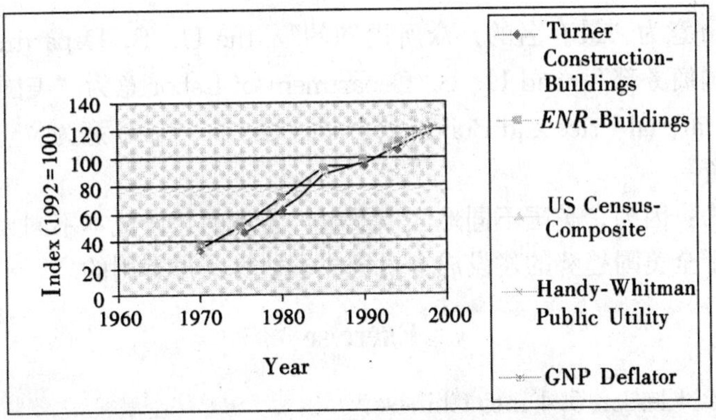

Figure 5-2 Trends for US price indices

Since construction costs vary in different regions of the United States and in all parts of the world, *locational indices* showing the construction cost at a specific location relative to the national trend are useful for cost estimation[3]. *ENR* publishes periodically the indices of

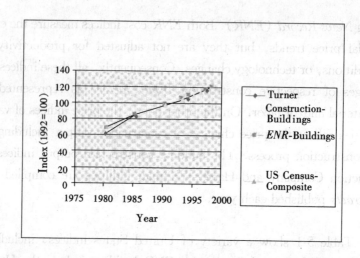

Figure 5-3 Price and cost indices for construction

local construction costs at the major cities in different regions of the United States as percentages of local to national costs, as is shown in Figure 5-3.

Words

Cost Indices　成本指数
productivity of construction　建筑生产率
deflators　通货紧缩指数
Engineering News-Record　《工程新闻记录》
price deflator　价格紧缩指数
Utilities Buildings　公用事业建筑

inflation　通货膨胀
GDP　国内生产总值
consumer price index　消费价格指数
Gross National Product　国民生产总值
building index　建筑指数
construction costs　建设成本

Notes

[1]　best-known 意为"最有名的，众所周知的"。the U. S. Department of Commerce 意为"美国商务部"。and U. S. Department of Labor 意为"美国劳工部"。

[2]　Building Material Price and Building Trades Union Wages 意为"建筑材料价格和建筑工会工资"。

[3]　全句可译为：因为，美国不同地区以及世界各地的建设成本不同，所以，反映具体地区相对于全美国趋势的建设成本对于成本估算是很有用的。

Exercise

Translate the text of lesson 5.4 into Chinese.

Chapter 6 Economic Evaluation of Facility Investments

6.1 Basic Concepts of Economic Evaluation

A systematic approach for economic evaluation of facilities consists of the following major steps:
1. Generate a set of projects or purchases for investment consideration.
2. Establish the planning horizon for economic analysis.
3. Estimate the cash flow profile for each project.
4. Specify the minimum attractive rate of return (MARR).
5. Establish the criterion for accepting or rejecting a proposal, or for selecting the best among a group of mutually exclusive proposals, on the basis of the objective of the investment.
6. Perform sensitivity or uncertainty analysis.
7. Accept or reject a proposal on the basis of the established criterion.

It is important to emphasize that many assumptions and policies, some implicit and some explicit, are introduced in economic evaluation by the decision maker. The decision making process will be influenced by the subjective judgment of the management as much as by the result of systematic analysis[1].

The period of time to which the management of a firm or agency wishes to look ahead is referred to as the *planning horizon*[2]. Since the future is uncertain, the period of time selected is limited by the ability to forecast with some degree of accuracy. For capital investment, the selection of the planning horizon is often influenced by the useful life of facilities, since the disposal of usable assets, once acquired, generally involves suffering financial losses[3].

In economic evaluations, project alternatives are represented by their cash flow profiles over the n years or periods in the planning horizon. Thus, the interest periods are normally assumed to be in years ($t = 0, 1, 2, \cdots, n$), $t = 0$ representing the present time. Let $B_{t,x}$ be the annual benefit at the end of year t for a investment project x where $x = 1, 2, \cdots$ refer to projects No.1, No.2, etc., respectively. Let $C_{t,x}$ be the annual cost at the end of year t

for the same investment project x. The net annual cash flow is defined as the annual benefit in excess of the annual cost, and is denoted by $A_{t,x}$ at the end of year t for an investment project x[4]. Then, for $t = 0,1,\cdots,n$:

$$A_{t,x} = B_{t,x} - C_{t,x} \tag{6.1}$$

where $A_{t,x}$ is positive, negative or zero depends on the values of $B_{t,x}$ and $C_{t,x}$, both of which are defined as positive quantities.

Once the management has committed funds to a specific project, it must forego other investment opportunities which might have been undertaken by using the same funds[5]. The *opportunity cost* reflects the return that can be earned from the best alternative investment opportunity foregone. The foregone opportunities may include not only capital projects but also financial investments or other socially desirable programs. Management should invest in a proposed project only if it will yield a return at least equal to the minimum attractive rate of return (MARR) from foregone opportunities as envisioned by the organization.

In general, the MARR specified by the top management in a private firm reflects the *opportunity cost of capital* of the firm, the market interest rates for lending and borrowing, and the risks associated with investment opportunities[6]. For public projects, the MARR is specified by a government agency, such as the Office of Management and Budget or the Congress of the United States. The public MARR thus specified reflects social and economic welfare considerations, and is referred to as the *social rate of discount*.

Regardless of how the MARR is determined by an organization, the MARR specified for the economic evaluation of investment proposals is critically important in determining whether any investment proposal is worthwhile from the standpoint of the organization[7]. Since the MARR of an organization often cannot be determined accurately, it is advisable to use several values of the MARR to assess the sensitivity of the potential of the project to variations of the MARR value.

Words

economic evaluation 经济评价	social rate of discount 社会折现率
sensitivity 灵敏度	investment consideration 投资分析
planning horizon 规划周期	decision maker 决策者
project alternative 备择项目	cash flow profile 现金流分布形态
opportunity cost 机会成本	net annual cash flow 年净现金流
financial investment 金融投资	capital project 资本项目
minium attractive rate of return 最低收益率	socially desirable programs 社会公益项目

the Office of Management and Budget 财政部门   government agency 政府部门

Notes

[1] emphasize 意为"强调，注意"。some implicit and some explicit 意为"有些是有意，有些是无意"。全句可译为：必须注意的是：决策者在经济评价中有意或无意地加入了许多假设和方针，而管理者的主观判断对决策过程的影响不亚于系统分析的结果。

[2] The period of time to which…此句是定语从句，整个定语从句作主语。look ahead 意为"预测"。is referred to as 意为"称为……"。

[3] 全句可译为：对资本投资来讲，设施使用寿命影响着规划周期的选择，因为有用资产在取得之后再行处置，一般都会蒙受财务损失。

[4] is denoted by…意为"用……表示"。全句可译为：投资项目 x 在 t 年末的年净现金流就是年收益减年费用得到，用 $A_{t,x}$ 表示。

[5] forego 意为"放弃"。全句可译为：管理者一旦将资金投入一个具体项目，他就必须放弃把这笔资金投入其中的其他投资机会，这就是机会成本。

[6] private firm 意为"私营企业"。全句可译为：一般来讲，由私营企业的最高管理人员指定的 MARR 值反映了这个公司资本的机会成本和市场的借贷利息，以及投资机会带有的风险。

[7] Regardless of 意为"不管，无论"。from the standpoint of…意为"从……角度看"。全句可译为：不管组织如何确定 MARR 值，从企业的角度来看，为投资建议经济评价指定的 MARR，在判断任何一个投资建议是否值得时，是极端重要的。

6.2 Investment Profit Measures

A *profit measure* is defined as an indicator of the desirability of a project from the standpoint of a decision maker. A profit measure may or may not be used as the basis for project selection. Since various profit measures are used by decision makers for different purposes, the advantages and restrictions for using these profit measures should be fully understood.

There are several profit measures that are commonly used by decision makers in both private corporations and public agencies. Each of these measures is intended to be an indicator of profit or net benefit for a project under consideration. Some of these measures indicate the size of the profit at a specific point in time; others give the rate of return per period when the capital is in use or when reinvestments of the early profits are also included[1]. If a decision maker understands clearly the meaning of the various profit measures for a given project, there is no reason why one cannot use all of them for the restrictive purposes for which they are appropriate. With the availability of computer based analysis and commercial software, it takes only a few seconds to compute these profit measures. However, it is important to define these measures precisely:

1. **Net Future Value and Net Present Value.** When an organization makes an investment, the decision maker looks forward to the gain over a planning horizon, against what might be gained if the money were invested elsewhere. A minimum attractive rate of return (MARR) is adopted to reflect this opportunity cost of capital. The MARR is used for compounding the estimated cash flows to the end of the planning horizon, or for discounting the cash flow to the present. The profitability is measured by the net future value (NFV) which is the net return at the end of the planning horizon above what might have been gained by investing elsewhere at the MARR[2]. The net present value (NPV) of the estimated cash flows over the planning horizon is the discounted value of the NFV to the present. A positive NPV for a project indicates the present value of the net gain corresponding to the project cash flows.

2. **Equivalent Uniform Annual Net Value.** The equivalent uniform annual net value (NUV) is a constant stream of benefits less costs at equally spaced time periods over the intended planning horizon of a project. This value can be calculated as the net present value multiplied by an appropriate "capital recovery factor." It is a measure of the net return of a project on an annualized or amortized basis. The equivalent uniform annual cost (EUAC) can be obtained by multiplying the present value of costs by an appropriate capital recovery factor[3]. The use of EUAC alone presupposes that the discounted benefits of all potential projects over the planning horizon are identical and therefore only the discounted costs of various projects need be considered. Therefore, the EUAC is an indicator of the negative attribute of a project which should be minimized.

3. **Benefit Cost Ratio.** The benefit-cost ratio (BCR), defined as the ratio of discounted benefits to the discounted costs at the same point in time, is a profitability index based on discounted benefits per unit of discounted costs of a project. It is sometimes referred to as the savings-to-investment ratio (SIR) when the benefits are derived from the reduction of undesirable effects. Its use also requires the choice of a planning horizon and a MARR. Since some savings may be interpreted as a negative cost to be deducted from the denominator or as a positive benefit to be added to the numerator of the ratio, the BCR or SIR is not an absolute numerical measure[4]. However, if the ratio of the present value of benefit to the present value of cost exceeds one, the project is profitable irrespective of different interpretations of such benefits or costs.

4. **Internal Rate of Return.** The internal rate of return (IRR) is defined as the discount rate which sets the net present value of a series of cash flows over the planning horizon equal to zero. It is used as a profit measure since it has been identified as the "marginal efficiency of capital" or the "rate of return over cost"[5]. The IRR gives the return of an investment

when the capital is in use as if the investment consists of a single outlay at the beginning and generates a stream of net benefits afterwards. However, the IRR does not take into consideration the reinvestment opportunities related to the timing and intensity of the outlays and returns at the intermediate points over the planning horizon[6]. For cash flows with two or more sign reversals of the cash flows in any period, there may exist multiple values of IRR; in such cases, the multiple values are subject to various interpretations.

5. Adjusted Internal Rate of Return. If the financing and reinvestment policies are incorporated into the evaluation of a project, an adjusted internal rate of return (AIRR) which reflects such policies may be a useful indicator of profitability under restricted circumstances. Because of the complexity of financing and reinvestment policies used by an organization over the life of a project, the AIRR seldom can reflect the reality of actual cash flows. However, it offers an approximate value of the yield on an investment for which two or more sign reversals in the cash flows would result in multiple values of IRR. The adjusted internal rate of return is usually calculated as the internal rate of return on the project cash flow modified so that all costs are discounted to the present and all benefits are compounded to the end of the planning horizon[7].

6. Return on Investment. When an accountant reports income in each year of a multi-year project, the stream of cash flows must be broken up into annual rates of return for those years. The return on investment (ROI) as used by accountants usually means the accountant's rate of return for each year of the project duration based on the ratio of the income (revenue less depreciation) for each year and the undercoated asset value (investment) for that same year[8]. Hence, the ROI is different from year to year, with a very low value at the early years and a high value in the later years of the project.

7. Payback Period. The payback period (PBP) refers to the length of time within which the benefits received from an investment can repay the costs incurred during the time in question while ignoring the remaining time periods in the planning horizon[9]. Even the discounted payback period indicating the "capital recovery period" does not reflect the magnitude or direction of the cash flows in the remaining periods. However, if a project is found to be profitable by other measures, the payback period can be used as a secondary measure of the financing requirements for a project.

Words

profit measure 盈利能力测度	desirability 吸引力
private corporations 私人公司	public agencies 公共机构
net benefit 净收益	negative （数或值）负数的
Net Present Value 净现值	Net Future Value 净终值

profitability　赢利能力
capital recovery factor　资本回收系数
savings-to-investment ratio　存款投资比率
Return on Investment　投资回收率

Annual Net Value　净年值
Benefit Cost Ratio　成本收益率
Internal Rate of Return　内部收益率
Payback Period　投资回收期

Notes

[1]　at a specific point in time 意为"具体时点"。the rate of return 意为"收益率"。全句可译为：某些测度表示某具体时点的利润是多少，而另外一些则是某时间段内投入资本或追加投资的收益率。

[2]　is measured by… 意为"用……表示"。net return 意为"净收益"。全句可译为：一个项目的赢利能力用净终值 NFV 衡量，即，若按照该 MARR 将资金投入别处而在规划周期结束时本来可以得到的净收益。

[3]　The equivalent uniform annual cost (EUAC) 意为"等值年费用"。全句可译为：等值年费用 EUAC 也可以用费用的现去乘上一个资本回收系数求得。

[4]　be interpreted as… 意为"被解释为……"。the denominator 意为"分母"。the numerator 意为"分子"。全句可译为：因为有时将一些节省当作费用的一种节约而从分母中减掉或者当作一种收益加在分子之中，所以 BCR 和 SIR 不是一种绝对的数值。

[5]　been identified as… 意为"被看作为……"。marginal efficiency of capital 意为"资本的边际收益率"。rate of return over cost 意为"成本回收率"。

[6]　take into consideration 意为"考虑"。全句译为"然而，内部收益率不考虑追加投资的时机和规划周期内各中间时点的开销和收益的大小"。

[7]　are discounted to… 意为"折现……"。are compounded to… 意为"按复利折算……"。planning horizon 意为"规划周期"。全句可译为：一般是为经过调整的项目现金流计算内部收益率，办法是计算所有费用的现值，所有的收益率都计算为规划周期末的终值，这样计算出来的内部收益率就是经过调整的内部收益率。

[8]　revenue less depreciation 意为"扣除折旧的年收入"。全句可译为：会计师使用的投资收益率 RO 一般是项目生命周期内各年的会计收益率，是根据每一年的利润率（扣除折旧的年收入）和未贬值资产价值得到的。

[9]　全句可译为：投资回收期指从投资中获得的收益可以偿还因此付出的费用需要经历的时间，不考虑规划周期内剩余的时间。

6.3　Methods of Economic Evaluation

The objective of facility investment in the private sector is generally understood to be profit maximization within a specific time frame. Similarly, the objective in the public sector is the maximization of net social benefit which is analogous to profit maximization in private organizations. Given this objective, a method of economic analysis will be judged by the reliability and ease with which a correct conclusion may be reached in project selection[1].

The basic principle underlying the decision for accepting and selecting investment projects is that if an organization can lend or borrow as much money as it wishes at the MARR, the goal of profit maximization is best served by accepting all independent projects whose net present values based on the specified MARR are nonnegative, or by selecting the project with the maximum nonnegative net present value among a set of mutually exclusive proposals[2]. The net present value criterion reflects this principle and is most straightforward and unambiguous when there is no budget constraint. Various methods of economic evaluation, when properly applied, will produce the same result if the net present value criterion is used as the basis for decision. For convenience of computation, a set of tables for the various compound interest factors is given in Appendix A.

Net Present Value Method

Let BPV_x be the present value of benefits of a project x and CPV_x be the present value of costs of the project x. Then, for MARR $= i$ over a planning horizon of n years,

$$BVP_x = \sum_{t=0}^{n} B_{t,x}(1+i)^{-t} = \sum_{t=0}^{n} B_{t,x}(P \mid F, i, t) \qquad (6.2)$$

$$CPV_x = \sum_{t=0}^{n} C_{t,x}(1+i)^{-t} = \sum_{t=0}^{n} C_{t,x}(P \mid F, i, t) \qquad (6.3)$$

where the symbol $(P \mid F, i, t)$ is a discount factor equal to $(1+i)^{-t}$ and reads as follows: "To find the present value P, given the future value $F = 1$, discounted at an annual discount rate i over a period of t years." When the benefit or cost in year t is multiplied by this factor, the present value is obtained. Then, the net present value of the project x is calculated as:

$$NPV_x = BPV_x - CPV_x \qquad (6.4)$$

or

$$NPV_x = \sum_{t=0}^{n}(B_{t,x} - C_{t,x})(P \mid F, i, t) = \sum_{t=0}^{n} A_{t,x}(P \mid F, i, t) \qquad (6.5)$$

If there is no budget constraitnt, then all independent projects having net present values greater than or equal to zero are acceptable. That is, project x is acceptable as long as

$$NPV_x \geqslant 0 \qquad (6.6)$$

For mutually exclusive proposals ($x = 1, 2, \cdots, m$), a proposal j should be selected if it has the maximum nonnegative net present value among all m proposals, i.e.

$$NPV_j = \max_{x \in m} \{NPV_x\} \qquad (6.7)$$

provided that $NPV_j \geqslant 0$.

Net Future Value Method

Since the cash flow profile of an investment can be represented by its equivalent value at any specified reference point in time, the net future value (NFV_x) of a series of cash flows $A_{t,x}$ (for $t = 0, 1, 2, \cdots, n$) for project x is as good a measure of economic potential as the net present value[3]. Equivalent future values are obtained by multiplying a present value by the compound interest factor $(F|P, i, n)$ which is $(1+i)^n$. Specifically,

$$NFV_x = NPV_x(1+i)^n = NPV_x(F \mid P, i, n) \qquad (6.8)$$

Consequently, if $NPV_x \geqslant 0$, it follows that $NFV_x \geqslant 0$, and vice versa.

Net Equivalent Uniform Annual Value Method

The net equivalent uniform annual value (NUV_x) refers to a uniform series over a planning horizon of n years whose net present value is that of a series of cash flow $A_{t,x}$ (for $t = 1, 2, \cdots, n$) representing project x. That is,

$$NUV_x = NPV_x \frac{i(1+i)^n}{(1+i)^n - 1} = NPV_x(U \mid P, i, n) \qquad (6.9)$$

where the symbol $(U|P, i, n)$ is referred to as the *capital recovery factor* and reads as follows: "To find the equivalent annual uniform amount U, given the present value $P = 1$, discounted at an annual discount rate i over a period of t years." Hence, if $NPV_x \geqslant 0$, it follows that $NUV_x \geqslant 0$, and vice versa.

Benefit-Cost Ratio Method

The benefit-cost ratio method is not as straightforward and unambiguous as the net present value method but, if applied correctly, will produce the same results as the net present value method[4]. While this method is often used in the evaluation of public projects, the results may be misleading if proper care is not exercised in its application to mutually exclusive proposals.

The *benefit-cost ratio* is defined as the ratio of the discounted benefits to the discounted cost at the same point in time. In view of Eq. 6.4 and Eq. 6.6, it follows that the criterion for accepting an *independent* project on the basis of the benefit-cost ratio is whether or not the benefit-cost ratio is greater than or equal to one:

$$\frac{BPV_x}{CPV_x} \geqslant 1 \qquad (6.10)$$

However, a project with the maximum benefit-cost ratio among a group of *mutually exclusive* proposals generally does not necessarily lead to the maximum net benefit. Consequently, it is necessary to perform incremental analysis through pairwise comparisons of such proposals in selecting the best in the group. In effect, pairwise comparisons are used to determine if incremental increases in costs between projects yields larger incremental increases in benefits. This approach is not recommended for use in selecting the best among mutually exclusive proposals.

Internal Rate of Return Method

The term *internal rate of return method* has been used by different analysts to mean somewhat different procedures for economic evaluation. The method is often misunderstood and misused, and its popularity among analysts in the private sector is undeserved even when the method is defined and interpreted in the most favorable light[5]. The method is usually applied by comparing the MARR to the internal rate of return value(s) for a project or a set of projects.

A major difficulty in applying the internal rate of return method to economic evaluation is the possible existence of multiple values of IRR when there are two or more changes of sign in the cash flow profile $A_{t,x}$ (for $t = 0, 1, 2, \cdots, n$)[6]. When that happens, the method is generally not applicable either in determining the acceptance of independent projects or for selection of the best among a group of mutually exclusive proposals unless a set of well defined decision rules are introduced for incremental analysis. In any case, no advantage is gained by using this method since the procedure is cumbersome even if the method is correctly applied. This method is not recommended for use either in accepting independent projects or in selecting the best among mutually exclusive proposals.

Words

profit maximization 利润最大化
exclusive proposals 互斥方案
Net Future Value Method 净终值法
Net Equivalent Uniform Annual Value Method 净等额年值法
Internal Rate of Return Method 内部收益率法
cash flow profile 现金流量图
incremental analysis 增量分析
Economic Evaluation 经济评价
Net Present Value Method 净现值法
Benefit-Cost Ratio Method 成本收益比率法
cumbersome 复杂的, 累赘的

Notes

[1] 全句可译为：在这样的投资目标下，一种项目的经济评价方法的好坏就取决于它是否能够正确可靠地估计出这个项目前景。

[2] 全句可译为：接受或选定投资项目的基本决策原则是，在组织能够以相当于 MARR 的利率借入足够资金时，对于独立项目，只要按照上述 MARR 计算出来的净现值大于等于零；而对于互斥项目，选择其中非负净现值最大者。这样做就可以实现取得最大利润的目标。

[3] be represented by…意为"用……表示"。at any specified reference point in time 意为"任意指定的参考时点"。

[4] straightforward and unambiguous 意为"直接且不含混"。not as … as 意为"不

像……一样"。if applied correctly 为插入语。全句可译为：成本收益比率法虽然没有净现值法那样一目了然，但若用得恰当，可以得到同样结论。

[5] popularity 意为"广泛性"。undeserved 意为"不应得的，不该的"。全句可译为：这个方法往往为人们曲解和误用，在民间部门分析人员中间很是流行，然而，即使往最好处想，这一方法也不应得到如此滥用。

[6] 全句可译为：在使用内部收益比率法时最为困难的地方就是由于现金流量表中存在两次以上的上下变化所造成的会出现多个内部收益率值的这种现象。

6.4 Public versus Private Ownership of Facilities

In recent years, various organizational ownership schemes have been proposed to raise the level of investment in constructed facilities. For example, independent authorities are assuming responsibility for some water and sewer systems, while private entrepreneurs are taking over the ownership of public buildings such as stadiums and convention centers in joint ventures with local governments[1]. Such ownership arrangements not only can generate the capital for new facilities, but also will influence the management of the construction and operation of these facilities. In this section, we shall review some of these implications.

A particular organizational arrangement or financial scheme is not necessarily superior to all others in each case. Even for similar facilities, these arrangements and schemes may differ from place to place or over time. For example, U.S. water supply systems are owned and operated both by relatively large and small organizations in either the private or public sector. Modern portfolio theory suggest that there may be advantages in using a variety of financial schemes to spread risks. Similarly, small or large organizations may have different relative advantages with respect to personnel training, innovation or other activities.

Differences in Required Rates of Return

A basic difference between public and private ownership of facilities is that private organizations are motivated by the expectation of profits in making capital investments. Consequently, private firms have a higher minimum attractive rate of return (MARR) on investments than do public agencies. The MARR represents the desired return or profit for making capital investments. Furthermore, private firms often must pay a higher interest rate for borrowing than public agencies because of the tax exempt or otherwise subsidized bonds available to public agencies. International loans also offer subsidized interest rates to qualified agencies or projects in many cases. With higher required rates of return, we expect that private firms will require greater receipts than would a public agency to make a particular investment desirable[2].

In addition to different minimum attractive rates of return, there is also an important distinction between public and private organizations with respect to their evaluation of investment benefits. For private firms, the returns and benefits to cover costs and provide profit are *monetary revenues*. In contrast, public agencies often consider *total* social benefits in evaluating projects. Total social benefits include monetary user payments plus users' surplus (e.g., the value received less costs incurred by users), external benefits (e.g., benefits to local businesses or property owners) and no quantifiable factors (e.g., psychological support, unemployment relief, etc.). Generally, total social benefits will exceed monetary revenues.

While these different valuations of benefits may lead to radically different results with respect to the extent of benefits associated with an investment, they do not necessarily require public agencies to undertake such investments directly[3]. First, many public enterprises must fund their investments and operating expenses from user fees. Most public utilities fall into this category, and the importance of user fee financing is increasing for many civil works such as waterways. With user fee financing, the required returns for the public and private firms to undertake the aforementioned investment are, in fact, limited to monetary revenues. As a second point, it is always possible for a public agency to contract with a private firm to undertake a particular project.

All other things being equal, we expect that private firms will require larger returns from a particular investment than would a public agency. From the users or taxpayers point of view, this implies that total payments would be *higher* to private firms for identical services[4]. However, there are a number of mitigating factors to counterbalance this disadvantage for private firms.

Tax Implications of Public Versus Private Organizations

Another difference between public and private facility owners is in their relative liability for taxes. Public entities are often exempt from taxes of various kinds, whereas private facility owners incur a variety of income, property and excise taxes[5]. However, these private tax liabilities can be offset, at least in part, by tax deductions of various kinds.

For private firms, income taxes represent a significant cost of operation. However, taxable income is based on the gross revenues less all expenses and allowable deductions as permitted by the prevalent tax laws and regulations. The most significant allowable deductions are depreciation and interest. By selecting the method of depreciation and the financing plan which are most favorable, a firm can exert a certain degree of control on its taxable income and, thus, its income tax.

Another form of relief in tax liability is the *tax credit* which allows a direct deduction for income tax purposes of a small percentage of the value of certain newly acquired assets[6]. Although the provisions for investment tax credit for physical facilities and equipment had been introduced at different times in the US federal tax code, they were eliminated in the 1986 Tax Reformation Act except a tax credit for low-income housing.

Effects of Financing Plans

Major investments in constructed facilities typically rely upon borrowed funds for a large portion of the required capital investments. For private organizations, these borrowed funds can be useful for leverage to achieve a higher return on the organizations' own capital investment.

For public organizations, borrowing costs which are larger than the MARR results in increased "cost" and higher required receipts. Incurring these costs may be essential if the investment funds are not otherwise available: capital funds must come from somewhere. But it is not unusual for the borrowing rate to exceed the MARR for public organizations. In this case, reducing the amount of borrowing lowers costs, whereas increasing borrowing lowers costs whenever the MARR is greater than the borrowing rate.

Effects of Capital Grant Subsidies

An important element in public investments is the availability of capital grant subsidies from higher levels of government. For example, interstate highway construction is eligible for federal capital grants for up to 90% of the cost. Other programs have different matching amounts, with 50/50 matching grants currently available for wastewater treatment plants and various categories of traffic systems improvement in the U.S.

Implications for Design and Construction

Different perspectives and financial considerations also may have implications for design and construction choices[7]. For example, an important class of design decisions arises relative to the trade-off between capital and operating costs. It is often the case that initial investment or construction costs can be reduced, but at the expense of a higher operating costs or more frequent and extensive rehabilitation or repair expenditures. It is this trade-off which has led to the consideration of "life cycle costs" of alternative designs. The financial schemes reviewed earlier can profoundly effect such evaluations.

For financial reasons, it would often be advantageous for a public body to select a more capital intensive alternative which would receive a larger capital subsidy and, thereby, reduce the project's local costs[8]. In effect, the capital grant subsidy would distort the trade-off between capital and operating costs in favor of more capital intensive projects.

The various tax and financing considerations will also affect the relative merits of relatively capital intensive projects. For example, as the borrowing rate increases, more capital intensive alternatives become less attractive. Tax provisions such as the investment tax credit or accelerated depreciation are intended to stimulate investment and thereby make more capital intensive projects relatively more desirable[9]. In contrast, a higher minimum attractive rate of return tends to make more capital intensive projects less attractive.

Words

constructed facilities　建成设施
joint ventures　联营体
public agencies　公共机构
subsidized bonds　补贴债券
user fee financing　用户融资
tax deductions　税款抵减额
life cycle costs　全寿命期成本
sewer systems　污水排放系统
modern portfolio theory　现代投资组合理论
tax exempt　免税
monetary revenues　货币收入
tax credit　税款减除额
tax shields　避税

Notes

[1] independent authorities 意为"独立的权利机构"。private entrepreneurs 意为"私人企业家"。taking over 意为"接管"。stadiums and convention centers 意为"体育场和会馆"。

[2] 全句可译为：如果要求提高收益率，我们会想到，私人公司对于具体投资收益的要求自然要比公共机构高。

[3] lead to 意为"导致"。associated with…意为"与……有关"。全句可译为：对于投资收益的范围和数量，这些不同的效益评价结果虽然会得出截然不同的结论，但这些评价结果不一定要求公共机构直接承担这类投资活动。

[4] From…point of view 意为"从……观点"。identical services 在这里指"同样的服务"。

[5] Public entities 意为"公共机构"。exempt from 是"免除"的意思。全句可译为：公共机构经常可以免交各种税，但是民间设施所有者却需要缴纳各种收入、财产和消费税。

[6] 全句可译为：纳税责任另一种减免是税款免除额，就收入税而言，允许按某些新购置资产价值直接扣减一个不大的百分比数额。

[7] perspectives 意为"视角，角度"。financial considerations 意为"财务计划"。have implications for…指"对……有影响"。

[8] it would often be advantageous for…意为"将更有利于……"。capital intensive 意为"资本密集型"。alternative which…为定语从句。

[9] the investment tax credit or accelerated depreciation 意为"投资税抵减或加速折旧"。are intended to 意为"打算，将要"。全句可译为：纳税条款（如投资税抵减或加速折旧）的用意是鼓励投资，进而使资本密集项目更具有吸引力。

Exercise

Translate the text of lesson 6.4 into Chinese.

Chapter 7   Financing of Constructed Facilities

7.1   The Financing Problem

Investment in a constructed facility represents a cost in the short term that returns benefits only over the long term use of the facility. Thus, costs occur earlier than the benefits, and owners of facilities must obtain the capital resources to finance the costs of construction[1]. A project cannot proceed without adequate financing, and the cost of providing adequate financing can be quite large. For these reasons, attention to project finance is an important aspect of project management. Finance is also a concern to the other organizations involved in a project such as the general contractor and material suppliers. Unless an owner immediately and completely covers the costs incurred by each participant, these organizations face financing problems of their own.

At a more general level, project finance is only one aspect of the general problem of corporate finance. If numerous projects are considered and financed together, then the net cash flow requirements constitutes the corporate financing problem for capital investment[2]. Whether project finance is performed at the project or at the corporate level does not alter the basic financing problem[3].

In essence, the project finance problem is to obtain funds to bridge the time between making expenditures and obtaining revenues. Based on the conceptual plan, the cost estimate and the construction plan, the cash flow of costs and receipts for a project can be estimated. Normally, this cash flow will involve expenditures in early periods. Covering this negative cash balance in the most beneficial or cost effective fashion is the project finance problem[4]. During planning and design, expenditures of the owner are modest, whereas substantial costs are incurred during construction. Only after the facility is complete do revenues begin. In contrast, a contractor would receive periodic payments from the owner as construction proceeds. However, a contractor also may have a negative cash balance due to delays in payment and *retainage* of profits or cost reimbursements on the part of the owner[5].

Plans considered by owners for facility financing typically have both long and short term aspects. In the long term, sources of revenue include sales, grants, and tax revenues. Borrowed funds must be eventually paid back from these other sources. In the short term, a wider variety of financing options exist, including borrowing, grants, corporate investment funds, payment delays and others[6]. Many of these financing options involve the participation of third parties such as banks or bond underwriters. For private facilities such as office buildings, it is customary to have completely different financing arrangements during the construction period and during the period of facility use[7]. During the latter period, mortgage or loan funds can be secured by the value of the facility itself. Thus, different arrangements of financing options and participants are possible at different stages of a project, so the practice of financial planning is often complicated[8].

On the other hand, the options for borrowing by contractors to bridge their expenditures and receipts during construction are relatively limited. For small or medium size projects, overdrafts from bank accounts are the most common form of construction financing. Usually, a maximum limit is imposed on an overdraft account by the bank on the basis of expected expenditures and receipts for the duration of construction[9]. Contractors who are engaged in large projects often own substantial assets and can make use of other forms of financing which have lower interest charges than overdrafting.

In recent years, there has been growing interest in design-build-operate projects in which owners prescribe functional requirements and a contractor handles financing[10]. Contractors are repaid over a period of time from project revenues or government payments. Eventually, ownership of the facilities is transferred to a government entity. An example of this type of project is the Confederation Bridge to Prince Edward Island in Canada.

In this chapter, we will first consider facility financing from the owner's perspective, with due consideration for its interaction with other organizations involved in a project[11]. Later, we discuss the problems of construction financing which are crucial to the profitability and solvency of construction contractors.

Words

aspect   方面
constitute   构成,组成
financing   融资
net cash flow   净现金流量
expenditure   支出
payment   支付
account   账户
financing options   融资方式
mortgage   抵押

incur   导致
corporate   企业的
project finance   项目融资
revenues   收入
negative cash balance   负现金结余
reimbursement   偿还
receipt   收据
bond underwriter   债券认购者
overdraft   透支

bank account 银行账号
transfer 移交
solvency 清偿

interest charge 收取利息,费用
entity 实体,单位

Notes

[1] to finance…为动词不定式短语作目的状语,译为"满足建设成本的资金要求"。

[2] the net cash flow 是指"净现金流量"。全句可译为:如果同时考虑多个项目并为之筹集资金,那么净现金流量反映的资金要求问题就构成了资本投资中的公司融资问题。

[3] at the corporate level 意为"在公司层面"。全句可译为:不管是在项目层面还是在公司层面,项目融资所面临的最基本的资金问题都是相同的。

[4] negative cash balance 意为"负现金结余"。全句可译为:如何以最有利或最有效的开支方式来平衡负现金结余就是项目融资问题。

[5] cost reimbursement 是指"成本补偿"。全句可译为:然而,承包商也可能会遇到现金负结余的问题,主要原因是业主的延期支付、考虑适当的利润及业主方可能的索赔要求。

[6] financing options 意为"融资方式"。全句可译为:短期融资有多种方式,包括借贷、拨款、公司投资基金以及延期支付等。

[7] 全句可译为:对于私营项目(和写字楼)来说,建设阶段和使用阶段的融资安排迥然不同乃是司空见惯的做法。

[8] 全句可译为:这样一来,在项目的不同阶段就可能有不同的融资方案和参与者,所以融资规划实际做起来常常很复杂。

[9] overdraft account 指"透支账户"。expected expenditures 意为"预期支出"。全句可译为:通常,银行会以建设期间的收支为依据,为透支账户设一个限额。

[10] design-build-operate projects 是指"设计——建造——运营项目"。in which…为定语从句,修饰前面的 design-build-operate projects。全句可译为:近几年,设计——建造——运营项目的运用越来越多,在这种项目类型当中,业主提出功能需求,而承包商进行融资操作。

[11] 全句可译为:在这一章,我们会首先从业主的角度来研究项目融资问题,并充分考虑项目融资与项目中其他参与方之间的相互影响。

7.2 Institutional Arrangements for Facility Financing

Financing arrangements differ sharply by type of owner and by the type of facility construction. As one example, many municipal projects are financed in the United States with *tax exempt bonds* for which interest payments to a lender are exempt from income taxes[1]. As a result, tax exempt municipal bonds are available at lower interest charges. Different institutional arrangements have evolved for specific types of facilities and organizations.

A private corporation which plans to undertake large capital projects may use its retained earnings, seek equity partners in the project, issue bonds, offer new stocks in the financial markets, or seek borrowed funds in another fashion[2]. Potential sources of funds would include pension funds, insurance companies, investment trusts, commercial banks and others. Developers who invest in real estate properties for rental purposes have similar sources, plus quasi-governmental corporations such as urban development authorities[3]. Syndicators for investment such as real estate investment trusts (REITs) as well as domestic and foreign pension funds represent relatively new entries to the financial market for building mortgage money[4].

Public projects may be funded by tax receipts, general revenue bonds, or special bonds with income dedicated to the specified facilities. General revenue bonds would be repaid from general taxes or other revenue sources, while special bonds would be redeemed either by special taxes or user fees collected for the project[5]. Grants from higher levels of government are also an important source of funds for state, county, city or other local agencies.

Despite the different sources of borrowed funds, there is a rough equivalence in the actual cost of borrowing money for particular types of projects[6]. Because lenders can participate in many different financial markets, they tend to switch towards loans that return the highest yield for a particular level of risk. As a result, borrowed funds that can be obtained from different sources tend to have very similar costs, including interest charges and issuing costs.

As a general principle, however, the costs of funds for construction will vary inversely with the risk of a loan[7]. Lenders usually require security for a loan represented by a tangible asset[8]. If for some reason the borrower cannot repay a loan, then the "lender" can take possession of the loan security. To the extent that an asset used as security is of uncertain value, then the lender will demand a greater return and higher interest payments. Loans made for projects under construction represent considerable risk to a financial institution. If a lender acquires an unfinished facility, then it faces the difficult task of re-assembling the project team. Moreover, a default on a facility may result if a problem occurs such as foundation problems or anticipated unprofitability of the future facility. As a result of these uncertainties, construction lending for unfinished facilities commands a premium interest charge of several percent compared to mortgage lending for completed facilities[9].

Financing plans will typically include a reserve amount to cover unforeseen expenses, cost increases or cash flow problems. This reserve can be represented by a special reserve or a contingency amount in the project budget. In the simplest case, this reserve might represent a borrowing agreement with a financial institution to establish a *line of credit* in case of need. For publicly traded bonds, specific reserve funds administered by a third party may be established. The cost of these reserve funds is the difference between the interest paid to bondholders and the interest received on the reserve funds plus any administrative costs[10].

Finally, arranging financing may involve a lengthy period of negotiation and review. Particularly for publicly traded bond financing, specific legal requirements in the issue must be met. A typical seven month schedule to issue revenue bonds would include the various steps outlined in Table 7-1. In many cases, the speed in which funds may be obtained will determine a project's financing mechanism.

Table 7-1 Illustrative Process and Timing for Issuing Revenue Bonds

Activities	Time of Activities
Analysis of financial alternatives	Weeks 0~4
Preparation of legal documents	Weeks 1~17
Preparation of disclosure documents	Weeks 2~20
Forecasts of costs and revenues	Weeks 4~20
Bond Ratings	Weeks 20~23
Bond Marketing	Weeks 21~24
Bond Closing and Receipt of Funds	Weeks 23~26

Example 7-1: Example of financing options
Suppose that you represent a private corporation attempting to arrange financing for a new headquarters building. These are several options that might be considered:

- Use corporate equity and retained earnings: The building could be financed by directly committing corporate resources. In this case, no other institutional parties would be involved in the finance. However, these corporate funds might be too limited to support the full cost of construction.
- Construction loan and long term mortgage: In this plan, a loan is obtained from a bank or other financial institution to finance the cost of construction. Once the building is complete, a variety of institutions may be approached to supply mortgage or long term funding for the building[11]. This financing plan would involve both short and long term borrowing, and the two periods might involve different lenders. The long term funding would have greater security since the building would then be complete. As a result, more organizations might be interested in providing funds (including pension funds) and the interest charge might be lower. Also, this basic financing plan might be supplemented by other sources such as corporate retained earnings or assistance from a local development agency[12].
- Lease the building from a third party: In this option, the corporation would

contract to lease space in a headquarters building from a developer. This developer would be responsible for obtaining funding and arranging construction. This plan has the advantage of minimizing the amount of funds borrowed by the corporation. Under terms of the lease contract, the corporation still might have considerable influence over the design of the headquarters building even though the developer was responsible for design and construction[13].

- Initiate a Joint Venture with Local Government: In many areas, local governments will help local companies with major new ventures such as a new headquarters. This help might include assistance in assembling property, low interest loans or proerty tax reductions. In the extreme, local governments may force sale of land through their power of *eminent domain* to assemble necessary plots.

Words

financing arrangement 融资安排	low interest loan 低息贷款
tax exempt bond 免税债券	eminent 知名的,著名的
retained earning 留存收益,保留盈余	municipal project 市政项目
equity 公平,公正	private corporation 民营公司
developer 开发商	stock 股票
quasi-governmental corporation 国营公司	insurance 保险
syndicator 联合体,辛迪加	real estate 房地产
real estate investment trusts(REITs) 房地产信托(基金)	mortgage 抵押
	security 有价证券
pension 养老基金	redeem 赎回
equivalence (时间、数量)相等	tangible asset 有形资产
public project 公共项目	default 违约,未履约
financial market 金融市场	reserve 准备金,后备金
loan security 贷款担保	bondholder 债券持有人
unforeseen expense 不可预见费用	joint venture 合资公司,联营体
contingency 突发事件,不可预见事件	supplement 追加,补遗
corporate equity 公司权益	

Notes

[1] municipal projects 指"市政项目"。tax exempt bonds 指"免税债券"。for which…为定语从句,修饰前面的 tax exempt bonds。全句可译为:作为一个例子,在美国,许多市政工程都通过免税债券的方式进行融资,即提供贷款的人所获得的收入是不用交纳所得税的。

[2] issue bonds 指"发行债券"。全可译为:计划大型资本项目的民营公司可以使用自

[3] 　　有的保留盈余，寻求为项目提供权益资金的合作伙伴，在金融市场上发行债券，增派新股，或以其他形式借入资金。

[3]　　real estate properties 指"房地产"。全句可译为：开发商投资房地产用于出租时，资金有相似的来源，类似的情况还出现在国营公司，比如城市开发部门。

[4]　　全句可译为：开发项目时，投资联合组织（如 REITs）以及国内外养老基金代表了一种相对较为新型的建筑市场融资方式。

[5]　　general revenue bonds 指"联邦政府债券"。全句可译为：联邦政府债券可以用联邦收入或其他来源收入赎回，而二种债券可以用专门为项目征收的税款或为用户使用费赎回。

[6]　　a rough equivalence 意为"大体相同"。全句可译为：尽管资金来源不同，但是对于某一具体的项目来说，资金的使用成本是大体相等的。

[7]　　a general principle 意为"一个总的原则"。

[8]　　tangible asset 指"有形资产"。相应地，intangible asset 指"无形资产"。

[9]　　premium interest charge 意为"额外的利息费"。compared to…过去分词短语，修饰 several percent。全句可译为：
这些不确定性导致的结果就是，未完工程的贷款与竣工项目的抵押贷款相比需要支付几个百分点的额外利息费。

[10]　　reserve funds 意为"准备金"。administrative costs 意为"管理费"。全句可译为：准备金的使用费用等于债券持有人应得利息和准备金应收利息之间的差额再加上一些筹资费用。

[11]　　全句可译为：一旦工程竣工，就可以同多种机构接洽使其为工程提供抵押或长期贷款。

[12]　　local development agency 指"当地开发机构"。全句可译为：同样，这种基本的融资计划可以通过其他的渠道来辅助，比如说，公司留存收益或当地开发机构的协助等。

[13]　　under terms of the lease contract 意为"根据租赁合同条款"。全句可译为：根据租赁合同条款，虽然开发商负责了设计和施工，但是公司本来可以对总公司大楼的设计施加更大的影响。

7.3 Project versus Corporate Finance

We have focused so far on problems and concerns at the project level. While this is the appropriate viewpoint for project managers, it is always worth bearing in mind that projects must fit into broader organizational decisions and structures[1]. This is particularly true for the problem of project finance, since it is often the case that financing is planned on a corporate or agency level, rather than a project level[2]. Accordingly, project managers should be aware of the concerns at this level of decision making.

A construction project is only a portion of the general capital budgeting problem faced by an owner. Unless the project is very large in scope relative to the owner, a particular construction project is only a small portion of the capital budgeting problem. Numerous construction projects may be lumped together as a single category in the allocation of investment funds. Construction projects would compete for attention with equipment purchases or other investments in a private corporation.

Financing is usually performed at the corporate level using a mixture of long term corporate debt and retained earnings[3]. A typical set of corporate debt instruments would include the different bonds and notes discussed in this chapter. Variations would typically include different maturity dates, different levels of security interests, different currency denominations, and, of course, different interest rates[4].

Grouping projects together for financing influences the type of financing that might be obtained. As noted earlier, small and large projects usually involve different institutional arrangements and financing arrangements. For small projects, the fixed costs of undertaking particular kinds of financing may be prohibitively expensive. For example, municipal bonds require fixed costs associated with printing and preparation that do not vary significantly with the size of the issue[5]. By combining numerous small construction projects, different financing arrangements become more practical.

While individual projects may not be considered at the corporate finance level, the problems and analysis procedures described earlier are directly relevant to financial planning for groups of projects and other investments[6]. Thus, the net present values of different financing arrangements can be computed and compared. Since the net present values of different subsets of either investments or financing alternatives are additive, each project or finance alternative can be disaggregated for closer attention or aggregated to provide information at a higher decision making level[7].

Example 7-2: Basic types of repayment schedules for loans
Coupon bonds are used to obtain loans which involve no payment of principal until the maturity date[8]. By combining loans of different maturities, however, it is possible to achieve almost any pattern of principal repayments. However, the interest rates charged on loans of different maturities will reflect market forces such as forecasts of how interest rates will vary over time[9]. As an example, Table 7-2 illustrates the cash flows of debt service for a series of coupon bonds used to fund a municipal construction project; for simplicity not all years of payments are shown in the table.

In this financing plan, a series of coupon bonds were sold with maturity dates ranging from June 1988 to June 2012. Coupon interest payments on all outstanding bonds were to be paid every six months, on December 1 and June 1 of each year. The interest rate or "coupon rate" was larger on bonds with longer maturities, reflecting an assumption that inflation would increase during this period[10]. The total principal obtained for construction was $26,250,000 from sale of these bonds. This amount represented the gross sale amount before subtracting issuing costs or any sales discounts; the amount available to support construction would be lower[11]. The maturity dates for bonds were selected to require relative high repayment amounts until December 1995, with a declining repayment amount subsequently. By shifting the maturity dates and amounts of bonds, this pattern of repayments could be altered. The initial interest payment (of $819,760 on December 1, 1987), reflected a payment for only a portion of a six month period since the bonds were issued in late June of 1987.

Table 7-2 Illustration of a Twenty-five Year Maturity Schedule for Bonds

Date	Maturing Principal	Corresponding Interest Rate	Interest Due	Annual Debt Service
Dec. 1, 1987	$1,350,000	5.00(%)	$819,760 894,429	$819,760
Jun. 1, 1988	1,450,000	5.25	860,540 860,540	3,104,969
Dec. 1, 1988	1,550,000	5.50	822,480 822,480	3,133,020
Jun. 1, 1989	1,600,000	5.80	779,850 779,850	3,152,330
Dec. 1, 1989	1,700,000	6.00	733,450 733,450	3,113,300
Jun. 1, 1990	1,800,000	6.20	682,450 682,450	3,115,900
Dec. 1, 1990 Jun. 1, 1991	⋮	⋮	626,650 ⋮	3,109,100 ⋮
Dec. 1, 1991	880,000	8.00	68.000 36,000	984,000
Jun. 1, 1992	96,000	8.00	36,000	996,000
Dec. 1, 1992 Jun. 1, 1993 Dec. 1, 1993 ⋮ Jun. 1, 2011 Dec. 1, 2011 Jun. 1, 2012 Dec. 1, 2012				

Words

portion	比例	allocation	分派,分摊
lump…together	把(两个以上东西)放在一起	purchase	购买
debt	借贷	instruments	有价证券
denomination	(货币等的)单位	assumption	假设,假定
decision making	决策	construction project	施工项目
general capital budgeting	总资本金预算	corporate level	公司层面
issue	发行	net present value	净现值
disaggregate	细分,分解	aggregate	累加
coupon bonds	附息票,公司债券	maturity date	到期日
interest rate	利率	inflation	通货膨胀
gross sale amount	毛销售额	discount	折扣

Notes

[1] it is always…that…是主语从句,可译为"值得我们随时牢记在心的是,项目必须符合更广泛的组织决策和组织结构"。

[2] 全句可译为:这对解决项目的资金问题尤为重要,因为项目的资金计划一般是公司层面或政府层面做出的,而不是项目层面。

[3] long term corporate debt 指"公司长期债"。全句可译为:融资通常是在公司一级将公司长期债与留存权益两者结合起来进行。

[4] 全句可译为:其变化性主要体现在到期日期、风险等级、货币种类以及利率的不同上。

[5] associated with…是过去分词短语作定语,修饰 fixed costs。that do not…是定语从句,修饰 fixed costs,可译为"不会因发行量大小而有太大的变化"。

[6] while…引导的是一个让步状语从句。全句可译为:尽管单个项目的融资不会在公司财务中考虑,但前面介绍的问题和分析方法却同项目或其他投资活动的融资方案规划直接有关。

[7] 全句可译为:因为不同的分项投资或融资方案的净现值是可以相加的,所以每个项目方案既可以被分解开以便细致研究,也可以被累加起来向更高的层面提供决策信息。

[8] 全句可译为:用公司债券借款,在贷款到期日之前借款人不用偿还本金。

[9] charged on…是过去分词短语作定语,修饰 the interest rates。全句可译为:然而,到期日不同的贷款利率是不同的,这将会反映出一段时间内市场利率的变化趋势。

[10] 全句可译为:到期日越长的债券,其利率越高,这是因为在到期日之前的这段时间内通货膨胀率被假定是逐步变高的。

[11] 全句可译为:这个数字没有扣除发行费和所有销售折扣之前的毛收入,实际获得

的资金会比它少一点。

7.4 Shifting Financial Burdens

The different participants in the construction process have quite distinct perspectives on financing. In the realm of project finance, the revenues to one participant represent an expenditure to some other participant. Payment delays from one participant result in a financial burden and a cash flow problem to other participants. It is common occurrence in construction to reduce financing costs by delaying payments in just this fashion[1]. Shifting payment times does not eliminate financing costs, however, since the financial burden still exists.

Traditionally, many organizations have used payment delays both to shift financing expenses to others or to overcome momentary shortfalls in financial resources[2]. From the owner's perspective, this policy may have short term benefits, but it certainly has long term costs. Since contractors do not have large capital assets, they typically do not have large amounts of credit available to cover payment delays. Contractors are also perceived as credit risks in many cases, so loans often require a premium interest charge. Contractors faced with large financing problems are likely to add premiums to bids or not bid at all on particular work. For example, A. Maevis noted:

…there were days in New York City when city agencies had trouble attracting bidders; yet contractors were beating on the door to get work from Consolidated Edison, the local utility. Why? First, the city was a notoriously slow payer, COs (change orders) years behind, decision process chaotic, and payments made 60 days after close of estimate. Con Edison paid on the 20th of the month for work done to the first of the month. Change orders negotiated and paid within 30~60 days. If a decision was needed, it came in 10 days. The number of bids you receive on your projects are one measure of your administrative efficiency. Further, competition is bound to give you the lowest possible construction price.

Even after bids are received and contracts signed, delays in payments may form the basis for a successful claim against an agency on the part of the contractor[3].

The owner of a constructed facility usually has a better credit rating and can secure loans at a lower borrowing rate, but there are some notable exceptions to this rule, particularly for construction projects in developing countries[4]. Under certain circumstances, it is advisable for the owner to advance periodic payments to the contractor in return for some concession in the contract price. This is particularly true for large-scale construction projects with long durations for which financing costs and capital requirements are high. If the owner is willing to advance these amounts to the contractor, the gain in lower financing costs can be shared by both parties through prior agreement.

Unfortunately, the choice of financing during the construction period is often left to the contractor who cannot take advantage of all available options alone. The owner is often shielded from participation through the traditional method of price quotation for construction contracts. This practice merely exacerbates the problem by excluding the owner from participating in decisions which may reduce the cost of the project[5].

Under conditions of economic uncertainty, a premium to hedge the risk must be added to the estimation of construction cost by both the owner and the contractor[6]. The larger and longer the project is, the greater is the risk. For an unsophisticated owner who tries to avoid all risks and to place the financing burdens of construction on the contractor, the contract prices for construction facilities are likely to be increased to reflect the risk premium charged by the contractors[7]. In dealing with small projects with short durations, this practice may be acceptable particularly when the owner lacks any expertise to evaluate the project financing alternatives or the financial stability to adopt innovative financing schemes[8]. However, for large scale projects of long duration, the owner cannot escape the responsibility of participation if it wants to avoid catastrophes of run-away costs and expensive litigation. The construction of nuclear power plants in the private sector and the construction of transportation facilities in the public sector offer ample examples of such problems. If the responsibilities of risk sharing among various parties in a construction project can be clearly defined in the planning stage, all parties can be benefited to take advantage of cost saving and early use of the constructed facility[9].

Words

delay 延误	eliminate 排除
distinct 明显不同的	realm 领域
shift 转移	momentary shortfall 暂时短缺
credit risk 信用风险	bidder 投标人
notoriously 名声狼籍地	COs(change orders) 变更单
premium 奖金,保险费	asset 资产
chaotic 混乱的	concession 让步,妥协
concession 让步	duration 持续时间
exacerbate 变坏,变糟	hedge 防范
unsophisticated 不熟练的	expertise 专业知识

option 选择权 quotation 报价
innovative 创造性的 litigation 诉讼
transportation facility 交通设施

Notes

[1] common occurrence 意为"常见的事"。全句可译为：工程中用这种延期支付的方法来减少财务费用是很常见的。

[2] to shift financing expenses 意为"转移财务支出"。momentary shortfalls 意为"短期的不足"。全句可译为：在过去，许多组织惯用延期支付的方法，一方面转移了财务负担，另一方面也克服了资金的短期不足。

[3] 全句可译为：即使在中标并签订了合同之后，支付延误也会成为承包商方面向某机构索赔成功的根据。

[4] credit rating 意为"信用等级"。brrowing rate 指"借款利率"。全句可译为：建设项目的业主一般拥有良好的信誉等级，可以以较低的贷款利率获得贷款，但是也会存在明显的例外，特别是对于发展中国家的建设项目。

[5] 全句可译为：这种做法只会使问题恶化，因为在做出可能会降低工程造价的决策时，业主被排除在外了。

[6] to hedge the risk 意为"规避风险"。全句可译为：在不确定的经济条件下，业主和承包商都在工程成本的估算中添加一笔金额用以规避风险。

[7] an unsophisticated owner 意为"一个缺乏经验的业主"。全句可译为：一个没有经验的业主，企图回避所有的风险并把建设融资的压力转移到承包商身上，但建筑设施的合同价就可能提高。

[8] 全句可译为：对于规模小、工期短的项目，这种做法是可以接受的，特别是当业主缺乏专业知识来对项目的融资方案进行评价或缺乏采用创新融资计划的能力的时候。

[9] risk sharing 意为"风险分担"。全句可译为：如果一个建设项目中各方要承担的风险责任能够在项目的规划阶段被清晰地界定出来，那么项目中的各方都可以因造价的节省和设施的尽早投入使用而从中获益。

7.5 Construction Financing for Contractors

For a general contractor or subcontractor, the cash flow profile of expenses and incomes for a construction project typically follows the work in progress for which the contractor will be paid periodically[1]. The markup by the contractor above the estimated expenses is included in the total contract price and the terms of most contracts generally call for monthly reimbursements of work completed less retainage[2]. At time period 0, which denotes the beginning of the construction contract, a considerable sum may have been spent in preparation. The contractor's expenses which occur more or less continuously for the

101

project duration are depicted by a piecewise continuous curve while the receipts (such as progress payments from the owner) are represented by a step function as shown in Figure. 7-1[3]. The owner's payments for the work completed are assumed to lag one period behind expenses except that a withholding proportion or remainder is paid at the end of construction[4]. This method of analysis is applicable to realistic situations where a time period is represented by one month and the number of time periods is extended to cover delayed receipts as a result of retainage.

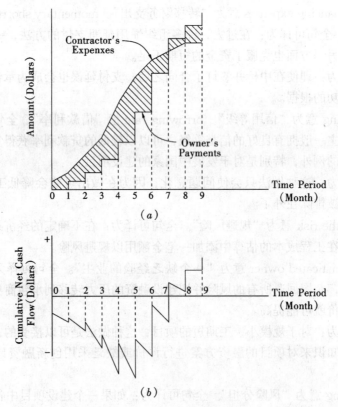

Figure 7-1 Contractor's Expenses and Owner's Payments
(a)Expenses and Payments;(b)Cumulative Net Cash Flow of Contractor

While the cash flow profiles of expenses and receipts are expected to vary for different projects, the characteristics of the curves depicted in Figure 7-1 are sufficiently general for most cases[5]. Let E_t represent the contractor's expenses in period t, and P_t represent owner's payments in period t, for $t = 0, 1, 2, \cdots, n$ for $n = 5$ in this case. The net operating cash flow at the end of period t for $t \geqslant 0$ is given by:

$$A_t = P_t - E_t \tag{7.1}$$

where A_t is positive for a surplus and negative for a shortfall.

The cumulative operating cash flow at the end of period t just before receiving payment P_t

(for $t \geqslant 1$) is:
$$F_t = N_{t-1} - E_t \tag{7.2}$$
where N_{t-1} is the cumulative net cash flows from period 0 to period $(t-1)$. Furthermore, the cumulative net operating cash flow after receiving payment P_t at the end of period t (for $t \geqslant 1$) is:
$$N_t = F_t + P_t = N_{t-1} + A_t \tag{7.3}$$
The gross operating profit G for a n-period project is defined as net operating cash flow at $t = n$ and is given by:
$$G = \sum_{t=0}^{n}(P_t - E_t) = \sum_{t=0}^{n} A_t = N_n \tag{7.4}$$
The use of N_n as a measure of the gross operating profit has the disadvantage that it is not adjusted for the time value of money[6].

Since the net cash flow A_t (for $t = 0, 1, \cdots, n$) for a construction project represents the amount of cash required or accrued after the owner's payment is plowed back to the project at the end of period t, the internal rate of return (IRR) of this cash flow is often cited in the traditional literature in construction as a profit measure[7]. To compute IRR, let the net present value (NPV) of A_t discounted at a discount rate i per period be zero, i.e.,
$$NPV = \sum_{t=0}^{n} A_t(1+i)^{-t} = 0 \tag{7.5}$$
The resulting i (if it is unique) from the solution of Eq. 7.5 is the IRR of the net cash flow A_t. Aside from the complications that may be involved in the solution of Eq. 7.5, the resulting $i =$ IRR has a meaning to the contractor only if the firm finances the entire project from its own equity. This is seldom if ever the case since most construction firms are highly *leveraged*, i.e. they have relatively small equity in fixed assets such as construction equipment, and depend almost entirely on borrowing in financing individual construction projects[8]. The use of the IRR of the net cash flows as a measure of profit for the contractor is thus misleading. It does not represent even the IRR of the bank when the contractor finances the project through overdraft since the gross operating profit would not be given to the bank[9].

Words

profile 轮廓	leverage 杠杆作用
denote 表示	markup 涨价
piecewise 分段	depict （用图形）表示
surplus 剩余,盈余	proportion 比例
remainder 剩余部分	receipt 收据
curve 曲线	cumulative 累计的

overdraft 透支

Notes

[1] 全句可译为：对于总承包商或分包商来说，一个建设项目支出与收入的现金流量曲线一般同工程的进度是相符的，因为承包商的款项是被定期支付的。

[2] 全句可译为：承包商在费用估算额之外添加的数额列在合同总价之内，大多数合同的条款一般规定按月支付已完工作的价值减去保留金后的数额。

[3] 全句可译为：项目建设期中承包商的支出或多或少带有连续性，它表现为分段的连续曲线，而收入（如业主的进度付款）则表现为阶梯函数，如图7-1所示。

[4] 全句可译为：假设业主对完工工程的付款比承包商实际支出延期一个时段，预留部分在建设结束时支付。

[5] depicted in…是过去分词短语作定语，修饰 the curves。全句可译为：虽然各个项目收支现金流曲线不同，但是图7-1中所绘出的曲线的特点还是符合大多数项目的。

[6] 全句可译为：用 N_n 来衡量总运营收益的缺点是其没有考虑货币的时间价值。

[7] the internal rate of return（IRR）指"内部收益率"。全句可译为：由于建设项目的净现金流量 A_t（$t=0, 1, \cdots, n$）表示 t 时段末，业主支付的款项回到项目后项目需要的或应当得到的现金数量，所以建设书籍常引用这个现金流的内部收益率IRR衡量收益情况。

[8] 全句可译为：这种情况是很少见的，因为对于大多数建筑公司来讲，其资产净值中有很大比例的融资租赁部分，比如，在他们的固定资产中只有很小一部分自有资产，例如施工设备等，而当进行单个建设项目施工的时候他们的资金基本上依赖借款。

[9] 全句可译为：即使承包商以透支方式为项目筹措资金，这个数字也不是银行的内部收益率，因为经营毛利润并不会送给银行。

Exercise

Translate the text of lesson 7.4 into Chinese.

Chapter 8   Construction Pricing and Contracting

8.1   Pricing for Constructed Facilities

Because of the unique nature of constructed facilities, it is almost imperative to have a separate price for each facility. The construction contract price includes the direct project cost including field supervision expenses plus the markup imposed by contractors for general overhead expenses and profit[1]. The factors influencing a facility price will vary by type of facility and location as well. Within each of the major categories of construction such as residential housing, commercial buildings, industrial complexes and infrastructure, there are smaller segments which have very different environments with regard to price setting[2]. However, all pricing arrangements have some common features in the form of the legal documents binding the owner and the supplier(s) of the facility. Without addressing special issues in various industry segments, the most common types of pricing arrangements can be described broadly to illustrate the basic principles[3].

Competitive Bidding

The basic structure of the bidding process consists of the formulation of detailed plans and specifications of a facility based on the objectives and requirements of the owner, and the invitation of qualified contractors to bid for the right to execute the project[4]. The definition of a qualified contractor usually calls for a minimal evidence of previous experience and financial stability. In the private sector, the owner has considerable latitude in selecting the bidders, ranging from open competition to the restriction of bidders to a few favored contractors. In the public sector, the rules are carefully delineated to place all qualified contractors on an equal footing for competition, and strictly enforced to prevent collusion among contractors and unethical or illegal actions by public officials[5].

Detailed plans and specifications are usually prepared by an architectural/engineering firm which oversees the bidding process on behalf of the owner[6]. The final bids are normally submitted on either a lump sum or unit price basis, as stipulated by the owner. A lump sum bid represents the total price for which a contractor offers to complete a facility according to the detailed plans and specifications. Unit price bidding is used in projects for which the quantity of materials or the amount of labor involved in some key tasks is particularly uncertain. In such cases, the contractor is permitted to submit a list of unit prices for those tasks, and the final price used to determine the lowest bidder is based on the lump sum price computed by multiplying the quoted unit price for each specified task by the corresponding quantity in the owner's estimates for quantities[7]. However, the total payment to the winning contractor will be based on the actual quantities multiplied by the respective quoted unit prices[8].

Negotiated Contracts

Instead of inviting competitive bidding, private owners often choose to award construction contracts with one or more selected contractors. A major reason for using negotiated contracts is the flexibility of this type of pricing arrangement, particularly for projects of large size and great complexity or for projects which substantially duplicate previous facilities sponsored by the owner[9]. An owner may value the expertise and integrity of a particular contractor who has a good reputation or has worked successfully for the owner in the past. If it becomes necessary to meet a deadline for completion of the project, the construction of a project may proceed without waiting for the completion of the detailed plans and specifications with a contractor that the owner can trust[10]. However, the owner's staff must be highly knowledgeable and competent in evaluating contractor proposals and monitoring subsequent performance.

Generally, negotiated contracts require the reimbursement of direct project cost plus the contractor's fee as determined by one of the following methods:
1. Cost plus fixed percentage.
2. Cost plus fixed fee.
3. Cost plus variable fee.
4. Target estimate.

Guaranteed maximum price or cost

The fixed percentage or fixed fee is determined at the outset of the project, while variable fee and target estimates are used as an incentive to reduce costs by sharing any cost savings[11]. A guaranteed maximum cost arrangement imposes a penalty on a contractor for cost overruns and failure to complete the project on time. With a guaranteed maximum price contract, amounts below the maximum are typically shared between the owner and the contractor, while the contractor is responsible for costs above the maximum[12].

Speculative Residential Construction

In residential construction, developers often build houses and condominiums in anticipation of the demand of home buyers. Because the basic needs of home buyers are very similar and home designs can be standardized to some degree, the probability of finding buyers of good housing units within a relatively short time is quite high[13]. Consequently, developers are willing to undertake speculative building and lending institutions are also willing to finance such construction. The developer essentially set the price for each housing unit as the market will bear, and can adjust the prices of remaining units at any given time according to the market trend[14].

Force-Account Construction

Some owners use in-house labor forces to perform a substantial amount of construction, particularly for addition, renovation and repair work. Then, the total of the force-account charges including in-house overhead expenses will be the pricing arrangement for the construction[15].

Words

impose 施加
quote 引用
imperative 不可避免的
markup 添价
competitive bidding 公开招标
Cost plus fixed percentage 成本加固定百分比
Cost plus variable fee 成本加变动酬金
Guaranteed maximum price or cost 保证最大价格或成本
delineate 描绘,描写
oversee 监督
lump sum 总价
incentive 激励

overrun 超支
lending institution 贷款机构
principle 规则,原理
deadline 截止期
contract price 合同价格
legal documents 法律文件
qualified contractor 合格的承包商
Cost plus fixed fee 成本加固定酬金
Target estimate 目标成本估算
collusion 串通,合谋
submit 提交,递交
unit price 单价
penalty 惩罚
condominium 公寓

Notes

[1] the direct project cost 指"项目直接费"。field supervision expenses 指"现场监督费"。overhead expenses 指"管理费"。全句可译为：建设工程合同价格由包括现场管理费用在内的直接工程费和承包商添加的包括间接费和利润在内的增加值这两大部分所组成。

[2] 全句可译为：在建设工程的每一主要类型中（如居住用房、商业建筑、工业设施或基础设施），只有少部分有着特别不同环境条件的专业，其相应价格的确定有所不同。

[3] to illustrate the basic principles 是动词不定式短语作目的状语。全句可译为：若不考虑本行业各个局部的特殊情况，最常用的定价办法可以根据概括介绍如下，并说

明其基本原则。

[4] based on…是过去分词补语作定语，修饰前面的 the formulation 和 specifications。全句可译为：招标过程的主要安排由根据业主的目标和要求而编制实施的详细图纸和技术要求说明书，以及邀请合格的承包商参加该项目施工权利的投标两部分组成。

[5] 全句可译为：在公共项目领域，需谨慎地进行规则，以使得所有合格的承包商均有一个相同的竞争平台和基础，同时也必须严格地执行规则，以防止承包商之间的相互串通以及公共机构及其人员的败德或违法行为。

[6] on behalf of 意为"代表"。全句可译为：详细图纸和技术要求说明书通常由一家建筑\工程设计（A\E）公司编制，A\E公司代表业主监督投标过程。

[7] 全句可译为：在这种情况下，允许承包商提交这些分部分项工程的单价表，而用于确定最低投标人的最终价格仍与总价投标时所用的计算方法相同，即将承包商对每一具体分部分项工程所报的单价乘以业主估算的相应工程量。

[8] multiplied by…是过去分词短语作定语，修饰前面的 quantities。the respective quoted unit prices 意为"相应的单价"。全句可译为：然而，最终支付给中标承包商的价款将根据其实际完成的工程量与他投标时所报的相应单价的乘积来确定。

[9] 全句可译为：采用协议合同的一个主要原因是在于这种计价方式的灵活性，尤其是对于规模较大和复杂程度高的工程，或者是与业主以前发起的项目十分类似的工程。

[10] 全句可译为：如果必须满足项目建设工期的期限要求，工程的施工可能让一个业主信任的承包商在工程设计文件及其说明完成之前就开始进行。

[11] 全句可译为：固定百分比或固定酬金在项目的开始阶段被确定下来，而可变酬金和目标估算是以分享成本节余的方式鼓励降低成本的手段。

[12] guaranteed maximum price contract 是指"保证最大价格（或成本）合同"。全句可译为：采用保证最大成本方式，低于最大成本值的部分通常由业主和承包商分享，而承包商则对超过最大成本值以外的费用负责。

[13] 全句可译为：因为购房者的基本需要都非常类似，因此住房的设计可以在一定程度上标准化，所以好的房子在短时间内找到购买者的可能性非常高。

[14] 全句可译为：开发商先是根据市场承受力确定每套居住单元的价格，然后可以根据市场的趋势在任何某一特定的时间调整剩余居住单元的价格。

[15] force-account charges 意为"自营工程费"。in-house overhead expenses 指"内业管理费"。全句可译为：
这样以来，包括内业管理费用在内的自营总费用的计算就成为工程的计价方式。

8.2　Contract Provisions for Risk Allocation

Provisions for the allocation of risk among parties to a contract can appear in numerous areas in addition to the total construction price. Typically, these provisions assign responsibility for covering the costs of possible or unforeseen occurances. A partial list of responsibilities with concomitant risk that can be assigned to different parties would include:

- Force majeure (i.e., this provision absolves an owner or a contractor for payment for costs due to "Acts of God" and other external events such as war or labor strikes)[1].
- Indemnification (i.e., this provision absolves the indemified party from any payment for losses and damages incurred by a third party such as adjacent property owners)[2].
- Liens (i.e., assurances that third party claims are settled such as "mechanics liens" for worker wages)[3].
- Labor laws (i.e., payments for any violation of labor laws and regulations on the job site).
- Differing site conditions (i.e., responsibility for extra costs due to unexpected site conditions).
- Delays and extensions of time.
- Liquidated damages (i.e., payments for any facility defects with payment amounts agreed to in advance)[4].
- Consequential damages (i.e., payments for actual damage costs assessed upon impact of facility defects)[5].
- Occupational safety and health of workers.
- Permits, licenses, laws, and regulations.
- Equal employment opportunity regulations.
- Termination for default by contractor.
- Suspension of work.
- Warranties and guarantees[6].

The language used for specifying the risk assignments in these areas must conform to legal requirements and past interpretations which may vary in different jurisdictions or over time. Without using standard legal language, contract provisions may be unenforceable. Unfortunately, standard legal language for this purpose may be difficult to understand. As a result, project managers often have difficulty in interpreting their particular responsibilities. Competent legal counsel is required to advise the different parties to an agreement about their respective responsibilities[7].

Standard forms for contracts can be obtained from numerous sources, such as the American Institute of Architects (AIA) or the Associated General Contractors (AGC)[8]. These standard forms may include risk and responsibility allocations which are unacceptable to one or more of the contracting parties. In particular, standard forms may be biased to reduce the risk and responsibility of the originating organization or group[9]. Parties to a contract should read and review all contract documents carefully.

The three examples appearing below illustrate contract language resulting in different risk assignments between a contractor (CONTRACTOR) and an owner (COMPANY). Each contract provision allocates different levels of indemnification risk to the contractor.

Example 8-1: A Contract Provision Example with High Contractor Risk
"Except where the sole negligence of COMPANY is involved or alleged, CONTRACTOR shall indemnify and hold harmless COMPANY, its officers, agents and employees, from and against any and all loss, damage, and liability and from any and all claims for damages on account of or by reason of bodily injury, including death, not limited to the employees of CONTRACTOR, COMPANY, and of any subcontractor or CONTRACTOR, and from and against any and all damages to property, including property of COMPANY and third parties, direct and/or consequential, caused by or arising out of, in while or in part, or claimed to have been caused by or to have arisen out of, in whole or in part, an act of omission of CONTRACTOR or its agents, employees, vendors, or subcontractors, of their employees or agents in connection with the performance of the Contract Documents, whether or not insured against; and CONTRACTOR shall, at its own cost and expense, defend any claim, suit, action or proceeding, whether groundless or not, which may be commenced against COMPANY by reason thereof or in connection therewith, and CONTRACTOR shall pay any and all judgments which may be recovered in such action, claim, proceeding or suit, and defray any and all expenses, including costs and attorney's fees which may be incurred by reason of such actions, claims, proceedings, or suits."

Comment: This is a very burdensome provision for the contractor. It makes the contractor responsible for practically every conceivable occurrence and type of damage, except when a claim for loss or damages is due to the sole negligence of the owner[10]. As a practical matter, sole negligence on a construction project is very difficult to ascertain because the work is so inter-twined. Since there is no dollar limitation to the contractor's exposure, sufficient liability coverage to cover worst scenario risks will be difficult to obtain. The best the contractor can do is to obtain as complete and broad excess liability insurance coverage as can be purchased. This insurance is costly, so the contractor should insure the contract price is sufficiently high to cover the expense.

Example 8-2: An Example Contract Provision with Medium Risk Allocation to Contractor
"CONTRACTOR shall protect, defend, hold harmless, and indemnify COMPANY from and against any loss, damage, claim, action, liability, or demand whatsoever (including,

with limitation, costs, expenses, and attorney's fees, whether for appeals or otherwise, in connection therewith), arising out of any personal in jury (including, without limitation, in jury to any employee of COMPANY, CONTRACTOR or any subcontractor), arising out of any personal injury (including, without limitation, injury to any employee of COMPANY, CONTRACTOR, or any subcontractor), including death resulting therefrom or out of any damage to or loss or destruction of property, real and or personal (including property of COMPANY, CONTRACTOR, and any subcontractor, and including tools and equipment whether owned, rented, or used by CONTRACTOR, any subcontractor, or any workman) in any manner based upon, occasioned by, or attributable or related to the performance, whether by the CONTRACTOR or any subcontractor, of the Work or any part thereof, and CONTRACTOR shall at its own expense defend any and all actions based thereon, except where said personal injury or property damage is caused by the negligence of COMPANY or COMPANY'S employees. Any loss, damage, cost expense or attorney's fees incurred by COMPANY in connection with the foregoing may, in addition to other remedies, be deducted from CONTRACTOR'S compensation, then due or thereafter to become due[11]. COMPANY shall effect for the benefit of CONTRACTOR a waiver of subrogation on the existing facilities, including consequential damages such as, but not by way of limitation, loss of profit and loss of product or plant downtime but excluding any deductibles which shall exist as at the date of this CONTRACT; provided, however, that said waiver of subrogation shall be expanded to include all said deductible amounts on the acceptance of the Work by COMPANY."

Comment: This clause provides the contractor considerable relief. He still has unlimited exposure for injury to all persons and third party property but only to the extent caused by the contractor's negligence[12]. The "sole" negligence issue does not arise. Furthermore, the contractor's liability for damages to the owner's property-a major concern for contractors working in petrochemical complexes, at times worth billions-is limited to the owner's insurance deductible, and the owner's insurance carriers have no right of recourse against the contractor. The contractor's limited exposure regarding the owner's facilities ends on completion of the work.

Example 8-3: An Example Contract Provision with Low Risk Allocation to Contractor
"CONTRACTOR hereby agrees to indemnify and hold COMPANY and/or any parent, subsidiary, or affiliate, or COMPANY and/or officers, agents, or employees of any of them, harmless from and against any loss or liability arising directly or indirectly out of any claim or cause of action for loss or damage to property including, but not limited to, CONTRACTOR'S property and COMPANY'S property and for injuries to or death of persons including but not limited to CONTRACTOR'S employees, caused by or resulting

from the performance of the work by CONTRACTOR, its employees, agents, and subcontractors and shall, at the option of COMPANY, defend COMPANY at CONTRACTOR'S sole expense in any litigation involving the same regardless of whether such work is performed by CONTRACTOR, its employees, or by its subcontractors, their employees, or all or either of them. In all instances, CONTRACTOR'S indemnity to COMPANY shall be limited to the proceeds of CONTRACTOR'S umbrella liability insurance coverage."

Comment: With respect to indemnifying the owner, the contractor in this provision has minimal out-of-pocket risk[13]. Exposure is limited to whatever can be collected from the contractor's insurance company.

Words

contract provisions 合同条文
concomitant 附随的
indemnification 免责保护
liquidated damages 先约赔偿金
warranty 保证(书),担保(书)
interpretations 解释
unenforceable 无法执行的
American institute of architects(AIA) 美国建筑师协会
indemnify 保护……使其不……
employee 雇员
attorney 律师
subrogation 代位清偿

petrochemical 石油化工的
risk allocation 风险分担
force majeurre 不可抗力
liens 留置
consequential damages 后果赔偿金
guarantee 担保
jurisdiction 司法,裁判权
legal counsel 法律顾问
negligence 疏忽,粗心
agent 代理人
defray 支付
inter-twined 相互纠葛的
clause 条款

Notes

[1] absolve 指"豁免"。全句可译为：不可抗力（这项条款免除业主或承包商支付由于"上帝的安排"以及诸如战争或罢工等其他外部事件所产生的费用）。

[2] incurred by…是过去分词短语作定语，修饰 losses and damages，可译为"由邻近物业业主等第三方所招致的"。全句可译为：损失赔偿（这一条款免除受损失方支付由第三方如相邻物业业主所造成的损失和损害而发生的费用）。

[3] 全句可译为：留置权（即，第三方要求得到实现作出的保证，如为保证工人领到工资而设的"技工留置权"）。

[4] 全句可译为：先约赔偿金（事先同意支付的为任何工程缺陷而支付的费用）。

[5] 全句可译为：后果赔偿金（即，由工程缺陷引起的经济评估的实际损失费用的支付）。

[6] warranties and guarantees 指"保证和担保"。

[7] 全句可译为：这就要求由胜任的法律顾问，向合同双方解释和说明他们各自的责任。

[8] the American Institute of Architects（AIA）指"美国建筑师协会"。the Associated General Contractors（AGC）指"美国总承包商会"。

[9] the originating organization or group 意为"发起组织或团体"。全句可译为：特别要注意的是，合同标准格式可能会有降低发起组织或团体的风险和责任的倾向。

[10] 全句可译为：这项规定使得承包商实际上对所有可能发生的损害情况以及类型承担责任，除非损害或损失赔偿完全是由业主的疏忽所致。

[11] attorney's fees 指"律师费"。then due or there after to become clue 应译为"彼时应付或其后应付"。全句可译为：由业主引起的的与上述事件相关的任何损失、损害、成本支出或律师费用，包括相应的调整，将从承包商的赔偿中扣除，彼时应付或其后应付。

[12] unlimited exposure 意为"无限的责任"。全句可译为：承包商仍须对所有人员和第三方财产承担无限责任，但只限于因承包商疏忽而造成者。

[13] with respect to 是"关于、有关"的意思。out-of-pocket risk 意为"额外风险"。全句可译为：关于对业主的赔偿，在这个条款下的承包商只有最小的额外风险。

8.3 Types of Construction Contracts

While construction contracts serve as a means of pricing construction, they also structure the allocation of risk to the various parties involved[1]. The owner has the sole power to decide what type of contract should be used for a specific facility to be constructed and to set forth the terms in a contractual agreement[2]. It is important to understand the risks of the contractors associated with different types of construction contracts.

Lump Sum Contract

In a lump sum contract, the owner has essentially assigned all the risk to the contractor, who in turn can be expected to ask for a higher markup in order to take care of unforeseen contingencies[3]. Beside the fixed lump sum price, other commitments are often made by the contractor in the form of submittals such as a specific schedule, the management reporting system or a quality control program[4]. If the actual cost of the project is underestimated, the underestimated cost will reduce the contractor's profit by that amount. An overestimate has an opposite effect, but may reduce the chance of being a low bidder for the project.

Unit Price Contract

In a unit price contract, the risk of inaccurate estimation of uncertain quantities for some key tasks has been removed from the contractor[5]. However, some contractors may submit an "unbalanced bid" when it discovers large discrepancies between its estimates and the owner's estimates of these quantities. Depending on the confidence of the contractor on its own estimates and its propensity on risk, a contractor can slightly raise the unit prices on the underestimated tasks while lowering the unit prices on other tasks[6]. If the contractor is correct in its assessment, it can increase its profit substantially since the payment is made on the actual quantities of tasks; and if the reverse is true, it can lose on this basis[7]. Furthermore, the owner may disqualify a contractor if the bid appears to be heavily unbalanced. To the extent that an underestimate or overestimate is caused by changes in the quantities of work, neither error will effect the contractor's profit beyond the markup in the unit prices.

Cost Plus Fixed Percentage Contract

For certain types of construction involving new technology or extremely pressing needs, the owner is sometimes forced to assume all risks of cost overruns[8]. The contractor will receive the actual direct job cost plus a fixed percentage, and have little incentive to reduce job cost. Furthermore, if there are pressing needs to complete the project, overtime payments to workers are common and will further increase the job cost[9]. Unless there are compelling reasons, such as the urgency in the construction of military installations, the owner should not use this type of contract.

Cost Plus Fixed Fee Contract

Under this type of contract, the contractor will receive the actual direct job cost plus a fixed fee, and will have some incentive to complete the job quickly since its fee is fixed regardless of the duration of the project[10]. However, the owner still assumes the risks of direct job cost overrun while the contractor may risk the erosion of its profits if the project is dragged on beyond the expected time.

Cost Plus Variable Percentage Contract

For this type of contract, the contractor agrees to a penalty if the actual cost exceeds the estimated job cost, or a reward if the actual cost is below the estimated job cost[11]. In return for taking the risk on its own estimate, the contractor is allowed a variable percentage of the direct job-cost for its fee. Furthermore, the project duration is usually specified and the contractor must abide by the deadline for completion. This type of contract allocates considerable risk for cost overruns to the owner, but also provides incentives to contractors to reduce costs as much as possible.

Target Estimate Contract

This is another form of contract which specifies a penalty or reward to a contractor, depending on whether the actual cost is greater than or less than the contractor's estimated direct job cost[12]. Usually, the percentages of savings or overrun to be shared by the owner and the contractor are predetermined and the project duration is specified in the contract. Bonuses or penalties may be stipulated for different project completion dates.

Guaranteed Maximum Cost Contract

When the project scope is well defined, an owner may choose to ask the contractor to take all the risks, both in terms of actual project cost and project time[13]. Any work change orders from the owner must be extremely minor if at all, since performance specifications are provided to the owner at the outset of construction. The owner and the contractor agree to a project cost guaranteed by the contractor as maximum. There may be or may not be additional provisions to share any savings if any in the contract. This type of contract is particularly suitable for *turnkey* operation.

Words

Lump Sum Contract　总价合同
Cost Plus Fixed Percentage Contract　成本加固定百分比合同
Cost Plus Fixed Fee Contract　成本加固定酬金合同
Cost Plus Variable Percentage Cost　成本加可变百分比合同
Target Estimate Contract　目标估算合同
Guaranteed Maximum Cost Contract　保证最大成本合同
assign　分派
commitment　承诺、保证
overestimate　高估
discrepancy　差异
assume　承担
additional provision　附加条款
Unit Price Contract　单价合同
contingency　偶然事件
underestimate　低估
unbalanced bid　不平衡报价
propensity　倾向
erosion　侵蚀

Notes

[1]　全句可译为：工程合同是工程定价的手段，还安排了各参与方之间的风险分担。

[2]　全句可译为：业主拥有决定应该为建设一个特定的工程而采取哪种合同形式的单独的权利，并将其在合同中用条款予以阐明。

[3]　who…是定语从句，修饰前面的 the contractor。全句可译为：在总价合同中，业主实质上将所有的风险都交给了承包商，但承包商会反过来会在合同价中添加更大的数额用以应付不可预见事件费用。

[4]　全句可译为：除固定总价外，承包商通常以提供其他文件的形式做出另外的承诺，例如某一特定的进度计划、管理报告系统或质量控制计划。

[5]　全句可译为：在单价合同中，承包商不再因某些主要分项工程量的不准确而承担估

[6]　全句可译为：基于对自己估算的信心以及对风险承担的态度，承包商可能在被低估数量的分项工程上略微提高相应的单价，而将其他分项工程的单价降低。

[7]　全句可译为：如果承包商估算正确，就可以大大增加利润，因为业主是根据实际的工程量支付款项；如果情况相反，则承包商利润可能因此而减少。

[8]　全句可译为：对于一些采用新技术或有迫切需求的特定工程，业主有时候被迫承担成本超支的所有风险。

[9]　全句可译为：而且，如果对于工程完成时间有急迫的要求，所以工人超时工作费用的支付是普遍的，这也将进一步提高工程成本。

[10]　regardless of 指"不考虑"。全句可译为：根据合同，承包商的实际成本会得到补偿，此外再加上一笔固定酬金，并有积极性尽快完成工程，因为不管工期多长，酬金是固定不变的。

[11]　全句可译为：对于这种合同，承包商同意当实际成本超过估算成本时受罚，而当实际成本低于估算成本时得奖。

[12]　depencling on…为现在分词短语作状语，可译为"取决于实际成本是高于或者低于承包商估算的直接成本"。

[13]　in terms of 意为"依据"。全句可译为：当项目范围明确之后，业主可能会要求承包商承担项目实际成本和工期方面的全部风险。

8.4　Resolution of Contract Disputes

Once a contract is reached, a variety of problems may emerge during the course of work. Disputes may arise over quality of work, over responsibility for delays, over appropriate payments due to changed conditions, or a multitude of other considerations[1]. Resolution of contract disputes is an important task for project managers. The mechanism for contract dispute resolution can be specified in the original contract or, less desirably, decided when a dispute arises[2].

The most prominent mechanism for dispute resolution is adjudication in a court of law. This process tends to be expensive and time consuming since it involves legal representation and waiting in queues of cases for available court times[3]. Any party to a contract can bring a suit. In adjudication, the dispute is decided by a neutral, third party with no necessary specialized expertise in the disputed subject[4]. After all, it is not a prerequisite for judges to be familiar with construction procedures! Legal procedures are highly structured with rigid, formal rules for presentations and fact finding. On the positive side, legal adjudication strives for consistency and predictability of results[5]. The results of previous cases are published and can be used as precedents for resolution of new disputes.

Negotiation among the contract parties is a second important dispute resolution mechanism. These negotiations can involve the same sorts of concerns and issues as with the original contracts. Negotiation typically does not involve third parties such as judges. The negotiation process is usually informal, unstructured and relatively inexpensive. If an agreement is not reached between the parties, then adjudication is a possible remedy.

A third dispute resolution mechanism is the resort to arbitration or mediation and conciliation[6]. In these procedures, a third party serves a central role in the resolution. These outside parties are usually chosen by mutually agreement of the parties involved and will have specialized knowledge of the dispute subject[7]. In arbitration, the third party may make a decision which is binding on the participants. In mediation and conciliation, the third party serves only as a facilitator to help the participants reach a mutually acceptable resolution[8]. Like negotiation, these procedures can be informal and unstructured.

Finally, the high cost of adjudication has inspired a series of non-traditional dispute resolution mechanisms that have some of the characteristics of judicial proceedings[9]. These mechanisms include:

- Private judging in which the participants hire a third party judge to make a decision.
- Neutral expert fact-finding in which a third party with specialized knowledge makes a recommendation.
- Mini-trial in which legal summaries of the participants' positions are presented to a jury comprised of principals of the affected parties[10].

Some of these procedures may be court sponsored or required for particular types of disputes.

While these various disputes resolution mechanisms involve varying costs, it is important to note that the most important mechanism for reducing costs and problems in dispute resolution is the reasonableness of the initial contract among the parties as well as the competence of the project manager[11].

Words

due to 由于	dispute resolution mechanism 争端解决机制
resolution 解决	contract dispute 合同纠纷
prominent 显著的	adjudication 判决,裁判
suit 诉讼	case 案件

consistency	一致性	prerequisite	先决条件,必要条件,前提
precedent	先例	predictability	可预见性
mediation	调解	arbitration	仲裁
resort to	诉诸	conciliation	调节
binding	有约束力的		

Notes

[1] 全句可译为:可能在工程质量、延误责任、由于条件变化而应支付的款项和其他请诸多事项上发生争议。

[2] 全句可译为:合同争议的解决机制可以在最初的合同中规定,或并不希望当争议出现后再行决定。

[3] 全句可译为:但这一过程因为涉及到法律陈述且要服从法庭审理时间安排等而耗时且代价高昂。

[4] 全句可译为:在法庭裁决中,争端是由对纠纷事项不具有必要专门知识的中立的第三方判定的。

[5] 全句可译为:从积极的角度来看,法律的判决是力争取得一致性和可预见的结果。

[6] 全句可译为:第三种争端解决机制是诉诸仲裁、调解或调节。

[7] 全句可译为:这些外部人士通常是由合同各方共同选定的,他们具有解决纠纷事项的专门知识。

[8] 全句可译为:在调解和调节中,第三方只是作为一个推动者,帮助参与方达成一个都可以接受的解决方案。

[9] non-traditional 意为"非传统的"。judicial proceedings 意为"司法程序"。全句可译为:最后,昂贵的法院判决逼出一系列非传统但带有某些司法程序特点的争端解决机制。

[10] 全句可译为:微型判决——各方立场的法律概要要呈送给由相关方主要负责人构成的陪审团裁决。

[11] 全句可译为:虽然各种争端解决机制会费用不同,但值得注意的是,双方签订合同之初就做到合理,项目经理胜任,才是降低成本和减少纠纷的最重要的机制。

8.5 Negotiation Simulation: An Example

This construction negotiation game simulates a contract negotiation between a utility, "CMG Gas" and a design/construct firm, "Pipeline Constructors, Inc." The negotiation involves only two parties but multiple issues. Participants in the game are assigned to represent one party or the other and to negotiate with a designated partner. In a class setting, numerous negotiating partners are created. The following overview from the CMG Gas participants' instructions describes the setting for the game:

CMG Gas has the opportunity to provide natural gas to an automobile factory under construction. Service will require a new sixteen mile pipeline through farms and light forest. The terrain is hilly with moderate slopes, and equipment access is relatively good. The pipeline is to be buried three feet deep. Construction of the pipeline itself will be contracted to a qualified design/construction firm, while required compression stations and ancillary work will be done by CMG Gas[1]. As project manager for CMG Gas, you are about to enter negotiations with a local contractor, "Pipeline Constructors, Inc." This firm is the only local contractor qualified to handle such a large project. If a suitable contract agreement cannot be reached, then you will have to break off negotiations soon and turn to another company[2].

The Pipeline Constructors, Inc. instructions offers a similar overview.

To focus the negotiations, the issues to be decided in the contract are already defined:

- Duration
  The final contract must specify a required completion date.
- Penalty for Late Completion
  The final contract may include a daily penalty for late project completion on the part of the contractor.
- Bonus for Early Completion
  The final contract may include a daily bonus for early project completion.
- Report Format
  Contractor progress reports will either conform to the traditional CMG Gas format or to a new format proposed by the state.
- Frequency of Progress Reports
  Progress reports can be required daily, weekly, bi-weekly or monthly.
- Conform to Pending Legislation Regarding Pipeline Marking
  State legislation is pending to require special markings and drawings for pipelines. The parties have to decide whether to conform to this pending legislation.
- Contract Type
  The construction contract may be a flat fee, a cost plus a percentage profit, or a guaranteed maximum with cost plus a percentage profit below the maximum[3].
- Amount of Flat Fee
  If the contract is a flat fee, the dollar amount must be specified.
- Percentage of Profit
  If the contract involves a percentage profit, then the percentage must be agreed upon.
- CMG Gas Clerk on Site

The contract may specify that a CMG Gas Clerk may be on site and have access to all accounts or that only progress reports are made by Pipeline Constructors, Inc[4].

- Penalty for Late Starting Date
CMG Gas is responsible for obtaining right-of-way agreements for the new pipeline. The parties may agree to a daily penalty if CMG Gas cannot obtain these agreements.

A final contract requires an agreement on each of these issues, represented on a form signed by both negotiators.

As a further aid, each participant is provided with additional information and a scoring system to indicate the relative desirability of different contract agreements. Additional information includes items such as estimated construction cost and expected duration as well as company policies such as desired reporting formats or work arrangements[5]. This information may be revealed or withheld from the other party depending upon an individual's negotiating strategy. The numerical scoring system includes point totals for different agreements on specific issues, including interactions among the various issues. For example, the amount of points received by Pipeline Constructors, Inc. for a bonus for early completion *increases* as the completion date become *later*. An earlier completion becomes more likely with a later completion date, and hence the probability of receiving a bonus increases, so the resulting point total likewise increases[6].

The two firms have differing perceptions of the desirability of different agreements. In some cases, their views will be directly conflicting. For example, increases in a flat fee imply greater profits for Pipeline Constructors, Inc. and greater costs for CMG Gas. In some cases, one party may feel strongly about a particular issue, whereas the other is not particularly concerned. For example, CMG Gas may want a clerk on site, while Pipeline Constructors, Inc. may not care. As described in the previous section, these differences in the evaluation of an issue provide opportunities for negotiators. By conceding an unimportant issue to the other party, a negotiator may trade for progress on an issue that is more important to his or her firm[7]. Examples of instructions to the negotiators appear below.

Instructions to the Pipelines Constructors, Inc. Representative

After examining the project site, your company's estimators are convinced that the project can be completed in thirty-six weeks. In bargaining for the duration, keep two things in mind; the longer past thirty-six weeks the contract duration is, the more money that can be made off the "bonuses for being early" and the chances of being late are reduced[8]. That reduces the risk of paying a "penalty for lateness".

Throughout the project the gas company will want progress reports. These reports take time to compile and therefore the fewer you need to submit, the better. In addition, State law dictates that the Required Standard Report be used unless the contractor and the owner agree otherwise. These standard reports are even more time consuming to produce than more traditional reports.

The State Legislature is considering a law that requires accurate drawings and markers of all pipelines by all utilities. You would prefer not to conform to this uncertain set of requirements, but this is negotiable.

What type of contract and the amount your company will be paid are two of the most important issues in negotiations. In the Flat Fee contract, your company will receive an agreed amount from *CMG Gas*. Therefore, when there are any delay or cost overruns, it will be the full responsibility of your company. With this type of contract, your company assumes all the risk and will in turn want a higher price[9]. Your estimators believe a cost and contingency amount of 4,500,000 dollars. You would like a higher fee, of course.

With the Cost Plus Contract, the risk is shared by the gas company and your company. With this type of contract, your company will bill *CMG Gas* for all of its costs, plus a specified percentage of those costs. In this case, cost overruns will be paid by the gas company. Not only does the percentage above cost have to be decided upon but also whether or not your company will allow a Field Clerk from the gas company to be at the job site to monitor reported costs[10]. Whether or not he is around is of no concern to your company since its policy is not to inflate costs. this point can be used as a bargaining weapon.

Finally, your company is worried whether the gas company will obtain the land rights to lay the pipe. Therefore, you should demand a penalty for the potential delay of the project starting date.

Instructions to the CMG Gas Company Representative

In order to satisfy the auto manufacturer, the pipeline must be completed in forty weeks. An earlier completion date will not result in receiving revenue any earlier. Thus, the only reason to bargain for shorter duration is to feel safer about having the project done on time. If the project does exceed the forty week maximum, a penalty will have to be paid to the auto manufacturer. Consequently, if the project exceeds the agreed upon duration, the contractor should pay you a penalty. The penalty for late completion might be related to the project duration. For example, if the duration is agreed to be thirty-six weeks, then the penalty for being late need not be so severe. Also, it is normal that the contractor get a bonus for early completion. of course, completion before forty weeks doesn't yield any benefit other than your own peace of mind. Try to keep the early bonus as low as possible.

Throughout the project you will want progress reports. The more often these reports are received, the better to monitor the progress. State law dictates that the Required Standard Report be used unless the contractor and the owner agree otherwise. These reports are very detailed and time consuming to review. You would prefer to use the traditional *CMG Gas* reports.

The state legislature is considering a law that requires accurate drawings and markers of all pipelines by all utilities[11]. For this project it will cost an additional $250,000 to do this now, or $750,000 to do this when the law is passed.

One of the most important issues is the type of contract, and the amount of be paid. The Flat Fee contract means that *CMG Gas* will pay the contractor a set amount. Therefore, when there are delays and cost overruns, the contractor assumes full responsibility for the individual costs. However, this evasion of risk has to be paid for and results in a higher price. If Flat Fee is chosen, only the contract price is to be determined. Your company's estimators have determined that the project should cost about $5,000,000.

The Cost Plus Percent contract may be cheaper, but the risk is shared. With this type of contract, the contractor will bill the gas company for all costs, plus a specified percentage of those costs. In this case, cost overruns will be paid by the gas company. If this type of contract is chosen, not only must the profit percentage be chosen, but also whether or not a gas company representative will be allowed on site all of the time acting as a Field Clerk, to ensure that a proper amount of material and labor is billed[12]. The usual percentage agreed upon is about ten percent.

Contractors also have a concern whether or not they will receive a penalty if the gas right-of-way is not obtained in time to start the project. In this case, *CMG Gas* has already secured the right-of-ways. But, if the penalty is too high, this is a dangerous precedent for future negotiations. However, you might try to use this as a bargaining tool.

Words

negotiation　谈判　　　　　　　　　　　　simulate　模拟

issue	争论	overview	总览
participant	参与方	pipeline	管线
scoring system	评分系统	concede	让步，妥协
ancillary	辅助的	handle	处理
submit	提交	bonus	奖金
frequency	频率	clerk	职员
strategy	策略	conflict	冲突
bargain	讨价还价	compile	编辑
evasion	逃避，籍口	revenue	收入

Notes

[1] 全句可译为：管道工程施工交给一家合格的设计/施工公司承包，而所需的压缩站及辅助设施将由 CMG 燃气公司负责建造。

[2] break off… 是"终止……"的意思。全句可译为：如果不能签订合理的合同，就必须马上终止谈判，寻找另一家承包商。

[3] a flat fee 是指"固定酬金合同"。a cost plus a percentage profit 是指"成本加百分比利润合同"。a guaranteed maximum with cost plus a percentage profit below the maximum 是指"保证最大成本加最大限额以下百分比利润合同"。

[4] 全句可译为：合同或许会规定一位 CMG 燃气公司的人员被派驻现场，有权使用、查阅所有文件或者只能是管道工程有限公司制定的进度报告。

[5] 全句可译为：附加信息包括这样一些事项，如工程成本估算、预期的完工日期以及公司诸如报告格式和工作部署等方针。

[6] 全句可译为：规定的完工日期越晚，那么工程较早完成的可能性就越大，因而获得奖金的可能性也随之增加，则评分结果的总值也会同样增加。

[7] 全句可译为：通过在非重要事项上向另一方让步，谈判人或许能换取在对本公司更为重要事项上的进展。

[8] 全句可译为：在工期的谈判中应牢记两件事：合同工期在 36 周以后拉得越长，则获取提前完工奖金的金额就越大；另一方面，工期延误的可能性也就越小。

[9] 全句可译为：因此，当出现进度拖延或成本超支时，你们的公司将承担因采用此类合同所产生的风险以及相应的责任，而反过来你们就会要求一个较高的合同价格作为补偿。

[10] 全句可译为：因此不但必须决定超过成本部分的酬金比例，还需要决定你们公司是否允许燃气公司的现场人员到现场监督所报告的成本。

[11] the state legislature 是指"州立法机关"。全句可译为：州立法机关正在考虑制订一法律，要求用作所有公用设施的管道必须有准确的图案和标志。

[12] 全句可译为：如果选用此类合同，不但必须选择利润率，还要确定是否允许燃气公司代表作为现场人员在所有的时间均在现场，以保证材料和人工的支付是恰当的。

Exercise

Translate the text of lesson 8.4 into Chinese.

Chapter 9   Construction Planning

9.1   Basic Concepts in the Development of Construction Plans

Construction planning is a fundamental and challenging activity in the management and execution of construction projects. It involves the choice of technology, the definition of work tasks, the estimation of the required resources and durations for individual tasks, and the identification of any interactions among the different work tasks[1]. A good construction plan is the basis for developing the budget and the schedule for work. Developing the construction plan is a critical task in the management of construction, even if the plan is not written or otherwise formally recorded[2]. In addition to these technical aspects of construction planning, it may also be necessary to make organizational decisions about the relationships between project participants and even which organizations to include in a project[3]. For example, the extent to which sub-contractors will be used on a project is often determined during construction planning.

Forming a construction plan is a highly challenging task. As Sherlock Holmes noted:

Most people, if you describe a train of events to them, will tell you what the result would be. They can put those events together in their minds, and argue from them that something will come to pass. There are few people, however, who, if you told them a result, would be able to evolve from their own inner consciousness what the steps were which led up to that result[4]. This power is what I mean when I talk of reasoning backward[5].

Like a detective, a planner begins with a result (i.e. a facility design) and must synthesize the steps required to yield this result[6]. Essential aspects of construction planning include the *generation* of required activities, *analysis* of the implications of these activities, and *choice* among the various alternative means of performing activities[7]. In contrast to a detective discovering a single train of events, however, construction planners also face the normative problem of choosing the best among numerous alternative plans[8]. Moreover, a detective is faced with an observable result, whereas a planner must imagine the final facility as described in the plans and specifications.

In developing a construction plan, it is common to adopt a primary emphasis on either cost control or on schedule control as illustrated in Figure 9-1. Some projects are primarily divided into expense categories with associated costs. In these cases, construction planning is cost or expense oriented. Within the categories of expenditure, a distinction is made between costs incurred directly in the performance of an activity and indirectly for the accomplishment of the project[9]. For example, borrowing expenses for project financing

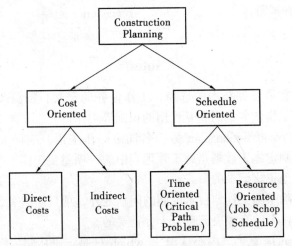

Figure 9-1 Alternative Emphases in Construction Planning

and overhead items are commonly treated as indirect costs. For other projects, scheduling of work activities over time is critical and is emphasized in the planning process. In this case, the planner insures that the proper precedence among activities are maintained and that efficient scheduling of the available resources prevails[10]. Traditional scheduling procedures emphasize the maintenance of task precedence (resulting in *critical path scheduling* procedures) or efficient use of resources over time (resulting in *job shop scheduling* procedures)[11]. Finally, most complex projects require consideration of both cost and scheduling over time, so that planning, monitoring and record keeping must consider both dimensions. In these cases, the integration of schedule and budget information is a major concern.

In this chapter, we shall consider the functional requirements for construction planning such as technology choice, work breakdown, and budgeting[12]. Construction planning is not an activity which is restricted to the period after the award of a contract for construction. It should be an essential activity during the facility design. Also, if problems arise during construction, re-planning is required.

Words

construction planning 施工计划   consciousness 意识
critical 关键的   synthesize 综合

implication 含义
primary 基本的，首要的
job shop scheduling procedure 工作现场进度计划程序
distinction 区别
evolve 演化，进化，推断
event 事件

detective 侦探
yield 产生，生产
normative 规范的
critical path scheduling procedure 关键路径进度计划程序
precedence 先导

Notes

[1] 全句可译为：它涉及到技术的选择、工作任务的定义、资源和工作持续时间的估算，以及不同工作任务之间相互作用的识别等工作。

[2] developing the construction plan 为动名词短语作主语，应译为"制定施工计划"。全句可译为：制定施工计划是施工管理当中的一项重要工作，即使这个施工计划不是书面的或其他正式记录的形式。

[3] 全句可译为：除了施工计划技术层面的问题之外，项目组织关于项目参与方之间在沟通和联系所作出的有关决策也是十分重要的。

[4] inner consciousness 意为"内心认识"。which… 是定语从句，修饰前面的 steps. 全句可译为：但是如果你仅仅告诉他们结果，很少有人能够从内心深处认识到造成这一结果的各个步骤到底是什么。

[5] reasoning backward 意为"逆向推理"。

[6] 全句可译为：如同一个侦探，计划人员通常由结果入手（例如，一个设施的设计），并且必须将产生这一结果所需要的步骤综合起来。

[7] 全句可译为：施工计划的基本内容包括定义所需要的各项活动，分析这些活动之间的内在联系和选择适当的方法来完成这些活动。

[8] numerous alternative plans 意为"众多的备选方案"。全句可译为：但是和侦探的不同之处在于，侦探可以发现一系列事件，而建设项目的计划人员遇到的是在多个备选方案中如何选择最好的这样一个规范性问题。

[9] 全句可译为：在划分支出类别时，我们将对执行一项活动所发生的直接成本和整个项目完成所需的间接成本予以特殊地对待。

[10] proper precedences among activities 意为"工作间适当的前导关系"。全句可译为：在这种情况下，施工计划人员遇到的是确保维持各项工作间的前导关系，保证对各项资源得到有效安排。

[11] critical path scheduling 意为"关键线路进度计划"，job shop scheduling 意为"施工现场进度安排"。

[12] technology choice 意为"技术选择"。work breakdown 是指"工作分解"。

9.2 Choice of Technology and Construction Method

As in the development of appropriate alternatives for facility design, choices of appropriate technology and methods for construction are often ill-structured yet critical ingredients in the success of the project[1]. For example, a decision whether to pump or to transport concrete in buckets will directly affect the cost and duration of tasks involved in building construction[2]. A decision between these two alternatives should consider the relative costs, reliabilities, and availability of equipment for the two transport methods. Unfortunately, the exact implications of different methods depend upon numerous considerations for which information may be sketchy during the planning phase, such as the experience and expertise of workers or the particular underground condition at a site[3].

In selecting among alternative methods and technologies, it may be necessary to formulate a number of construction plans based on alternative methods or assumptions[4]. Once the full plan is available, then the cost, time and reliability impacts of the alternative approaches can be reviewed. This examination of several alternatives is often made explicit in bidding competitions in which several alternative designs may be proposed or *value engineering* for alternative construction methods may be permitted[5]. In this case, potential constructors may wish to prepare plans for each alternative design using the suggested construction method as well as to prepare plans for alternative construction methods which would be proposed as part of the value engineering process.

In forming a construction plan, an useful approach is to simulate the construction process either in the imagination of the planner or with a formal computer based simulation technique[6]. By observing the result, comparisons among different plans or problems with the existing plan can be identified. For example, a decision to use a particular piece of equipment for an operation immediately leads to the question of whether or not there is sufficient access space for the equipment. Three dimensional geometric models in a computer aided design (CAD) system may be helpful in simulating space requirements for operations and for identifying any interferences[7]. Similarly, problems in resource availability identified during the simulation of the construction process might be effectively forestalled by providing additional resources as part of the construction plan[8].

Example 9-1: A roadway rehabilitation
An example from a roadway rehabilitation project in Pittsburgh, PA can serve to illustrate the importance of good construction planning and the effect of technology choice[9]. In this project, the decks on overpass bridges as well as the pavement on the highway itself were to be replaced. The initial construction plan was to work outward from each end of the overpass bridges while the highway surface was replaced below the bridges. As a result, access of equipment and concrete trucks to the overpass bridges was a considerable problem. However, the highway work could be staged so that each overpass bridge was accessible

from below at prescribed times. By pumping concrete up to the overpass bridge deck from the highway below, costs were reduced and the work was accomplished much more quickly[10].

Example 9-2: Laser Leveling

An example of technology choice is the use of laser leveling equipment to improve the productivity of excavation and grading. In these systems, laser surveying equipment is erected on a site so that the relative height of mobile equipment is known exactly[11]. This height measurement is accomplished by flashing a rotating laser light on a level plane across the construction site and observing exactly where the light shines on receptors on mobile equipment such as graders. Since laser light does not disperse appreciably, the height at which the laser shines anywhere on the construction site gives an accurate indication of the height of a receptor on a piece of mobile equipment[12]. In turn, the receptor height can be used to measure the height of a blade, excavator bucket or other piece of equipment. Combined with electro-hydraulic control systems mounted on mobile equipment such as bulldozers, graders and scrapers, the height of excavation and grading blades can be precisely and automatically controlled in these systems. This automation of blade heights has reduced costs in some cases by over 80% and improved quality in the finished product, as measured by the desired amount of excavation or the extent to which a final grade achieves the desired angle. These systems also permit the use of smaller machines and less skilled operators. However, the use of these semi-automated systems require investments in the laser surveying equipment as well as modification to equipment to permit electronic feedback control units[13]. Still, laser leveling appears to be an excellent technological choice in many instances.

Words

reliability　可靠性
implication　含义
sketchy　概略的
assumption　假设
simulation　模拟
forestall　提前制订
deck　甲板，面层
pavement　人行道
concrete　混凝土
excavation　开掘
laser　镭射激光
bucket　桶

electro-hydraulic　电动水压的
scraper　刮刀
availability　可得性
value engineering　价值工程
formulate　制订
explicit　明显的
geometric　几何的
rehabilitation　修复
overpass　立交桥
highway　公路
access　方法、途径
survey　测量

receptor 接受装置 bulldozer 推土机
blade 叶片，刀口 feedback 反馈

Notes

[1] 全句可译为：如同建筑设计中的合理方案选择一样，施工中合理的技术与方法的选择通常也是项目成功中棘手但却关键的因素。

[2] involved in building construction 是过去分词短语作定语，修饰 tasks。全句可译为：例如，用泵送混凝土还是用吊斗浇注混凝土的决定将直接影响建筑物施工各项任务的成本和时间。

[3] 全句可译为：遗憾的是，诸如劳动者的经验和技能以及现场的条件等我们在比选不同方案时所需考虑的信息，在计划阶段却往往是粗略的。

[4] based on…是过去分词短语作定语，修饰 construction plans。全句可译为：选择施工方法和技术时，有必要根据各种备选的施工方法和假设提出若干套施工计划。

[5] 全句可译为：这种对几个备选方案之间的评比在公开招标中表现的十分明显：在设计招标中会要求提交数个设计方案，而在施工招标中则会用到价值工程。

[6] simulation technique 指"模拟技术"。全句可译为：在制定施工计划时，非常有用的办法是根据施工计划人员的想像或利用以电脑为工具的仿真技术对施工过程进行模拟。

[7] three dimensional geometric model 指"三维图形模拟"。computer aided design (CAD) 指"计算机辅助设计"。全句可译为：这时使用计算机辅助设计系统中的三维图形模型对施工中的空间进行模拟，并对干扰因素进行识别就能够帮助我们解决这个问题。

[8] 全句可译为：类似地，我们还可以用计算机对施工过程中的资源使用情况进行模拟，并根据模拟结果提前制定资源供应计划。

[9] 全句可译为：本例引自宾夕法尼亚州匹兹堡市的一个道路修复项目，该项目可用来说明好的施工计划的重要性以及施工技术选择的效果。

[10] 全句可译为：通过在立交桥下方的公路使用泵送混凝土来完成立交桥的路面修复施工，不仅成本得以降低而且工做也会很快被完成。

[11] laser surveying equipment 指"激光测量装置"。全句可译为：在这套系统中，将激光测量装置架设在现场的某个位置上，以便测量移动设备的相对高度。

[12] 全句可译为：由于激光束不易发散，我们使用这种方法便可以精确地测量施工现场中任何安装激光接受装置的移动设备的高度。

[13] semi-automated 意为"半自动化的"。electronic feedback control unit 指"电子反馈控制器"。全句可译为：然而，使用这种自动化程度较高的系统却不仅需要在激光测距装置上进行一次性的初始投资，同时为了保证电子反馈遥控器的正常运行，还需经常性地对设备进行校正调试。

9.3 Defining Work Tasks

At the same time that the choice of technology and general method are considered, a parallel step in the planning process is to define the various work tasks that must be accomplished[1]. These work tasks represent the necessary framework to permit *scheduling* of construction activities, along with estimating the *resources* required by the individual work tasks, and any necessary *precedence* or required sequence among the tasks[2]. The terms "work", "tasks" or "activities" are often used interchangeably in construction plans to refer to specific, defined items of work[3]. In job shop or manufacturing terminology, a project would be called a "job" and an activity called an "operation", but the sense of the terms is equivalent. The *scheduling problem* is to determine an appropriate set of activity start time, resource allocations and completion times that will result in completion of the project in a timely and efficient fashion[4]. Construction planning is the necessary forerunner to scheduling. In this planning, defining work tasks, technology and construction method is typically done either simultaneously or in a series of iterations.

The definition of appropriate work tasks can be a laborious and tedious process, yet it represents the necessary information for application of formal scheduling procedures[5]. Since construction projects can involve thousands of individual work tasks, this definition phase can also be expensive and time consuming. Fortunately, many tasks may be repeated in different parts of the facility or past facility construction plans can be used as general models for new projects. For example, the tasks involved in the construction of a building floor may be repeated with only minor differences for each of the floors in the building. Also, standard definitions and nomenclatures for most tasks exist. As a result, the individual planner defining work tasks does not have to approach each facet of the project entirely from scratch[6].

While repetition of activities in different locations or reproduction of activities from past projects reduces the work involved, there are very few computer aids for the process of defining activities[7]. Databases and information systems can assist in the storage and recall of the activities associated with past projects as described in Chapter 14. For the scheduling process itself, numerous computer programs are available. But for the important task of defining activities, reliance on the skill, judgment and experience of the construction planner is likely to continue.

More formally, an *activity* is any subdivision of project tasks. The set of activities defined for a project should be *comprehensive* or completely *exhaustive* so that all necessary work tasks are included in one or more activities[8]. Typically, each design element in the planned facility will have one or more associated project activities. Execution of an activity requires time and resources, including manpower and equipment, as described in the next section. The time required to perform an activity is called the *duration of* the activity. The beginning and the end of activities are signposts or *milestones*, indicating the progress of the project. Occasionally, it is useful to define activities which have no duration to mark important events. For example, receipt of equipment on the construction site may be defined as an activity since other activities would depend upon the equipment availability and the project manager might appreciate formal notice of the arrival[9]. Similarly, receipt of regulatory approvals would also be specially marked in the project plan.

The extent of work involved in any one activity can vary tremendously in construction project plans. Indeed, it is common to begin with fairly coarse definitions of activities and then to further sub-divide tasks as the plan becomes better defined. As a result, the definition of activities evolves during the preparation of the plan. A result of this process is a natural *hierarchy* of activities with large, abstract functional activities repeatedly sub-divided into more and more specific sub-tasks[10]. For example, the problem of placing concrete on site would have sub-activities associated with placing forms, installing reinforcing steel, pouring concrete, finishing the concrete, removing forms and others. Even more specifically, sub-tasks such as removal and cleaning of forms after concrete placement can be defined[11]. Even further, the sub-task "clean concrete forms" could be subdivided into the various operations:

- Transport forms from on-site storage and unload onto the cleaning station.
- Position forms on the cleaning station.
- Wash forms with water.
- Clean concrete debris from the form's surface.
- Coat the form surface with an oil release agent for the next use.
- Unload the form from the cleaning station and transport to the storage location.

This detailed task breakdown of the activity "clean concrete forms" would not generally be done in standard construction planning, but it is essential in the process of programming or designing a *robot* to undertake this activity since the various specific tasks must be well defined for a robot implementation[12].

It is generally advantageous to introduce an explicit *hierarchy* of work activities for the purpose of simplifying the presentation and development of a schedule. For example, the initial plan might define a single activity associated with "site clearance." Later, this single activity might be sub-divided into "re-locating utilities," "removing vegetation," "grading", etc. However, these activities could continue to be identified as sub-activities under the general activity of "site clearance." This hierarchical structure also facilitates the preparation of summary charts and reports in which detailed operations are combined into aggregate or "super"-activities[13].

More formally, a hierarchical approach to work task definition decomposes the work activity into component parts in the form of a tree. Higher levels in the tree represent decision nodes or summary activities, while branches in the tree lead to smaller components and work activities[14]. A variety of constraints among the various nodes may be defined or imposed, including precedence relationships among different tasks as defined below[15]. Technology choices may be *decomposed* to decisions made at particular nodes in the tree. For example, choices on plumbing technology might be made without reference to choices for other functional activities.

Of course, numerous different activity hierarchies can be defined for each construction plan. For example, upper level activities might be related to facility components such as foundation elements, and then lower level activity divisions into the required construction operations might be made[16]. Alternatively, upper level divisions might represent general types of activities such as electrical work, while lower work divisions represent the application of these operations to specific facility components. As a third alternative, initial divisions might represent different spatial locations in the planned facility. The choice of a hierarchy depends upon the desired scheme for summarizing work information and on the convenience of the planner. In computerized databases, multiple hierarchies can be stored so that different aggregations or views of the work breakdown structure can be obtained[17].

Words

interchangeable 可相互替换的	terminology 术语
tedious 单调而令人厌烦的	nomenclature 术语（表）
facet 面，方面	database 数据库
storage 存储	recall 记忆
subdivision 细分	manpower 人力
signpost 路标	milestone 里程碑
coarse 粗略的	hierarchy 层次结构
debris 建筑废弃物	node 节点
spatial 空间的	multiple 多样的

Notes

[1] that the choice of…是定语从句，修饰 the same time。全句可译为：在考虑技术和方法选择的同时，计划过程中同步进行的另一项工作是对项目中必须完成的各项工作任务进行定义。

[2] 全句可译为：这些工作任务为我们安排进度计划以及估算各项工作所需的资源和确定各项工作的先后顺序关系提供了必要的架构。

[3] 全句可译为：在施工计划中，工作，任务或活动等术语经常用来指称具体而又明确的工作，使用时可以互换。

[4] 全句可译为：进度计划中的问题就是确定能够使项目以一个及时有效的方式完成的各项活动合理的开始时间、资源配置和完成时间。

[5] formal scheduling procedures 意为"正式的进度计划程序"。全句可译为：尽管能够为进度计划的应用提供必要的信息，但定义工作本身却是一项繁复而又单调的事务。

[6] 全句可译为：这样一来，计划制定人员在定义工作任务时就无需考虑整个项目的所有细节。

[7] 全句可译为：尽管不同施工部位重复进行的工作以及过去已完工项目的工作任务可以减轻定义工作任务繁重的工作量，但我们在进行这项工作时却很少使用计算机来为我们帮忙。

[8] 全句可译为：在定义项目的这些工作时应尽可能完整和详尽，将所有必要的工作任务都列入一个或多个活动当中。

[9] 全句可译为：比方说，我们将施工现场对于设备的接受定义为一项工作，原因是其他工作可能要依赖这台设备，并且项目经理也会非常看重它的到场通知。

[10] a natural hierarchy 意为"关系自然的层次结构"。sub-tasks 是指"子任务"。

[11] 全句可译为：例如，施工现场的混凝土施工可以被细分成支设模板、绑扎钢筋、浇注混凝土、混凝土养护、拆模板等子任务。

[12] 全句可译为：在一般的标准施工计划中，通常是不会将"清理模板"这项工作划分到如此细的程度的，但如果是设计机器人来完成这项工作的话，就有必要这样做了，因为对于要由机器人来完成的工作，我们必须予以明确细致的定义。

[13] 全句可译为：为了简化进度计划的开发和表达，我们通常使用一种有明确等级的工作结构。

[14] decision node 指"决策节点"。全句可译为：树状图中的较高层级代表决策节点或综合性工作，而树状图中的枝干则用来指向较低层级的组成部分或工作。

[15] including…是现在分词短语作独立状语，应译为"其中包括如下定义的不同任务之间的前导关系"。

[16] 全句可译为：例如，上面各层活动可表示同设施基础工程这类组成的分部工程，而后可以将其进一步划分为必要的施工作业。

[17] computerized database 是指"计算机化的数据库"。全句可译为：在计算机的数据库中，我们可以将这多种工作分解的结构形式都储存下来以备用时之需。

9.4 Defining Precedence Relationships Among Activities

Once work activities have been defined, the relationships among the activities can be specified. *Precedence* relations between activities signify that the activities must take place in a particular sequence[1]. Numerous natural sequences exist for construction activities due to requirements for structural integrity, regulations, and other technical requirements. For example, design drawings cannot be checked before they are drawn. Diagramatically, precedence relationships can be illustrated by a *network or graph in* which the activities are represented by arrows as shown in Figure 9-2. The arrows in Figure 9-2 are called *branches or links* in the *activity network*, while the circles marking the beginning or end of each arrow are called *nodes or events*[2]. In this figure, links represent particular activities, while the nodes represent milestone events.

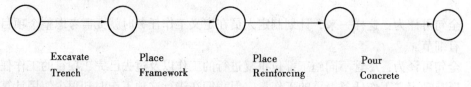

Figure 9-2 Illustrative Set of Four Activities with Precedence

More complicated precedence relationships can also be specified. For example, one activity might not be able to start for several days after the completion of another activity. As a common example, concrete might have to cure (or set) for several days before formwork is removed. This restriction on the removal of forms activity is called a *lag* between the completion of one activity (i.e., pouring concrete in this case) and the start of another activity (i.e., removing formwork in this case)[3]. Many computer based scheduling programs permit the use of a variety of precedence relationships.

Three mistakes should be avoided in specifying predecessor relationships for construction plans. First, a circle of activity precedence will result in an impossible plan. For example, if activity A precedes activity B, activity B precedes activity C, and activity C precedes activity A, then the project can never be started or completed! Figure 9-3 illustrates the resulting activity network. Fortunately, formal scheduling methods and good computer scheduling programs will find any such errors in the logic of the construction plan[4].

Forgetting a necessary precedence relationship can be more insidious. For example, suppose that installation of dry wall should be done prior to floor finishing. Ignoring this precedence relationship may result in both activities being scheduled at the same time. Corrections on the spot may result in increased costs or problems of quality in the completed project.

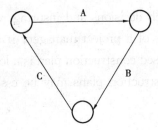

Figure 9-3 Example of an Impossible Work Plan

Unfortunately, there are few ways in which precedence omissions can be found other than with checks by knowledgeable managers or by comparison to comparable projects[5]. One other possible but little used mechanism for checking precedence is to conduct a physical or computer based simulation of the construction process and observe any problems[6].

Finally, it is important to realize that different types of precedence relationships can be defined and that each has different implications for the schedule of activities[7]:

- Some activities have a necessary technical or physical relationship that cannot be superseded. For example, concrete pours cannot proceed before formwork and reinforcement are in place.
- Some activities have a necessary precedence relationship over a continuous space rather than as discrete work task relationships[8]. For example, formwork may be placed in the first part of an excavation trench even as the excavation equipment continues to work further along in the trench. Formwork placement cannot proceed further than the excavation, but the two activities can be started and stopped independently within this constraint[9].
- Some "precedence relationships" are not technically necessary but are imposed due to implicit decisions within the construction plan. For example, two activities may require the same piece of equipment so a precedence relationship might be defined between the two to insure that they are not scheduled for the same time period[10]. Which activity is scheduled first is arbitrary. As a second example, reversing the sequence of two activities may be technically possible but more expensive. In this case, the precedence relationship is not physically necessary but only applied to reduce costs as perceived at the time of scheduling.

In revising schedules as work proceeds, it is important to realize that different types of precedence relationships have quite different implications for the flexibility and cost of changing the construction plan[11]. Unfortunately, many formal scheduling systems do not possess the capability of indicating this type of flexibility. As a result, the burden is placed upon the manager of making such decisions and insuring realistic and effective schedules. With all the other responsibilities of a project manager, it is no surprise that preparing or revising the formal, computer based construction plan is a low priority to a manager in such cases. Nevertheless, formal construction plans may be essential for good management of complicated projects.

Words

design drawing	设计图纸	sequence	顺序
integrity	完整	network	网络
milestone	里程碑	lag	时间间隔
predecessor	紧前活动	illustrate	用（图、表等）说明
logic	逻辑的	insidious	危险的
installation	安装	omission	省略，遗漏，忽略
check	检查	excavation	开挖
trench	沟槽	constraint	约束
reverse	颠倒	flexibility	灵活性
priority	优先顺序		

Notes

[1]　precedence relations 意为"先导关系"。全句可译为：工作之间的先后顺序关系规定了各工作必须按照一定顺序进行。

[2]　activity network 指"工作网络图"。全句可译为：图 9-2 中的箭杆表示一项工作，节点之间的连线代表具体的工作，节点则代表里程碑事件。

[3]　全句可译为：就一项工作完成（本例为浇注混凝土）和另一项工作开始（本例为拆除模板）之间在时间上的限制称为时间间隔。

[4]　全句可译为：幸好，正规的进度计划编制方法和良好的计算机进度计划编制程序均能识别出施工计划中的此类逻辑错误。

[5]　全句可译为：遗憾的是，除了依靠有经验的项目经理进行核对和通过与类似项目进行比较之外，还几乎没有能够发现工作之间先后顺序关系遗漏的有效方法。

[6]　checking precedence 意为"核对先导关系"。全句可译为：一种理论上可行但很少使用的核对先导关系的方法是对施工过程进行计算化的模拟，并从中观察和发现问题。

[7]　全句可译为：最后，还应当认识到，虽然我们定义了不同类型的先导关系，但每一种先导关系对于进度计划而言却有着不同的含义。

[8]　全句可译为：某些工作之间的顺序关系是根据工作空间而非工艺流程来确定的。

[9]　全句可译为：支设模板虽然不能先于沟槽开挖进行，但两项工作可以在不同的施工段上独立地进行。

[10]　全句可译为：例如，两项工作可能要使用同一台机械设备，这样就必须确定它们

之间的先导关系，以便这两项工作不会被安排在同一时间段内施工。

[11] In revising schedules as work proceeds 应译为"随着工作的进展对进度计划进行调整时"。全句可译为：在随着工作的进展对进度计划进行调整时，应当意识到不同类型的先导关系，在改变施工计划时灵活性不同。

Exercise

Translate the text of lesson 9.3 into Chinese.

Chapter 10   Fundamental Scheduling Procedures

10.1   Relevance of Construction Schedules

In addition to assigning dates to project activities, project scheduling is intended to match the resources of equipment, materials and labor with project work tasks over time. Good scheduling can eliminate problems due to production bottlenecks, facilitate the timely procurement of necessary materials, and otherwise insure the completion of a project as soon as possible[1]. In contrast, poor scheduling can result in considerable waste as laborers and equipment wait for the availability of needed resources or the completion of preceding tasks. Delays in the completion of an entire project due to poor scheduling can also create havoc for owners who are eager to start using the constructed facilities[2].

Attitudes toward the formal scheduling of projects are often extreme. Many owners require detailed construction schedules to be submitted by contractors as a means of monitoring the work progress. The actual work performed is commonly compared to the schedule to determine if construction is proceeding satisfactorily. After the completion of construction, similar comparisons between the planned schedule and the actual accomplishments may be performed to allocate the liability for project delays due to changes requested by the owner, worker strikes or other unforeseen circumstances[3].

In contrast to these instances of reliance upon formal schedules, many field supervisors disdain and dislike formal scheduling procedures. In particular, the *critical path method* of scheduling is commonly required by owners and has been taught in universities for over two decades, but is often regarded in the field as irrelevant to actual operations and a time consuming distraction[4]. The result is "seat-of-the-pants" scheduling that can be good or that can result in grossly inefficient schedules and poor productivity[5]. Progressive construction firms use formal scheduling procedures whenever the complexity of work tasks is high and the coordination of different workers is required.

Formal scheduling procedures have become much more common with the advent of personal computers on construction sites and easy-to-use software programs. Sharing schedule information via the internet has also provided a greater incentive to use formal scheduling methods. Savvy construction supervisors often carry schedule and budget information around with wearable or handheld computers[6]. As a result, the continued development of easy to use computer programs and improved methods of presenting schedules have overcome the practical problems associated with formal scheduling mechanisms[7]. But problems with the use of scheduling techniques will continue until managers understand their proper use and limitations.

A basic distinction exists between *resource oriented* and *time oriented* scheduling techniques. For resource oriented scheduling, the focus is on using and scheduling particular resources in an effective fashion[8]. For example, the project manager's main concern on a high-rise building site might to be insure that cranes are used effectively for moving materials; without effective scheduling in this case, delivery trucks might queue on the ground and workers wait for deliveries on upper floors. For time oriented scheduling, the emphasis is on determining the completion time of the project given the necessary precedence relationships among activities. Hybrid techniques for resource leveling or resource constrained scheduling in the presence of precedence relationships also exist. Most scheduling software is time-oriented, although virtually all of the programs have the capability to introduce resource constraints.

This chapter will introduce the fundamentals of scheduling methods. Our discussion will generally assume that computer based scheduling programs will be applied. Consequently, the wide variety of manual or mechanical scheduling techniques will not be discussed in any detail. These manual methods are not as capable or as convenient as computer based scheduling[9]. With the availability of these computer based scheduling programs, it is important for managers to understand the basic operations performed by scheduling programs. Moreover, even if formal methods are not applied in particular cases, the conceptual framework of formal scheduling methods provides a valuable reference for a manager. Accordingly, examples involving hand calculations will be provided throughout the chapter to facilitate understanding.

Words

production bottlenecks 生产瓶颈	constructed facilities 建成设施
construction schedules 施工计划	critical path method 关键线路法
construction sites 工地	budget 预算
resource oriented 以资源为导向的	hybrid techniques 混合计划方法
cranes 起重机	time oriented 以时间为导向的

Notes

[1] 全句可译为：一个好的计划可以消除生产瓶颈所带来的问题，同时也使各项必须的

物资得以及时的采购，因而尽可能地保证了工程如期的完工。

[2] havoc 本意为"大破坏，浩劫"，这里可理解为对业主造成的损失。全句可译为：因为进度计划拙劣而造成整个项目完成时间的拖延会给急于使用建成设施的业主造成灾害性的损失。

[3] due to 意为"由于"，本句结构比较复杂，主句为"similar comparisons may be performed to allocate the liability for project delays"。全句可译为：可以对计划进度和实际进度之间进行类似的的比较，以便查明由于业主的变更要求、工人罢工或者其他不可预见的情况所造成的工程延期责任。

[4] 全句可译为：尤其是业主普遍需要的进度计划中的关键线路法，尽管这种方法在大学里面已经被讲授了二十几年了，但在一些领域当中，这种方法经常不但被认为与一些工作是毫不相关的，而且是对时间和精力的一种浪费。

[5] seat-of-the-pants 本译为"闲坐，无所事事"，可引申为"派不上用场"。全句可译为：结果就是中看不中用的进度计划，若真照着办，效率并不高，甚至妨碍生产。

[6] Savvy construction supervisors 意为"聪明的施工监督人员"，全句可译为：聪明的施工监督人员常常随身携带电脑，存着工程计划和预算资料。

[7] 全句可译为：结果是，易于操作的计算机软件的不断发展和现有计划方法的改进，已经解决了与常规计划手段有关的一些实际问题。

[8] focus on 意为"集中，聚焦"，在这里 focus 用作名词，但与介词 on 的搭配关系不变。

[9] 本句为"as…as"句型，全句可译为：手工方法不如电脑编制那样高效和方便。

10.2 The Critical Path Method

The most widely used scheduling technique is the critical path method (CPM) for scheduling, often referred to as *critical path scheduling*. This method calculates the minimum completion time for a project along with the possible start and finish times for the project activities[1]. Indeed, many texts and managers regard critical path scheduling as the only usable and practical scheduling procedure. Computer programs and algorithms for critical path scheduling are widely available and can efficiently handle projects with thousands of activities.

The *critical path* itself represents the set or sequence of predecessor/successor activities which will take the longest time to complete[2]. The duration of the critical path is the sum of the activities' durations along the path. Thus, the critical path can be defined as the longest possible path through the "network" of project activities, as described in Chapter 9. The duration of the critical path represents the minimum time required to complete a project. Any delays along the critical path would imply that additional time would be required to complete the project.

There may be more than one critical path among all the project activities, so completion of the entire project could be delayed by delaying activities along any one of the critical paths[3]. For example, a project consisting of two activities performed in parallel that each requires three days would have each activity critical for a completion in three days.

Formally, critical path scheduling assumes that a project has been divided into activities of fixed duration and well defined predecessor relationships. A predecessor relationship implies that one activity must come before another in the schedule. No resource constraints other than those implied by precedence relationships are recognized in the simplest form of critical path scheduling[4].

To use critical path scheduling in practice, construction planners often represent a *resource constraint* by a precedence relation. A *constraint* is simply a restriction on the options available to a manager, and a *resource constraint* is a constraint deriving from the limited availability of some resource of equipment, material, space or labor[5]. For example, one of two activities requiring the same piece of equipment might be arbitrarily assumed to precede the other activity. This artificial precedence constraint insures that the two activities requiring the same resource will not be scheduled at the same time[6]. Also, most critical path scheduling algorithms impose restrictions on the generality of the activity relationships or network geometries which are used. In essence, these restrictions imply that the construction plan can be represented by a network plan in which activities appear as nodes in a network. Nodes are numbered, and no two nodes can have the same number or designation. Two nodes are introduced to represent the start and completion of the project itself.

With an activity-on-branch network, dummy activities may be introduced for the purposes of providing unique activity designations and maintaining the correct sequence of activities[7]. A *dummy activity* is assumed to have no time duration and can be graphically represented by a dashed line in a network. Several cases in which dummy activities are useful are illustrated in Figuer 10-1. In Figure 10-1part(a), the elimination of activity C would mean that both activities B and D would be identified as being between nodes 1 and 3. However, if a dummy activity X is introduced, as shown in part (b), the unique designations for activity B (node 1 to 2) and D (node 1 to 3) will be preserved. Furthermore, if the problem in part (a) is changed so that activity E cannot start until both C and D are completed but that F can start after D alone is completed, the order in the new sequence can be indicated by the addition of a dummy activity Y, as shown in part (c). In general, dummy activities may be necessary to meet the requirements of specific computer scheduling algorithms, but it is important to limit the number of such dummy link insertions to the extent possible[8].

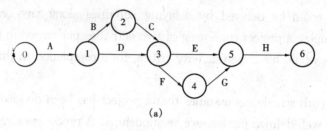

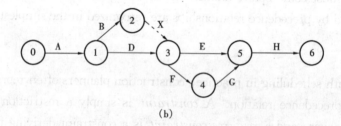

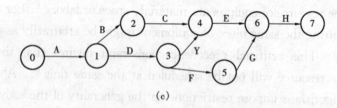

Figure 10-1 Dummy Activities in a Project Network

Many computer scheduling systems support only one network representation, either activity-on-branch or activity-on-node. A good project manager is familiar with either representation.

Words

algorithms　算法
recourses constrains　资源限制
screen menu　屏幕菜单
a dashed line　虚线
representation　表示方法

predecessor relationship　前后顺序关系
construction planners　施工计划编制人员
activity-on-branch network　双代号网络图
dummy activities　虚工作
activity-on-node network　单代号网络图

Notes

[1]　全句可译为：这种方法能够计算出项目的最短完成时间和项目各项活动可能的开始与结束时间。

[2]　全句可译为：关键线路本身由一系列有着先行后继顺序关系的活动组成，完成这些

[3]   全句可译为：在全部的项目活动当中，可能会有多条关键线路，所以整个工程的完成时间会因为任何一条关键线路上活动的延迟而拖后。

[4]   other than 意为"除了"，为常见短语。本句可译为：最简单的关键线路进度计划编制，除了时间先后关系的限制外，没有资源限制。

[5]   derive from 意为"源于"。全句可译为：制约因素就是对可供管理人员选择的一种限制，而资源制约因素来源于某些可用资源，如设备、材料、空间或劳动力。

[6]   artifical precedence constraints 意为"人为确定的先后顺序制约"。全句可译为：人为确定的先后顺序制约确保了两个需要同一资源的活动不被安排在同一时间。

[7]   全句可译为：在一个双代号网络图中，虚工作被用来提供特殊的工作安排和保持正确的工作间的逻辑关系。

[8]   全句可译为：通常情况下我们必须用虚工作来满足具体的计算机进度计算的要求，但在一定程度上尽可能的限制虚工作的数量也是非常重要的。

10.3 Activity Float and Schedules

A number of different activity schedules can be developed from the critical path scheduling procedure described in the previous section[1]. An *earliest time* schedule would be developed by starting each activity as soon as possible, at $ES(i,j)$. Similarly, a *latest time* schedule would delay the start of each activity as long as possible but still finish the project in the minimum possible time. This late schedule can be developed by setting each activity's start time to $LS(i,j)$.

Activities that have different early and late start times $[i.e., ES(i,j) < LS(i,j)]$ can be scheduled to start anytime between $ES(i,j)$ and $LS(i,j)$ as shown in Figure 10-2. The concept of *float* is to use part or all of this allowable range to schedule an activity without delaying the completion of the project. An activity that has the earliest time for its predecessor and successor nodes differing by more than its duration possesses a window in which it can be scheduled[2]. That is, if $E(i) + D_{ij} < L(j)$, then some float is available in which to schedule this activity.

Float is a very valuable concept since it represents the scheduling flexibility or "maneuvering room" available to complete particular tasks[3]. Activities on the critical path do not provide any flexibility for scheduling nor leeway in case of problems[4]. For activities with some float, the actual starting time might be chosen to balance work loads over time, to correspond with material deliveries, or to improve the project's cash flow.

Of course, if one activity is allowed to float or change in the schedule, then the amount of float available for other activities may decrease. Three separate categories of float are defined in critical path scheduling:

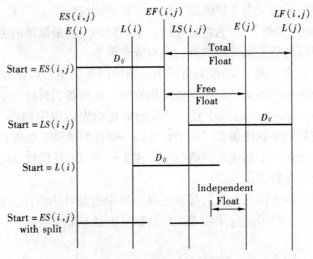

Figure 10-2 Illustration of Activity Float

1. *Free float* is the amount of delay which can be assigned to any one activity without delaying subsequent activities. The free float, $FF(i,j)$, associated with activity (i,j) is:

$$FF(i,j) = E(j) - E(i) - D_{ij} \qquad (10.1)$$

2. *Independent float* is the amount of delay which can be assigned to any one activity without delaying subsequent activities or restricting the scheduling of preceding activities. Independent float, $IF(i,j)$, for activity (i,j) is calculated as:

$$IF(i,j) = \begin{cases} 0 \\ E(j) - L(i) - D_{ij} \end{cases} \qquad (10.2)$$

3. *Total float* is the maximum amount of delay which can be assigned to any activity without delaying the entire project. The total float, $TF(i,j)$, for any activity (i, j) is calculated as:

$$TF(i,j) = L(j) - E(i) - D_{ij} \qquad (10.3)$$

Each of these "floats" indicates an amount of flexibility associated with an activity[5]. In all cases, total float equals or exceeds free float, while independent float is always less than or equal to free float. Also, any activity on a critical path has all three values of float equal to zero. The converse of this statement is also true, so any activity which has zero total float can be recognized as being on a critical path[6].

The various categories of activity float are illustrated in Figure 10-4 in which the activity is represented by a bar which can move back and forth in time depending upon its scheduling start. Three possible scheduled starts are shown, corresponding to the cases of starting each activity at the earliest event time, $E(i)$, the latest activity start time $LS(i,j)$, and at the latest event time $L(i)$[7]. The three categories of float can be found directly from this figure. Finally, a fourth bar is included in the figure to illustrate the possibility that an activity might start, be temporarily halted, and then re-start. In this case, the temporary halt was sufficiently short that it was less than the independent float time and thus would not interfere with other activities. Whether or not such work splitting is possible or economical depends upon the nature of the activity[8].

As we can see activity $D(1,3)$ has free and independent floats of 10 for the project shown in Figure 10-2. Thus, the start of this activity could be scheduled anytime between time 4 and 14 after the project began without interfering with the schedule of other activities or with the earliest completion time of the project. As the total float of 11 units indicates, the start of activity D could also be delayed until time 15, but this would require that the schedule of other activities be restricted. For example, starting activity D at time 15 would require that activity G would begin as soon as activity D was completed. However, if this schedule was maintained, the overall completion date of the project would not be changed.

Words

earliest start times 最早开始时间	latest start times 最迟开始时间
cash flow 现金流量	independent float 独立时差
free float 自由时差	total float 总时差
bar 横线	the temporary halt 暂时中断
preliminary design 初步设计	evaluation of design 设计评价
contract negotiation 合同谈判	preparation of fabrication plant 设备制作准备
final design 施工图设计	
shipment of product to owner 运交业主	fabrication of Product 生产制作

Notes

[1] described 为过去分词短语作定语，其完整结构为"which is described"，全句可译为：前节所述关键线路进度计划编制过程可以编制出多种活动时间不同的进度计划。

[2] in which 引导状语从句，全句可译为：如果一项工作的持续时间小于其前后节点间的最早时间之差，它就拥有了一段可供计划支配的时差。

[3] maneuvering room 指"回旋余地"，与 flexibility 有相同的含义。

[4] leeway 本意为"后路"，这里可以引申为"机动时间"。全句可译为：关键线路上的工作没有时间安排上的灵活性，在遇到问题时也没有退路。

[5] associated with … 意为"与……相联系"。全句可译为：每一种时差所表示的都是工作时间灵活性的大小。

[6] the converse of the statement 意思是"这一说法反过来"，可译为"反之"。全句可译为为：反之，任何总时差为零的工作必在关键线路上。

[7] corresponding to 意思是"与……相对应的"。全句可译为：有三种计划开始时间，分别是与工作最早开始时间相对应的事件最早时间为 $E(i)$，工作最迟开始时间为 $LS(i,j)$，以及事件最迟时间为 $L(i)$。

[8] whether 引导的从句作主语，全句可译为：这种工作暂时中断是否可行、经济，取决于工作本身的性质。

10.4 Presenting Project Schedules

Communicating the project schedule is a vital ingredient in successful project management. A good presentation will greatly ease the manager's problem of understanding the multitude of activities and their inter-relationships. Moreover, numerous individuals and parties are involved in any project, and they have to understand their assignments. *Graphical* presentations of project schedules are particularly useful since it is much easier to comprehend a graphical display of numerous pieces of information than to sift through a large table of numbers[1]. Early computer scheduling systems were particularly poor in this regard since they produced pages and pages of numbers without aids to the manager for understanding them. In practice, a project summary table would be much longer. It is extremely tedious to read a table of activity numbers, durations, schedule times, and floats and thereby gain an understanding and appreciation of a project schedule. In practice, producing diagrams manually has been a common prescription to the lack of automated drafting facilities.

Network diagrams for projects have already been introduced. These diagrams provide a powerful visualization of the precedence and relationships among the various project activities. They are a basic means of communicating a project plan among the participating planners and project monitors. Project planning is often conducted by producing network representations of greater and greater refinement until the plan is satisfactory.

A useful variation on project network diagrams is to draw a *time-scaled* network[2]. The activity diagrams shown in the previous section were topological networks in that only the relationship between nodes and branches were of interest[3]. The actual diagram could be distorted in any way desired as long as the connections between nodes were not changed. In time-scaled network diagrams, activities on the network are plotted on a horizontal axis measuring the time since project commencement. Figure 10-3 gives an example of a time-scaled activity-on-branch diagram for the nine activity project in Figure 10-2. In this time-scaled diagram, each node is shown at its earliest possible time. By looking over the horizontal axis, the time at which activity begin can be observed. Obviously, this time scaled diagram is produced as a display after activities are initially scheduled by the critical path method.

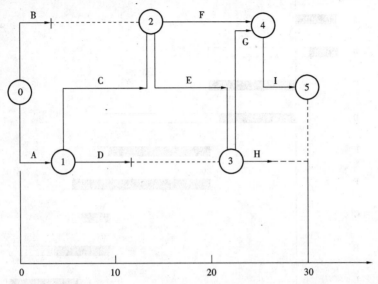

Figure 10-3 Illustration of a Time Scaled Network Diagram with Nine Activities

Another useful graphical representation tool is a bar or Gantt chart illustrating the scheduled time for each activity. The bar chart lists activities and shows their scheduled start, finish and duration. An illustrative bar chart for the nine activity project appearing in Figure 10-4 is shown in Figure 10-3. Activities are listed in the vertical axis of this figure, while time since project commencement is shown along the horizontal axis. During the course of *monitoring* a project, useful additions to the basic bar chart include a vertical line to indicate the current time plus small marks to indicate the current state of work on each activity. In Figure 10-4, a hypothetical project state after 4 periods is shown. The small "v" marks on each activity represent the current state of each activity.

Bar charts are particularly helpful for communicating the current state and schedule of activities on a project. As such, they have found wide acceptance as a project representation tool in the field. For planning purposes, bar charts are not as useful since they do not indicate the precedence relationships among activities[4]. Thus, a planner must remember or record separately that a change in one activity's schedule may require changes to successor activities. There have been various schemes for mechanically linking activity bars to represent precedence, but it is now easier to use computer based tools to represent such relationships.

Other graphical representations are also useful in project monitoring. Time and activity graphs are extremely useful in portraying the current status of a project as well as the

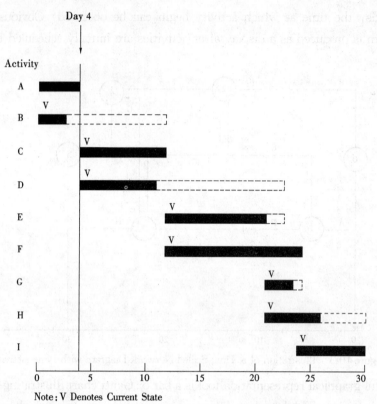

Figure 10-4 An Example Bar Chart for a Nine Activity Project

existence of activity float. For example, Figure 10-5 shows two possible schedules for the nine activity project described in Table 9-1 and shown in the previous figures. The first schedule would occur if each activity was scheduled at its earliest start time, $ES(i,j)$ consistent with completion of the project in the minimum possible time. With this schedule, Figure 10-5 shows the percent of project activity completed versus time. The second schedule in Figure 10-5 is based on latest possible start times for each activity, $LS(i,j)$. The horizontal time difference between the two feasible schedules gives an indication of the extent of possible float. If the project goes according to plan, the actual percentage completion at different times should fall between these curves. In practice, a vertical axis representing cash expenditures rather than percent completed is often used in developing a project representation of this type[5]. For this purpose, activity cost estimates are used in preparing a time versus completion graph. Separate "S-curves" may also be prepared for groups of activities on the same graph, such as separate curves for the design, procurement, foundation or particular sub-contractor activities[6].

Graphs of resource use over time are also of interest to project planners and managers. An example of resource use is shown in Figure 10-6 for the resource of total employment on the site of a project. This graph is prepared by summing the resource requirements for each activity at each time period for a particular project schedule. With limited resources of some kind, graphs of this type can indicate when the competition for a resource is too large to

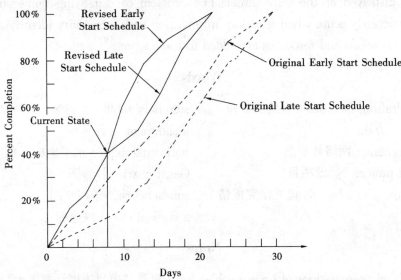

Figure 10-5 Illustration of Actual Percentage Completion versus Time for a Nine Activity Project Underway

accommodate; in cases of this kind, resource constrained scheduling would be very necessary. Even without fixed resource constraints, a scheduler tries to avoid extreme fluctuations in the demand for labor or other resources since these fluctuations typically incur high costs for training, hiring, transportation, and management. Thus, a planner might alter a schedule through the use of available activity floats so as to level or smooth out the demand for resources. Resource graphs such as Figure 10-6 provide an invaluable indication of the potential trouble spots and the success that a scheduler has in avoiding them[7].

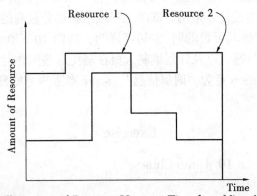

Figure 10-6 Illustration of Resource Use over Time for a Nine Activity Project

A common difficulty with project network diagrams is that too much information is available for easy presentation in a network. In a project with, say, five hundred activities, drawing activities so that they can be seen without a microscope requires a considerable expanse of paper. A large project might require the wall space in a room to include the entire diagram. On a computer display, a typical restriction is that less than twenty activities can be successfully displayed at the same time. The problem of displaying numerous activities becomes particularly acute when accessory information such as activity identifying numbers or phrases, durations and resources are added to the diagram[8].

Words

automated drafting facilities　自绘图设备　　summary table　汇总表
prescription　方法　　　　　　　　　　　　assignment　任务
network diagrams　网络计划图　　　　　　　horizontal axis　水平坐标
hypothetical project　假设项目　　　　　　　Gantt chart　甘特图
time and activity graphs　时间工作完成情　　sub-network　子网络图
况曲线图　　　　　　　　　　　　　　　　a vertical axis　纵坐标

Notes

[1] graphical presentations of project schedules 意思是"项目进度计划图示"，全句可译为：以图形将项目进度计划显示出来特别有用，因为用大量信息图形表现要比用罗列大量数据的表格容易理解得多。

[2] time-scaled network 意为"时标网络图"。全句可译为：项目网络图很有用的一种形式就是时标网络图。

[3] be of interest 意思是"值得注意的"。

[4] since 引导的原因状语从句，for planning purposes 意思是"就计划的目的而言"。

[5] 全句可译为：但在实际中，在以这种形式准备项目的介绍材料时，纵坐标表示资金的支出而不是完成的百分比。

[6] S-curves 表示"S-曲线图"。全句可译为：在一张图上，有时可以分别绘制各种活动的 S 曲线，比如设计、采购、基础工程或是特定分包商的各项工作。

[7] invaluable 意为"极其可贵的"，本句可译为：如图 10-6 所示的资源曲线对于揭示可能发生的潜在问题，以及计划编制人员在避免这些问题时的成功做法极有价值。

[8] accessory information 意为"附属信息"。acute 本意为"剧烈的、尖锐的"，在文章中可译为"棘手的"。

Exercise

Translate the text of lesson 10.4 into Chinese.

Chapter 11   Advanced Scheduling Techniques

11.1   Scheduling with Uncertain Durations

Section 10.3 described the application of *critical path scheduling* for the situation in which activity durations are fixed and known. Unfortunately, activity durations are estimates of the actual time required, and there is liable to be a significant amount of uncertainty associated with the actual durations. During the preliminary planning stages for a project, the uncertainty in activity durations is particularly large since the scope and obstacles to the project are still undefined[1]. Activities that are outside of the control of the owner are likely to be more uncertain. For example, the time required to gain regulatory approval for projects may vary tremendously. Other external events such as adverse weather, trench collapses, or labor strikes make duration estimates particularly uncertain[2].

Two simple approaches to dealing with the uncertainty in activity durations warrant some discussion before introducing more formal scheduling procedures to deal with uncertainty[3]. First, the uncertainty in activity durations may simply be ignored and scheduling done using the expected or most likely time duration for each activity[4]. Since only one duration estimate needs to be made for each activity, this approach reduces the required work in setting up the original schedule. Formal methods of introducing uncertainty into the scheduling process require more work and assumptions. While this simple approach might be defended, it has two drawbacks. First, the use of expected activity durations typically results in overly optimistic schedules for completion; a numerical example of this optimism appears below. Second, the use of single activity durations often produces a rigid, inflexible mindset on the part of schedulers. As field managers appreciate, activity durations vary considerable and can be influenced by good leadership and close attention[5]. As a result, field managers may lose confidence in the realism of a schedule based upon fixed activity durations. Clearly, the use of fixed activity durations in setting up a schedule makes a continual process of monitoring and updating the schedule in light of actual experience imperative[6]. Otherwise, the project schedule is rapidly outdated.

A second simple approach to incorporation uncertainty also deserves mention. Many managers recognize that the use of expected durations may result in overly optimistic schedules, so they include a contingency allowance in their estimate of activity durations[7].

For example, an activity with an expected duration of two days might be scheduled for a period of 2.2 days, including a ten percent contingency. Systematic application of this contingency would result in a ten percent increase in the expected time to complete the project. While the use of this rule-of-thumb or *heuristic* contingency factor can result in more accurate schedules, it is likely that formal scheduling methods that incorporate uncertainty more formally are useful as a means of obtaining greater accuracy or in understanding the effects of activity delays[8].

The most common formal approach to incorporate uncertainty in the scheduling process is to apply the critical path scheduling process (as described in Section 10.3) and then analyze the results from a probabilistic perspective[9]. This process is usually referred to as the PERT scheduling or evaluation method. As noted earlier, the duration of the critical path represents the minimum time required to complete the project. Using expected activity durations and critical path scheduling, a critical path of activities can be identified. This critical path is then used to analyze the duration of the project incorporating the uncertainty of the activity durations along the critical path. The expected project duration is equal to the sum of the expected durations of the activities along the critical path. Assuming that activity durations are independent random variables, the variance or variation in the duration of this critical path is calculated as the sum of the variances along the critical path[10]. With the mean and variance of the identified critical path known, the distribution of activity durations can also be computed.

While the PERT method has been made widely available, it suffers from three major problems. First, the procedure focuses upon a single critical path, when many paths might become critical due to random fluctuations[11]. For example, suppose that the critical path with longest expected time happened to be completed early. Unfortunately, this does not necessarily mean that the project is completed early since another path or sequence of activities might take longer. Similarly, a longer than expected duration for an activity not on the critical path might result in that activity suddenly becoming critical[12]. As a result of the focus on only a single path, the PERT method typically *underestimates* the actual project duration.

As a second problem with the PERT procedure, it is incorrect to assume that most construction activity durations are independent random variables. In practice, durations are *correlated* with one another. For example, if problems are encountered in the delivery of concrete for a project, this problem is likely to influence the expected duration of numerous activities involving concrete pours on a project[13]. Positive correlations of this type between activity durations imply that the PERT method *underestimates* the variance of the critical path and thereby produces over-optimistic expectations of the probability of meeting a particular project completion deadline[14].

Finally, the PERT method requires three duration estimates for each activity rather than the single estimate developed for critical path scheduling. Thus, the difficulty and labor of estimating activity characteristics is multiplied threefold.

Words

liable 有义务的
obstacle 障碍
collapse 倒塌
warrant 授权
uncertainty 不确定性
optimistic 乐观的
rigid 刚性的,僵硬的
incorporation 编入,融入
heuristic 凭经验与直觉的
random variables 随机变量
variance 差异,分歧
correlate 相关
imply 含有……的意思,暗示
probability 概率

trench 沟槽
adverse 不利的
approach 方法,途径
drawback 缺点
overly 过度的
mindset 心态
realism 现实
allowance 津贴,余地
probabilistic 概率的
mean 平均值
fluctuation 波动
positive correlation 正相关
over-optimistic 过于乐观的
threefold 三倍

Abbreviation（缩略语）

PERT（Program Evaluation and Review Technology）计划评审技术

Notes

[1] since…是原因状语从句,可译为"由于项目的范围和潜在的障碍还不明确"。

[2] adverse weather 意为"恶劣的天气"。trench collapse 指"沟槽塌方"。全句可译为：此外,恶劣的天气、沟槽塌方或工人罢工等都会使工作持续时间变得极不确定。

[3] 全句可译为：在我们深入讨论处理不确定性的进度计划方法之前,先介绍两种处理工作持续时间中不确定性的简单方法。

[4] 全句可译为：第一种方法是忽略工作持续时间中的不确定性,在编制进度计划过程中采用每项工作的期望或最可能持续时间。

[5] appreciate 指"体会、感受"。close attention 意为"随时注意,认真对待"。全句可译为：现场管理人员已经认识到,工作持续时间变化很大,领导有方,随时注意与认真对待也有很大影响。

[6] 全句可译为：显然,在制定进度计划时,使用固定的工作持续时间就必须时刻根据

实际情况对进度计划进行监控和更新。

[7] 全句可译为：许多项目经理意识到使用预期的工作持续时间会使进度计划变得过于乐观，因此他们在计算工作持续时间时常会在其中考虑一个应急准备的时间。

[8] rule-of-thumb 意为"领先的、先进的"。全句可译为：尽管考虑了应急时间在内的第二种处理不确定性的进度计划方法在精度上有所提高，但为了获得更高的精确性和为了了解进度拖延的影响及原因，我们通常会使用将在下面予以介绍的把不确定性因素考虑在内的进度计划方法。

[9] the critical path scheduling process 指"关键线路进度计划流程"。from a probabilistic perspective 意为"从概率分析的角度"。全句可译为：在进度计划中把不确定性考虑进去的最为常用的方法是在关键线路法（在 10.3 节中介绍过）的基础上再对计算结果进行概率分析。

[10] independent random variables 意为"独立随机变量"。variance 是指"方差"。全句可译为：假定工作持续时间是独立随机变量，关键线路上持续时间的方差可由对关键线路上各关键工作的方差进行求和计算而得出。

[11] a single critical path 意为"单一的关键路径"。random-fluctuation 意为"随机波动"。全句可译为：首先，当由于随机波动而有可能出现多条关键线路时，该方法仍然只关注于原有的单一关键线路。

[12] 全句可译为：同样地，某非关键线路上的工作持续时间的延长有可能使其突然变成关键线路。

[13] the delivery of concrete 意为"混凝土的运输"。全句可译为：例如，当一个项目遇到混凝土运输方面的问题时，那么该项目所有与混凝土浇灌有关工作的持续时间可能都会因此而受到影响。

[14] positive correlation 意为"正相关性"。全局可译为：由于没有考虑工作持续时间之间的这种正相关性，PERT 计划技术就有可能忽略了关键线路的变异性，因而对于一个项目能否满足工期要求就可能产生过于乐观的概率期望值。

11.2　Scheduling in Poorly Structured Problems

The previous discussion of activity scheduling suggested that the general structure of the construction plan was known in advance. With previously defined activities, relationships among activities, and required resources, the scheduling problem could be represented as a mathematical optimization problem[1]. Even in the case in which durations are uncertain, we assumed that the underlying probability distribution of durations is known and applied analytical techniques to investigate schedules[2].

While these various scheduling techniques have been exceedingly useful, they do not cover the range of scheduling problems encountered in practice. In particular, there are many cases in which costs and durations depend upon other activities due to congestion on the site[3]. In contrast, the scheduling techniques discussed previously assume that durations of activities are generally independent of each other. A second problem stems from the complexity of construction technologies. In the course of resource allocations, numerous additional constraints or objectives may exist that are difficult to represent analytically[4]. For example, different workers may have specialized in one type of activity or another. With greater experience, the work efficiency for particular crews may substantially increase. Unfortunately, representing such effects in the scheduling process can be very difficult. Another case of complexity occurs when activity durations and schedules are negotiated among the different parties in a project so there is no single overall planner[5].

A practical approach to these types of concerns is to insure that all schedules are reviewed and modified by experienced project managers before implementation. This manual review permits the incorporation of global constraints or consideration of peculiarities of workers and equipment. Indeed, interactive schedule revision to accommodate resource constraints is often superior to any computer based heuristic[6]. With improved graphic representations and information availability, man-machine interaction is likely to improve as a scheduling procedure.

More generally, the solution procedures for scheduling in these more complicated situations cannot be reduced to mathematical algorithms[7]. The best solution approach is likely to be a "generate-and-test" cycle for alternative plans and schedules. In this process, a possible schedule is hypothesized or generated. This schedule is tested for feasibility with respect to relevant constraints (such as available resources or time horizons) and desirability with respect to different objectives[8]. Ideally, the process of evaluating an alternative will suggest directions for improvements or identify particular trouble spots. These results are then used in the generation of a new test alternative. This process continues until a satisfactory plan is obtained.

Two important problems must be borne in mind in applying a "generate-and-test" strategy. First, the number of possible plans and schedules is enormous, so considerable insight to the problem must be used in generating reasonable alternatives[9]. Secondly, evaluating alternatives also may involve considerable effort and judgment. As a result, the number of actual cycles of alternative testing that can be accommodated is limited. One hope for computer technology in this regard is that the burdensome calculations associated with this type of planning may be assumed by the computer, thereby reducing the cost and required time for the planning effort[10].

Example 11-1: Man-machine Interactive Scheduling

An interactive system for scheduling with resource constraints might have the following characteristics :

- graphic displays of bar charts, resource use over time, activity networks and other graphic images available in different windows of a screen simultaneously.
- descriptions of particular activities including allocated resources and chosen technologies available in windows as desired by a user.
- a three dimensional animation of the construction process that can be stopped to show the progress of construction on the facility at any time.
- easy-to-use methods for changing start times and allocated resources, and
- utilities to run relevant scheduling algorithms such as the critical path method at any time.

Figure 11-1 shows an example of a screen for this system. In Figure 11-1, a bar chart

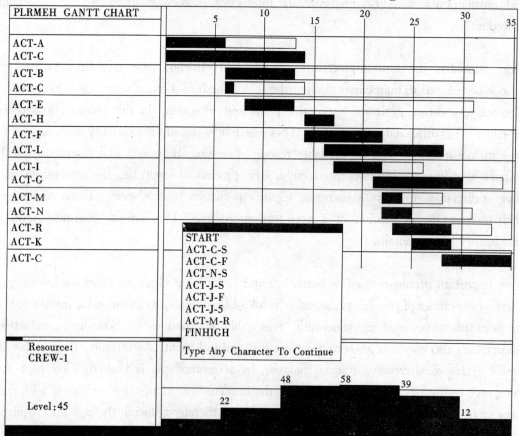

Figure 11-1 Example of a Bar Chart and Other Windows for Interactive Scheduling

156

appears in one window, a description of an activity in another window, and a graph of the use of a particular resource over time appears in a third window[11]. These different "windows" appear as sections on a computer screen displaying different types of information. With these capabilities, a project manager can call up different pictures of the construction plan and make changes to accomadate objectives or constraints that are not formally represented[12]. With rapid response to such changes, the effects can be immediately evaluated.

Words

optimization 优化	distribution 分布
encounter 遭遇	congestion 混淆,拥挤
crew 全体人员	revision 校订
review 检查	interactive 互动的,交互的
accommodate 适应	graphic 图形的
hypothesize 假设	insight 洞察,洞察力
burdensome 烦重的	simultaneously 同时地
animation 动画	algorithm 算法

Notes

[1] With…为介词短语作状语,可译为"在工作,工作之间逻辑关系以及工作所需资源已经确定的情况下"。mathematical optimization 意为"数学优化"。全句可译为:在工作,工作之间逻辑关系以及工作所需的资源已经确定的情况下,进度计划问题就可以被描述成为一个数学优化问题。

[2] 全句可译为:即使当工作持续时间不确定时,我们也可以假设工作持续时间的概率分布是已知的,从而运用相应的数学分析技术来解决进度计划中的问题。

[3] congestion on the site 意为"现场的拥挤"。全句可译为:尤其是,有许多情况是施工现场的拥挤使得工作持续时间和成本取决于其他工作。

[4] that are…是定语从句,修饰前面的 constraints or objectives。全句可译为:在资源配置过程中,有许多很难用数学式子表达的约束条件与目标。

[5] 全句可译为:此外,当项目由于没有一个总的计划安排者,而使得工作持续时间和进度计划需要在不同参与方之间谈判确定时,也会出现类似的问题。

[6] interactive schedule revision 意为"互动的进度计划检查"。be superior to 指"优于、强于"。全句可译为:事实上,这种为满足资源约束条件而进行的互动的进度计划检查通常比基于计算机的渐进调整方法更为贴近实际。

[7] 全句可译为:更为一般地,在这些更复杂的条件下编制进度计划的问题,不能简单地靠数学算法来解决。

[8] with respect to 指"关于"。time horizon 意为"时间基准"。全句可译为:我们根据相关的约束条件(如可获得的资源以及时间基准)和不同的目标对这种进度计划的

[9] 全句可译为：首先，由于可能的方案和进度计划的数目会很多，因此在生成合理的被选方案时，我们应当对问题有足够的调查。

[10] may be assumed by the computer 可译为"由计算机来承担"。全句可译为：在这方面寄托于电脑的希望是，这类计划工作中的繁琐计算由电脑完成，从而降低计划工作的成本，缩短编织计划所需的时间。

[11] 全句可译为：在图 11-1 中，横道图出现在一个视窗中，对于工作的描述出现在另一个视窗中，而资源的消耗量则显示在第三个视窗当中。

[12] 全句可译为：在这些功能的支持下，项目经理就可以调出施工计划中的不同画面并做出适当的调整，以满足目标或约束条件。

11.3 Calculations for Monte Carlo Schedule Simulation

In this section, we outline the procedures required to perform Monte Carlo simulation for the purpose of schedule analysis[1]. These procedures presume that the various steps involved in forming a network plan and estimating the characteristics of the probability distributions for the various activities have been completed. Given a plan and the activity duration distributions, the heart of the Monte Carlo simulation procedure is the derivation of a *realization* or synthetic outcome of the relevant activity durations[2]. Once these realizations are generated, standard scheduling techniques can be applied. We shall present the formulas associated with the generation of normally distributed activity durations, and then comment on the requirements for other distributions in an example[3].

To generate normally distributed realizations of activity durations, we can use a two step procedure. First, we generate uniformly distributed random variables, u_i in the interval from zero to one. Numerous techniques can be used for this purpose. For example, a general formula for random number generation can be of the form:

$$u_i = fractional\ part\ of[(\pi + u_{i-1})^5] \tag{11.1}$$

where $\pi = 3.14159265$ and u_{i-1} was the previously generated random number or a preselected beginning or seed number. For example, a seed of $u_0 = 0.215$ in Eq. 11.1 results in $u_1 = 0.0820$, and by applying this value of u_1, the result is $u_2 = 0.1029$. This formula is a special case of the mixed congruential method of random number generation. While Eq. 11.1 will result in a series of numbers that have the appearance and the necessary statistical properties of true random numbers, we should note that these are actually "pseudo" random numbers since the sequence of numbers will repeat given a long enough time[4].

With a method of generating uniformly distributed random numbers, we can generate normally distributed random numbers using two uniformly distributed realizations with the equations[5]:

$$x_k = u_x + s \sin t \qquad (11.2)$$

with

$$s = \sigma_x \sqrt{-2 \ln u_1}$$

$$t = 2\pi u_2$$

where x_k is the normal realization, μ_x is the mean of x, σ_x is the standard deviation of x, and u_1 and u_2 are the two uniformly distributed random variable realizations[6]. For the case in which the mean of an activity is 2.5 days and the standard deviation of the duration is 1.5 days, a corresponding realization of the duration is $s = 2.2365$, $t = 0.6465$ and $x_k = 2.525$ days, using the two uniform random numbers generated from a seed of 0.215 above.

Correlated random number realizations may be generated making use of conditional distributions. For example, suppose that the duration of an activity d is normally distributed and correlated with a second normally distributed random variable x which may be another activity duration or a separate factor such as a weather effect[7]. Given a realization x_k of x, the conditional distribution of d is still normal, but it is a function of the value x_k. In particular, the conditional mean $(\mu'_d \mid x = x_k)$ and standard deviation $(\sigma'_d \mid x = x_k)$ of a normally distributed variable given a realization of the second variable is:

$$\{\mu'_d \mid x = x_k\} = \rho_{dx}(\sigma_d/\sigma_x)(x_k - \mu_x) + \mu_d$$

$$\{\sigma'_d \mid x = x_k\} = \sigma_d \sqrt{1 - \rho_{dx}} \qquad (11.3)$$

where ρ_{dx} is the correlation coefficient between d and x. Once x_k is known, the conditional mean and standard deviation can be calculated from Eq. 11.3 and then a realization of d obtained by applying Eq. 11.2[8].

Correlation coefficients indicate the extent to which two random variables will tend to vary together. Positive correlation coefficients indicate one random variable will tend to exceed its mean when the other random variable does the same[9]. From a set of n historical observations of two random variables, x and y, the correlation coefficient can be estimated as:

$$\rho_{xy} = \frac{n \sum_{i=1}^{n} x_i y_i - \sum_{i=1}^{n} x_i \sum_{i=1}^{n} y_i}{\left[n \sum_{i=1}^{n} x_i^2 - \left(\sum_{i=1}^{n} x_i\right)^2\right]^{1/2} \left[n \sum_{i=1}^{n} y_i^2 - \left(\sum_{i=1}^{n} y_i\right)^2\right]^{1/2}} \qquad (11.4)$$

The value of ρ_{xy} can range from one to minus one, with values near one indicating a positive, near linear relationship between the two random variables[10].

It is also possible to develop formulas for the conditional distribution of a random variable correlated with numerous other variables; this is termed a multi-variable distribution. Random number generations from other types of distributions are also possible. Once a set of random variable distributions is obtained, then the process of applying a scheduling algorithm is required as described in previous sections[11].

Words

procedure　程序
probability　概率
realization　实得值
formula　公式
variable　变量
statistical　统计的
mean　均值
function　函数
linear　线性

presume　假设
derivation　方差
synthetic　综合的
random　随机的
pre-selected　预先选定的
property　特性
standard deviation　标准差
coefficient　系数

Notes

[1]　Monte Carlo simulation 指"蒙特卡罗模拟"。全句可译为：在这一节，我们介绍在进度分析中使用蒙特卡罗模拟的主要步骤。

[2]　全句可译为：对于给定的进度计划和工作持续时间概率分布，蒙特卡罗模拟的核心是取得相关工作持续时间的实得值或合成结果。

[3]　全句可译为：我们将首先介绍与正态分布的工作持续时间的生成有关的公式，然后通过例子来讨论其他分布类型所需要的条件。

[4]　"pseudo" random numbers 意为"'伪'随机数"。全句可译为：尽管公式11.1可以产生一系列的貌似真实随机数且具有真实随机数必要统计特征的数字，但我们应当注意当时间足够长时，这些数字列会出现重复，因而这些数字实际上是"伪"随机数。

[5]　全句可译为：按照生成一致性分布随机数的方法，根据下面的公式我们利用两个一致性分布的实得值就可以生成一致性正态分布随机数：

[6]　uniformly distributed random variable realizations 指"一致性分布随机变量实得值"。

[7]　which may be... 为定语从句，修饰前面的"x"。全句可译为：例如，假定工作 d 的持续时间服从正态分布，并且与第二个服从正态分布的随机变量 x 相关，x 可以是另外一个工作的持续时间，也可以是像天气影响这样一类的独立因素。

[8]　全句可译为：一旦 x_k 已知，我们用公式11.3就可以计算出条件分布的均值和标准差，应用公式11.2则可以计算出实得值。

[9]　positive correlation coefficients 意为"正相关系数"。全句可译为：而正相关系数则是指当另一个随机变量超过其均值时，某随机变量也往往会超过其均值。

[10] 全句可译为：ρ_{xy}取值范围在 1 到 -1 之间，如果ρ_{xy}趋近于 1，则说明 x 和 y 之间为正相关的线性关系。

[11] a set of random variable distribution 意为"一系列随机变量分布"。全句可译为：一旦得到了一组随机变量的分布，就可以应用前面各节已经介绍过的编制进度计划的计算方法了。

11.4　Improving the Scheduling Process

Despite considerable attention by researchers and practitioners, the process of construction planning and scheduling still presents problems and opportunities for improvement[1]. The importance of scheduling in insuring the effective coordination of work and the attainment of project deadlines is indisputable. For large projects with many parties involved, the use of formal schedules is indispensable.

The network model for representing project activities has been provided as an important conceptual and computational framework for planning and scheduling. Networks not only communicate the basic precedence relationships between activities, they also form the basis for most scheduling computations.

As a practical matter, most project scheduling is performed with the critical path scheduling method, supplemented by heuristic procedures used in project crash analysis or resource constrained scheduling[2]. Many commercial software programs are available to perform these tasks. Probabilistic scheduling or the use of optimization software to perform time/cost trade-offs is rather more infrequently applied, but there are software programs available to perform these tasks if desired.

Rather than concentrating upon more elaborate solution algorithms, the most important innovations in construction scheduling are likely to appear in the areas of data storage, ease of use, data representation, communication and diagnostic or interpretation aids[3]. Integration of scheduling information with accounting and design information through the means of database systems is one beneficial innovation; many scheduling systems do not provide such integration of information. The techniques discussed in Chapter 14 are particularly useful in this regard.

With regard to ease of use, the introduction of interactive scheduling systems, graphical output devices and automated data acquisition should produce a very different environment that has existed[4]. In the past, scheduling was performed as a batch operation with output contained in lengthy tables of numbers. Updating of work progress and revising activity duration was a time consuming manual task. It is no surprise that managers viewed scheduling as extremely burdensome in this environment. The lower costs associated with computer systems as well as improved software make "user friendly" environments a real possibility for field operations on large projects.

Finally, information representation is an area which can result in substantial improvements. While the network model of project activities is an extremely useful device to represent a project, many aspects of project plans and activity inter-relationships cannot or have not been represented in network models[5]. For example, the similarity of processes among different activities is usually unrecorded in the formal project representation. As a result, updating a project network in response to new information about a process such as concrete pours can be tedious. What is needed is a much more flexible and complete representation of project information.

Words

practitioner 实践工作者   indisputable   无可争议的
indispensable 不可或缺的   computational   运算的
innovation   创新   diagnostic   诊断
batch   批   lengthy   冗长的

Notes

[1] considerable attention 意为"相当的关注"。全句可译为：尽管施工计划和进度计划编制过程，已经得到研究与实践人员极大的关注，但仍然有提出问题并进行改进的余地。

[2] used in…为过去分词短语作定语，修饰 heuristic procedures。全句可译为：实际应用当中，大多数项目先用关键线路法编制基准进度计划，在此基础上再进行时间压缩或凭直觉和经验的资源限定分析。

[3] rather than 指"不再是，而非"。data storage 指"数据储存"。data representation 意为"数据表达"。

[4] with regard to 指"关于"。interactive scheduling system 意为"交互式进度计划编制系统"。graphical output device 意为"图形输出装置"。

[5] network model 指"网络模型"。全句可译为：尽管项目工作的网络模型是表达项目的极为有用的工具，但项目计划和工作之间的相互关系的很多方面不能或还没有用网络模型表示。

Exercise

Translate the text of lesson 11.4 into Chinese.

Chapter12　Cost Control, Monitoring and Accounting

12.1　The Cost Control Problem

During the execution of a project, procedures for project control and record keeping become indispensable tools to managers and other participants in the construction process. These tools serve the dual purpose of recording the financial transactions that occur as well as giving managers an indication of the progress and problems associated with a project[1]. The problems of project control are aptly summed up in an old definition of a project as "any collection of vaguely related activities that are ninety percent complete, over budget and late".[2] The task of project control systems is to give a fair indication of the existence and the extent of such problems.

In this chapter, we consider the problems associated with resource utilization, accounting, monitoring and control during a project. In this discussion, we emphasize the project management uses of accounting information. Interpretation of project accounts is generally not straightforward until a project is completed, and then it is too late to influence project management[3]. Even after completion of a project, the accounting results may be confusing. Hence, managers need to know how to interpret accounting information for the purpose of project management. In the process of considering management problems, however, we shall discuss some of the common accounting systems and conventions, although our purpose is not to provide a comprehensive survey of accounting procedures[4].

The limited objective of project control deserves emphasis. Project control procedures are primarily intended to identify deviations from the project plan rather than to suggest possible areas for cost savings[5]. This characteristic reflects the advanced stage at which project control becomes important. The time at which major cost savings can be achieved is during planning and design for the project. During the actual construction, changes are likely to delay the project and lead to inordinate cost increases. As a result, the focus of project control is on fulfilling the original design plans or indicating deviations from these plans, rather than on searching for significant improvements and cost savings[6]. It is only when a rescue operation is required that major changes will normally occur in the construction plan.

Finally, the issues associated with integration of information will require some discussion.

Project management activities and functional concerns are intimately linked, yet the techniques used in many instances do not facilitate comprehensive or integrated consideration of project activities[7]. For example, schedule information and cost accounts are usually kept separately. As a result, project managers themselves must synthesize a comprehensive view from the different reports on the project plus their own field observations. In particular, managers are often forced to infer the cost impacts of schedule changes, rather than being provided with aids for this process. Communication or integration of various types of information can serve a number of useful purposes, although it does require special attention in the establishment of project control procedures[8].

For cost control on a project, the construction plan and the associated cash flow estimates can provide the baseline reference for subsequent project monitoring and control[9]. For schedules, progress on individual activities and the achievement of milestone completions can be compared with the project schedule to monitor the progress of activities[10]. Contract and job specifications provide the criteria by which to assess and assure the required quality of construction. The final or detailed cost estimate provides a baseline for the assessment of financial performance during the project. To the extent that costs are within the detailed cost estimate, then the project is thought to be under *financial control*. Overruns in particular cost categories signal the possibility of problems and give an indication of exactly what problems are being encountered. Expense oriented construction planning and control focuses upon the categories included in the final cost estimation. This focus is particular relevant for projects with few activities and considerable repetition such as grading and paving roadways.

For control and monitoring purposes, the original detailed cost estimate is typically converted to a *project budget*, and the project budget is used subsequently as a guide for management[11]. Specific items in the detailed cost estimate become job cost elements. Expenses incurred during the course of a project are recorded in specific job cost accounts to be compared with the original cost estimates in each category. Thus, individual job cost accounts generally represent the basic unit for cost control. Alternatively, job cost accounts may be disaggregated or divided into *work elements* which are related both to particular scheduled activities and to particular cost accounts[12].

In addition to cost amounts, information on material quantities and labor inputs within each job account is also typically retained in the project budget. With this information, actual materials usage and labor employed can be compared to the expected requirements. As a result, cost overruns or savings on particular items can be identified as due to changes in unit prices, labor productivity or in the amount of material consumed[13].

Words

dual	双重的	transaction	交易活动
utilization	利用	accounting	会计
vaguely	含糊地	straightforward	直接的，明确的
inordinate	非正常的	fulfill	履行，实行
interpret	解释	convention	常规
comprehensive	广泛的，综合的	deviation	偏差
characteristic	特征	consume	消耗
reference	参考、索引	intimately	亲切地，亲密地
infer	推断	subsequent	后续的，随后的
criteria	准则	assess	评估
project budget	项目预算	work element	工作要素
productivity	生产率		

Notes

[1] as well as 所引导的部分和 recording…并列。全句可译为：这些工具有记录实际发生的财务交易和向项目经理提供有关项目进展与问题的双重作用。

[2] 全句可译为：项目控制所面临的问题可以用一个过去的关于项目的描述来恰如其分地予以总结，即一大堆虽以完成 90%，但超预算且进度拖延的、定义不明确的工作集合。

[3] not…until…指"直到……才"。straight forward 意为"直观的，明白的"。全句可译为：项目会计报告一般只有在项目完成时才会有明确的解释，而这对于项目管理而言，其作用显然是太迟了。

[4] 全句可译为：尽管我们的目的不在于详细介绍会计的程序，但从考虑管理问题的角度出发，我们应当讨论一下常用的会计系统和惯例。

[5] 全句可译为：项目控制程序的首要任务是识别项目偏差，而不是为节约成本提供参考建议。

[6] original design plans 指"原有设计图纸"。全句可译为：因此，项目控制的重点是实现原有设计图纸或识别偏离这些图纸之处，而不是寻求大的改进和节约成本上。

[7] 全句可译为：虽然现有的技术仍然无法便于让人对项目活动有综合且完整的认识和考虑，但项目管理活动和功能上的考虑是密不可分的。

[8] integration 意为"集成"。project control procedure 指"项目控制程序"。全句可译为：尽管需要在建立项目控制程序中予以特别的关注，沟通和各类不同信息的集成仍是服务于项目管理的有效方法。

[9] baseline reference 意为"参考基准"。全句可译为：对于项目成本控制，施工计划和有关的现金流量估算可以为后续的项目监督和控制提供参照基准。

[10] 全句可译为：对于进度控制，我们可以将项目活动的实际进度以及项目的里程碑

完工情况和项目的计划进度相比较，以监督项目的进度实施。

[11] the original detailed cost estimate 意为"初始的详细成本估算"。be converted to 指"转变为"。全句可译为：就控制和监督而言，初始的详细成本估算经常被转化为项目预算，并用作为以成本管理的指南。

[12] 全句可译为：另一方面，工作成本报告还可以分解成与具体的进度活动及具体的成本报告都有关的作业要素。

[13] cost overrun 指"成本超支"。全句可译为：这样一来，就可以识别具体活动成本超支或节约是由于单价，劳动生产率，还是材料消耗量的变化所造成的。

12.2 Forecasting for Activity Cost Control

For the purpose of project management and control, it is not sufficient to consider only the past record of costs and revenues incurred in a project. Good managers should focus upon future revenues, future costs and technical problems. For this purpose, traditional financial accounting schemes are not adequate to reflect the dynamic nature of a project. Accounts typically focus on recording routine costs and past expenditures associated with activities. Generally, past expenditures represent *sunk costs* that cannot be altered in the future and may or may not be relevant in the future[1]. For example, after the completion of some activity, it may be discovered that some quality flaw renders the work useless. Unfortunately, the resources expended on the flawed construction will generally be *sunk* and cannot be recovered for re-construction (although it may be possible to change the burden of who pays for these resources by financial withholding or charges; owners will typically attempt to have constructors or designers pay for changes due to quality flaws)[2]. Since financial accounts are historical in nature, some means of forecasting or projecting the future course of a project is essential for management control[3]. In this section, some methods for cost control and simple forecasts are described.

An example of forecasting used to assess the project status is shown in Table 12-1. In this example, costs are reported in five categories, representing the sum of all the various cost accounts associated with each category:

- Budgeted Cost
  The budgeted cost is derived from the detailed cost estimate prepared at the start of the project. The factors of cost would be referenced by cost account and by a prose description.
- Estimated total cost
  The estimated or forecast total cost in each category is the current best estimate of costs based on progress and any changes since the budget was formed[4]. Estimated

total costs are the sum of cost to date, commitments and exposure. Methods for estimating total costs are described below.

- Cost Committed and Cost Exposure

  Estimated cost to completion in each category in divided into firm commitments and estimated additional cost or *exposure*. Commitments may represent material orders or subcontracts for which firm dollar amounts have been committed.

- Cost to Date

  The actual cost incurred to date is recorded in column 6 and can be derived from the financial record keeping accounts[5].

- Over or (Under)

  A final column in Table 12-1 indicates the amount over or under the budget for each category. This column is an indicator of the extent of variance from the project budget; items with unusually large overruns would represent a particular managerial concern[6]. Note that *variance is* used in the terminology of project control to indicate a difference between budgeted and actual expenditures[7]. The term is defined and used quite differently in statistics or mathematical analysis. In Table 12-1, labor costs are running higher than expected, whereas subcontracts are less than expected.

The current status of the project is a forecast budget overrun of $5,950. with 23 percent of the budgeted project costs incurred to date.

Table 12-1 Illustration of a Job Status Report

Factor	Budgeted Cost	Estimated Total Cost	Cost Committed	Cost Exposure	Cost To Date	Over or (Under)
Labor	$99,406	$102,342	$49,596	—	$52,746	$2,936
Material	88,499	88,499	42,506	45,993	—	0
Subcontracts	198,458	196,323	83,352	97,832	15,139	(2,135)
Equipment	37,543	37,543	23,623	—	13,920	0
Other	72,693	81,432	49,356	—	32,076	8,739
Total	496,599	506,139	248,433	143,825	113,881	5,950

For project control, managers would focus particular attention on items indicating substantial deviation from budgeted amounts. In particular, the cost overruns in the labor and in the other expense category would be worthy of attention by a project manager in Table 12-1. A next step would be to look in greater detail at the various components of these categories. Overruns in cost might be due to lower than expected productivity, higher than expected wage rates, higher than expected material costs, or other factors[8]. Even further, low productivity might be caused by inadequate training, lack of required resources such as equipment or tools, or inordinate amounts of re-work to correct quality problems[9]. Review of a job status report is only the first step in project control.

Words

scheme　计划
routine　例行事务
sunk cost　沉没成本
render　使……（变为）……
status　状态
Cost Committed　承诺成本
Estimated total cost　预计总成本
dynamic　动态的
expenditure　支出
flaw　缺陷
forecast　预测
Budgeted Cost　预算成本
Cost Exposure　附加成本
Cost to Date　到期成本

Notes

[1] sunk cost 指 "沉没成本"。全句可译为：一般将过去已经发生，不管与将来的活动是否有关，只要将来无法改变的支出就称为沉没成本。

[2] 全句可译为：遗憾的是，耗费在有缺陷的建筑产品上的各种资源通常就"沉没了"，并且无法通过重建而得到恢复（尽管可以根据责任的归属来确定由谁承担所造成的损失，业主也会要求承包商或设计方来负担由于质量缺陷而产生的费用）。

[3] in nature 意为"天生的，本质的"。全句可译为：由于财务报告本质上记载的是历史，所以对于管理和控制，利用某些手段预测项目未来的进展是十分重要的。

[4] since 引导的是时间状语从句，应译为"在预算形成之后"。全句可译为：每一项类别的预计总成本是根据预算形成之后的项目进展和变化对当前这类成本作出的最为精确的估算。

[5] 全句可译为：到期发生的实际成本记录在表 12-1 的第 6 栏里，它可以由财务记录报告得到。

[6] 全句可译为：这一栏也是预算偏差的指示器；那些超出合理范围的成本偏差应当引起管理上的关注。

[7] 全句可译为：注意，被用在项目控制中的"偏差"一词指的是预算值和实际值之间的差异。

[8] be due to 指"起因于"。全句可译为：成本超支的原因可能是实际生产率低于预期，工资和材料成本超过预期，或者其他因素。

[9] re-work 意为"返工"。全句可译为：进一步而言，劳动生产率的降低又可能源于新来的工人未经培训、缺乏机器和设备等生产所需的资源、纠正质量问题的不当返工数量等原因。

12.3　Schedule and Budget Updates

Scheduling and project planning is an activity that continues throughout the lifetime of a project. As changes or discrepancies between the plan and the realization occur, the project schedule and cost estimates should be modified and new schedules devised[1]. Too often, the schedule is devised once by a planner in the central office, and then revisions or modifications are done incompletely or only sporadically[2]. The result is the lack of effective project monitoring and the possibility of eventual chaos on the project site.

On "fast track" projects, initial construction activities are begun even before the facility design is finalized[3]. In this case, special attention must be placed on the coordinated scheduling of design and construction activities. Even in projects for which the design is finalized before construction begins, *change orders* representing changes in the "final" design are often issued to incorporate changes desired by the owner[4].

Periodic updating of future activity durations and budgets is especially important to avoid excessive optimism in projects experiencing problems. If one type of activity experiences delays on a project, then related activities are also likely to be delayed unless managerial changes are made. Construction projects normally involve numerous activities which are closely related due to the use of similar materials, equipment, workers or site characteristics[5]. Expected cost changes should also be propagated throughout a project plan. In essence, duration and cost estimates for future activities should be revised in light of the actual experience on the job. Without this updating, project schedules slip more and more as time progresses. To perform this type of updating, project managers need access to original estimates and estimating assumptions.

Unfortunately, most project cost control and scheduling systems do not provide many aids for such updating. What is required is a means of identifying discrepancies, diagnosing the cause, forecasting the effect, and propagating this effect to all related activities. While these steps can be undertaken manually, computers aids to support interactive updating or even automatic updating would be helpful.

Beyond the direct updating of activity durations and cost estimates, project managers should have mechanisms available for evaluating any type of schedule change. Updating activity duration estimations, changing scheduled start times, modifying the estimates of resources required for each activity, and even changing the project network logic (by inserting new activities or other changes) should all be easily accomplished[6]. In effect, scheduling aids should be directly available to project managers. Fortunately, local computers are commonly available on site for this purpose.

Example 12-1: Schedule Updates in a Small Project

As an example of the type of changes that might be required, consider the nine activity project appearing in Figure 12-1. Also, suppose that the project is four days underway, with the current activity schedule and progress as shown in Figure 12-2. A few problems or changes that might be encountered include the following:

1. An underground waterline that was previously unknown was ruptured during the fifth day of the project. An extra day was required to replace the ruptured section, and another day will be required for clean-up. What is the impact on the project duration?

    - To analyze this change with the critical path scheduling procedure, the manager has the options of (1) changing the expected duration of activity C, General Excavation, to the new expected duration of 10 days or (2) splitting activity C into two tasks (corresponding to the work done prior to the waterline break and that to be done after) and adding a new activity representing repair and clean-up from the waterline break. The second approach has the advantage that any delays to other activities (such as activities D and E) could also be indicated by precedence constraints[7].

    - Assuming that no other activities are affected, the manager decides to increase the expected duration of activity C to 10 days. Since activity C is on the critical path, the project duration also increases by 2 days. Applying the critical path scheduling procedure would confirm this change and also give a new set of earliest and latest starting times for the various activities.

2. After 8 days on the project, the owner asks that a new drain be installed in addition to the sewer line scheduled for activity G. The project manager determines that a new activity could be added to install the drain in parallel with Activity G and requiring 2 days. What is the effect on the schedule?

    - Inserting a new activity in the project network between nodes 3 and 4 violates the activity-on-branch convention that only one activity can be defined between any two nodes[8]. Hence, a new node and a dummy activity must be inserted in addition to the drain installation activity. As a result, the nodes must be re-numbered and the critical path schedule developed again. Performing these operations reveals that no change in the project duration would occur and the new activity has a total float of 1 day.

    - To avoid the labor associated with modifying the network and re-numbering nodes, suppose that the project manager simply re-defined activity G as installation of sewer and drain lines requiring 4 days[9]. In this case, activity G would appear on the critical path and the project duration would increase. Adding an additional crew so that the two installations could proceed in parallel might reduce the duration of activity G back to 2 days and thereby avoid the increase in the project duration[10].

3. At day 12 of the project, the excavated trenches collapse during Activity E. An additional 5 days will be required for this activity. What is the effect on the project schedule? What changes should be made to insure meeting the completion deadline?

- Activity E has a total float of only 1 day. With the change in this activity's duration, it will lie on the critical path and the project duration will increase[11].
- Analysis of possible time savings in subsequent activities is now required.

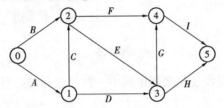

Figure 12-1 A Nine Activity Example Project

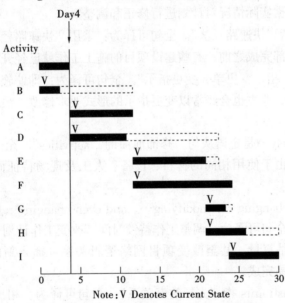

Figure 12-2 Current Schedule for an Example Project Presented as a Bar Chart

As can be imagined, it is not at all uncommon to encounter changes during the course of a project that require modification of durations, changes in the network logic of precedence relationships, or additions and deletions of activities[12]. Consequently, the scheduling process should be readily available as the project is underway.

words

discrepancy 差异
fast track 快速路径
initial 初始的
incorporate 整合

optimism	乐观	coordinated	协调的
propagate	传播	periodic	定期的
original	最初的	excessive	过度的
reinforcement	加强,强化	update	更新
forecast	预测	assumption	前提,假设
drain	排水管	diagnose	诊断
parallel	平行	undertake	承担
revision	修订	ruptured	破裂的
chaos	混乱	sewer	下水道

Notes

[1] 全句可译为：当计划和现实之间出现不一致和差异时，就应调整项目计划进度和费用估算。

[2] 全句可译为：更多的情形是，计划制定者往往只在中心办公室做出一个进度计划后，便疏于根据实际情况对计划进行修正和调整。

[3] "fast track"指"快速路径法"。全句可译为：采用"快速路径法"的项目，在建筑设计还没有全部完成之前，有些建设项目的施工工作就已经开始了。

[4] changes orders 指"变更单，变更指示"。全句可译为：即使施工开始前设计就已全部完成的项目，业主也会经常以变更指示的形式要求修改"最终"设计体现其希望的改变。

[5] which are closely…是定语从句，修饰前面的"activities"。全句可译为：建设项目通常会有大量由于使用相同的材料、设备、人工及现场特征而相互联系紧密的工作。

[6] Updating…, changing…, modifying…, and even changing…是并列的动名词短语共同作主语。全句可译为：调整工作持续时间、改变工作计划开始时间、修正每项工作必要资源估算量，甚至改变项目网络逻辑关系（插入新的工作或其他变化）等，都应当容易完成。

[7] precedence constraints 指"先导约束关系"。全句可译为：相比较之下，第二种办法的优点是利用先导约束关系还能查明对其他工作造成的延误（如工作 D 和工作 E）。

[8] activity-on-branch convention 指"双代号网络图规则"。全句可译为：在项目网络图的节点 3 和 4 之间插入一项新工作，就违反双代号网络图两个节点之间只能有一项工作的规定。

[9] 全句可译为：为了避免调整网络图和对节点进行重新编号，假定项目经理还有一种选择，即仅仅把下水道施工和排水关安装这两项工作合并为一项工作，且需要 4 天。

[10] 全句可译为：但假如另外增加一个工人班组，使得上面这两项工作可以平行施工的话，就可以把 G 工作的作业时间恢复到原来的 2 天，这样一来，就可以避免工

期的拖延。
[11] 全句可译为：随着工作持续时间的变化，该项工作将位于关键线路上并且项目工期也会延长。
[12] 全句可译为：可以想像，在一个项目的进展过程中几乎会碰到各种各样的变化，从而需要我们对项目的进度计划进行调整，这包括对作业时间的改变、网络图逻辑关系的变化以及工作的添加或删减等。

12.4 Relating Cost and Schedule Information

The previous sections focused upon the identification of the budgetary and schedule status of projects. Actual projects involve a complex inter-relationship between time and cost. As projects proceed, delays influence costs and budgetary problems may in turn require adjustments to activity schedules[1]. Trade-offs between time and costs were discussed in the former Section in the context of project planning in which additional resources applied to a project activity might result in a shorter duration but higher costs[2]. Unanticipated events might result in increases in both time and cost to complete an activity. For example, excavation problems may easily lead to much lower than anticipated productivity on activities requiring digging.

While project managers implicitly recognize the inter-play between time and cost on projects, it is rare to find effective project control systems which include both elements[3]. Usually, project costs and schedules are recorded and reported by separate application programs. Project managers must then perform the tedious task of relating the two sets of information.

The difficulty of integrating schedule and cost information stems primarily from the level of detail required for effective integration[4]. Usually, a single project activity will involve numerous cost account categories. For example, an activity for the preparation of a foundation would involve laborers, cement workers, concrete forms, concrete, reinforcement, transportation of materials and other resources. Even a more disaggregated activity definition such as erection of foundation forms would involve numerous resources such as forms, nails, carpenters, laborers, and material transportation. Again, different cost accounts would normally be used to record these various resources. Similarly, numerous activities might involve expenses associated with particular cost accounts. For example, a particular material such as standard piping might be used in numerous different schedule activities. To integrate cost and schedule information, the disaggregated charges for specific activities and specific cost accounts must be the basis of analysis[5].

A straightforward means of relating time and cost information is to define individual *work elements* representing the resources in a particular cost category associated with a particular project activity[6]. Work elements would represent an element in a two-dimensional matrix of activities and cost accounts as illustrated in Figure 12-3. A numbering or identifying system for work elements would include both the relevant cost account and the associated activity. In some cases, it might also be desirable to identify work elements by the responsible organization or individual. In this case, a three dimensional representation of work elements is required, with the third dimension corresponding to responsible individuals[7]. More generally, modern computerized databases can accommodate a flexible structure of data representation to support aggregation with respect to numerous different perspectives; this type of system will be discussed in Chapter 14[8].

With this organization of information, a number of management reports or views could be generated. In particular, the costs associated with specific activities could be obtained as the sum of the work elements appearing in any row in Figure 12-3[9]. These costs could be used to evaluate alternate technologies to accomplish particular activities or to derive the expected project cash flow over time as the schedule changes. From a management perspective, problems developing from particular activities could be rapidly identified since costs would be accumulated at such a disaggregated level. As a result, project control becomes at once more precise and detailed.

Project Activity Group	Cost Amount for Superstructure					
	204.1	204.2	204.3	204.4	204.5	204.6
First Floor	×	×		×		×
Second Floor		×		×		×
Third Floor		×	×	×		×
Fourth Floor		×	×			×
Fifth Floor		×	×		×	×

Figure 12-3 Illustration of a Cost Account and Project Activity Matrix

Unfortunately, the development and maintenance of a work element database can represent a large data collection and organization effort. As noted earlier, four hundred separate cost accounts and four hundred activities would not be unusual for a construction project. The result would be up to $400 \times 400 = 160,000$ separate work elements. Of course, not all activities involve each cost account. However, even a density of two percent (so that each activity would have eight cost accounts and each account would have eight associated activities on the average) would involve nearly thirteen thousand work elements. Initially preparing this database represents a considerable burden, but it is also the case that project bookkeepers must record project events within each of these various work elements.

Implementations of the "work element" project control systems have typically fondered on the burden of data collection, storage and book-keeping[10].

Until data collection is better automated, the use of work elements to control activities in large projects is likely to be difficult to implement. However, certain segments of project activities can profit tremendously from this type of organization. In particular, material requirements can be tracked in this fashion. Materials involve only a subset of all cost accounts and project activities, so the burden of data collection and control is much smaller than for an entire system. Moreover, the benefits from integration of schedule and cost information are particularly noticeable in materials control since delivery schedules are directly affected and bulk order discounts might be identified[11]. Consequently, materials control systems can reasonably encompass a "work element" accounting system.

In the absence of a work element accounting system, costs associated with particular activities are usually estimated by summing expenses in all cost accounts directly related to an activity plus a proportion of expenses in cost accounts used jointly by two or more activities[12]. The basis of cost allocation would typically be the level of effort or resource required by the different activities. For example, costs associated with supervision might be allocated to different concreting activities on the basis of the amount of work (measured in cubic yards of concrete) in the different activities. With these allocations, cost estimates for particular work activities can be obtained.

Words

budgetary 预算的
inter-relationship 相互关系
inter-play 相互作用
cement 水泥
straight forward 直接的
two-dimensional matrix 二维矩阵
density 浓度，密度
fonder 荒废

implicitly 暗示地，含蓄地
reinforcement 加强，增强
subset 子集
concrete 混凝土
illustrate 用（图）表示，用实例说明
accumulate 累计
bookkeeper 薄记员
track 跟踪、追踪

Notes

[1] 全句可译为：随着项目的进展，进度的拖延会影响到成本；反过来预算上的问题也需要对进度做出某些调整。

[2] in which…为定语从句，修饰 the context，应译为"在项目计划中，若为项目某个工作增加资源就会缩短时间，但同时会增加成本"。

[3] inter-play 意为"相互作用"。全句可译为：尽管项目经理也隐约意识到项目当中时

间和成本之间相互影响的关系，但却极少能找到考虑这两个要素的有效项目管理方法。

[4] stem from 意为"在于、源于"。the level of detail 指"详细程度"。全句可译为：综合进度和成本信息的困难之处主要在于为了有效地综合所需要的详细程度。

[5] specific cost account 意为"具体的成本报告"。全句可译为：为了综合成本和进度信息，必须把针对具体工作和具体成本报告而分散计算的数额当作分析的基础。

[6] representing…是现在分词短语作定语，修饰 work elements。associated with…是过去分词短语作定语，修饰 category。全句可译为：一个综合进度和成本信息的直观方法是定义一些单独的作业要素，它们被用来表示一个具体的项目工作按特定的成本类别所耗费的资源。

[7] 全句可译为：在这种情况下，作业要素就需要一个三维的表达方式，其中第三维对应于相关负责的组织或个人。

[8] 全句可译为：更为普遍的是，现代化的计算机数据库能够提供弹性的数据表达结构，用以支持和许多不同角度有关的信息集成，这种类型的系统将在第14章介绍。

[9] 全句可译为：尤其是，通过汇总出现在图12-3内任一行的作业要素，我们可以得到具体工作的相关成本。

[10] 全句可译为："作业要素"项目控制系统会因为不堪数据的采集、存储和记账之重负而常常半途而废。

[11] delivery schedule 指"运送计划"。bulk order discounts 意为"大宗定单折扣"。

[12] 全句可译为：在没有作业要素会计系统的情况下，首先汇总所有成本报告中与一项工作直接有关的费用，再按比例将成本报告两个或两个以上工作的共同费用估算同具体工作有关的成本。

Exercise

Translate the text of lesson 12.3 into Chinese.

Chapter 13   Quality Control and Safety During Construction

13.1   Quality and Safety Concerns in Construction

Quality control and safety represent increasingly important concerns for project managers. Defects or failures in constructed facilities can result in very large costs. Even with minor defects, re-construction may be required and facility operations impaired. Increased costs and delays are the result. In the worst case, failures may cause personal injuries or fatalities. Accidents during the construction process can similarly result in personal injuries and large costs. Indirect costs of insurance, inspection and regulation are increasing rapidly due to these increased direct costs. Good project managers try to ensure that the job is done right the first time and that no major accidents occur on the project[1].

As with cost control, the most important decisions regarding the quality of a completed facility are made during the design and planning stages rather than during construction. It is during these preliminary stages that component configurations, material specifications and functional performance are decided[2]. Quality control during construction consists largely of insuring *conformance* to these original design and planning decisions.

While conformance to existing design decisions is the primary focus of quality control, there are exceptions to this rule. First, unforeseen circumstances, incorrect design decisions or changes desired by an owner in the facility function may require re-evaluation of design decisions during the course of construction[3]. While these changes may be motivated by the concern for quality, they represent occasions for re-design with all the attendant objectives and constraints. As a second case, some designs rely upon informed and appropriate decision making during the construction process itself. For example, some tunneling methods make decisions about the amount of shoring required at different locations based upon observation of soil conditions during the tunneling process. Since such decisions are based on better information concerning actual site conditions, the facility design may be more cost effective as a result[4]. Any special case of re-design during construction requires the various considerations discussed in Chapter 3.

With the attention to conformance as the measure of quality during the construction process, the specification of quality requirements in the design and contract documentation becomes extremely important[5]. Quality requirements should be clear and verifiable, so that all parties in the project can understand the requirements for conformance. Much of the discussion in this chapter relates to the development and the implications of different quality requirements for construction as well as the issues associated with insuring conformance[6].

Safety during the construction project is also influenced in large part by decisions made during the planning and design process. Some designs or construction plans are inherently difficult and dangerous to implement, whereas other, comparable plans may considerably reduce the possibility of accidents[7]. For example, clear separation of traffic from construction zones during roadway rehabilitation can greatly reduce the possibility of accidental collisions. Beyond these design decisions, safety largely depends upon education, vigilance and cooperation during the construction process. Workers should be constantly alert to the possibilities of accidents and avoid taking unnecessary risks.

A variety of different organizations are possible for quality and safety control during construction. One common model is to have a group responsible for quality assurance and another group primarily responsible for safety within an organization. In large organizations, departments dedicated to quality assurance and to safety might assign specific individuals to assume responsibility for these functions on particular projects[8]. For smaller projects, the project manager or an assistant might assume these and other responsibilities. In either case, insuring safe and quality construction is a concern of the project manager in overall charge of the project in addition to the concerns of personnel, cost, time and other management issues[9].

Inspectors and quality assurance personnel will be involved in a project to represent a variety of different organizations. Each of the parties directly concerned with the project may have their own quality and safety inspectors, including the owner, the engineer/architect, and the various constructor firms. These inspectors may be contractors from specialized quality assurance organizations. In addition to on-site inspections, samples of materials will commonly be tested by specialized laboratories to insure compliance[10]. Inspectors to insure compliance with regulatory requirements will also be involved. Common examples are inspectors for the local government's building department, for environmental agencies, and for occupational health and safety agencies.

The US Occupational Safety and Health Administration (OSHA) routinely conducts site visits of work places in conjunction with approved state inspection agencies[11]. OSHA inspectors are required by law to issue citations for all standard violations observed. Safety standards prescribe a variety of mechanical safeguards and procedures; for example, ladder safety is covered by over 140 regulations. In cases of extreme non-compliance with standards, OSHA inspectors can stop work on a project. However, only a small fraction of construction sites are visited by OSHA inspectors and most construction site accidents are not caused by violations of existing standards[12]. As a result, safety is largely the responsibility of the managers on site rather than that of public inspectors.

While the multitude of participants involved in the construction process require the services of inspectors, it cannot be emphasized too strongly that inspectors are only a formal check on quality control[13]. Quality control should be a primary objective for all the members of a project team. Managers should take responsibility for maintaining and improving quality control. Employee participation in quality control should be sought and rewarded, including the introduction of new ideas. Most important of all, quality improvement can serve as a catalyst for improved productivity. By suggesting new work methods, by avoiding rework, and by avoiding long term problems, good quality control can pay for itself. Owners should promote good quality control and seek out contractors who maintain such standards.

In addition to the various organizational bodies involved in quality control, issues of quality control arise in virtually all the functional areas of construction activities. For example, insuring accurate and useful information is an important part of maintaining quality performance. Other aspects of quality control include document control (including changes during the construction process), procurement, field inspection and testing, and final checkout of the facility[14].

Words

concern	关心，关注	defect	缺点，缺陷
re-construction	返工，重修	regarding	关于
attendant	伴随的	ensure	确保
preliminary	预备的，初步的，开始的	configuration	配置
conformance	一致	tunnel	隧道
shoring	支撑	verifiable	可核实的，可验证的
rehabilitation	恢复，修复	collision	碰撞
vigilance	警惕性	alert	警觉的
assume	承担	inspector	检查人员
agency	机构	violation	违反
prescribe	规定	safeguard	安全保障
compliance	遵守，服从	check	检查

catalyst 催化剂

Notes

[1] that the job…与 that no major accidents…为由连词 and 连接的并列的定语从句修饰 ensure。全句可译为：称职的项目经理努力保证工作一次便符合要求，项目不出现大的事故。

[2] It is…that…是强调句型，强调"these preliminary stages"。全句可译为：正是在这几个前期阶段，决定了构件的布置、对材料规格与性能，以及建筑物使用功能要求。

[3] unforeseen circumstances 指"不可预见事件"。re-evaluation 意为"重新评价"。during the course of construction 应译为"在施工过程中"。

[4] 全句可译为：由于这样的决策是建立在有关现场实际条件的更为详尽的信息基础之上，所以设计方案会更加符合实际。

[5] design and contract documentation 意为"设计和合同文件"。全句可译为：如果把遵守设计作为施工过程中的质量保证手段，那么设计和合同文件中对于质量的标准和要求便显得极为重要。

[6] 全句可译为：在本章我们将详细讨论有关施工当中不同质量标准之间的联系，以及一味遵守设计所带来的一些问题。

[7] whereas 在这里是连词，意思同"while"，即"然而，但是"的意思。全句可译为：有些设计和施工计划本身难以实施，甚至危险执，但另外一些设计和施工计划却能够大大地降低发生意外事件的可能性。

[8] dedicated to…是过去分词短语作定语，修饰 departments。assign 指"分派、指派"。全句可译为：大型组织承担质量保证和安全生产责任的部门会指派专人负责具体项目当中的质量和安全职能。

[9] 全句可译为：而无论在哪种情形下，确保施工的质量和安全，是除了人力、成本和进度等管理问题之外，项目经理在项目整个过程中必须予以关注的事情。

[10] on-site inspection 指"现场检查"。全句可译为：除了现场的监督之外，材料的取样检测通常也会由专业实验室来完成，以保证施工符合要求。

[11] US Occupational Safety and Health Administration（OSHA）指"美国职业安全和健康署"。全句可译为：美国职业安全和健康署（OSHA）配合各州经联邦政府批准的检查机构对各个工作场所进行例行检查。

[12] 全句可译为：然而，OSHA 的检查人员所能查访到的施工现场毕竟有限，加之大多数施工现场的意外事件并非由于违反现行标准而引起。

[13] multitude 指"多数"。formal check 意为"正式检查"。全句可译为：尽管参与施工过程的各方人士数目众多，需要有检验人员的服务，但必须再三强调的是检验人员仅仅是质量控制中的一种官方环节。

[14] document control 意为"文档控制"。final checkout 指"最终的竣工验收"。全句可译为：质量控制的其他方面还包括文档控制（包括施工过程中的变更控制）、采购管理、现场的监督与检测和设施的最终检查验收等内容。

13.2　Total Quality Control

Quality control in construction typically involves insuring compliance with minimum standards of material and workmanship in order to insure the performance of the facility according to the design[1]. These minimum standards are contained in the specifications described in the previous section. For the purpose of insuring compliance, random samples and statistical methods are commonly used as the basis for accepting or rejecting work completed and batches of materials[2]. Rejection of a batch is based on non-conformance or violation of the relevant design specifications. Procedures for this quality control practice are described in the following sections.

An implicit assumption in these traditional quality control practices is the notion of an *acceptable quality level* which is a allowable fraction of defective items[3]. Materials obtained from suppliers or work performed by an organization is inspected and passed as acceptable if the estimated defective percentage is within the acceptable quality level[4]. Problems with materials or goods are corrected after delivery of the product.

In contrast to this traditional approach of quality control is the goal of *total quality control*. In this system, no defective items are allowed anywhere in the construction process. While the zero defects goal can never be permanently obtained, it provides a goal so that an organization is never satisfied with its quality control program even if defects are reduced by substantial amounts year after year[5]. This concept and approach to quality control was first developed in manufacturing firms in Japan and Europe, but has since spread to many construction companies. The best known formal certification for quality improvement is the International Organization for Standardization's ISO 9000 standard[6]. ISO 9000 emphasizes good documentation, quality goals and a series of cycles of planning, implementation and review.

Total quality control is a commitment to quality expressed in all parts of an organization and typically involves many elements. Design reviews to insure safe and effective construction procedures are a major element. Other elements include extensive training for personnel, shifting the responsibility for detecting defects from quality control inspectors to workers, and continually maintaining equipment[7]. Worker involvement in improved quality control is often formalized in *quality circles* in which groups of workers meet regularly to make suggestions for quality improvement[8]. Material suppliers are also required to insure zero defects in delivered goods. Initially, all materials from a supplier are inspected and batches of goods with any defective items are returned. Suppliers with good records can be certified and not subject to complete inspection subsequently.

The traditional microeconomic view of quality control is that there is an "optimum" proportion of defective items[9]. Trying to achieve greater quality than this optimum would substantially increase costs of inspection and reduce worker productivity. However, many companies have found that commitment to total quality control has substantial economic benefits that had been unappreciated in traditional approaches[10]. Expenses associated with inventory, rework, scrap and warranties were reduced. Worker enthusiasm and commitment improved. Customers often appreciated higher quality work and would pay a premium for good quality. As a result, improved quality control became a competitive advantage.

Of course, total quality control is difficult to apply, particular in construction. The unique nature of each facility, the variability in the workforce, the multitude of subcontractors and the cost of making necessary investments in education and procedures make programs of total quality control in construction difficult[11]. Nevertheless, a commitment to improved quality even without endorsing the goal of zero defects can pay real dividends to organizations.

Example 13-1: Experience with Quality Circles
Quality circles represent a group of five to fifteen workers who meet on a frequent basis to identify, discuss and solve productivity and quality problems[12]. A circle leader acts as liason between the workers in the group and upper levels of management. Appearing below are some examples of reported quality circle accomplishments in construction:
1. On a highway project under construction by Taisei Corporation, it was found that the loss rate of ready-mixed concrete was too high. A quality circle composed of cement masons found out that the most important reason for this was due to an inaccurate checking method[13]. By applying the circle's recommendations, the loss rate was reduced by 11.4%.
2. In a building project by Shimizu Construction Company, many cases of faulty reinforced concrete work were reported. The iron workers quality circle examined their work thoroughly and soon the faulty workmanship disappeared. A 10% increase in productivity was also achieved.

Words

workmanship　手艺，技巧　　　　　　　implicit　隐含的
total quality control　全面质量管理　　　permanently　永远地
random sample　随机抽样　　　　　　　quality circle　质量环

optimum 最佳的	notion 概念
unappreciated 未体会到的	certification 认证
dividend 股息	microeconomic 微观经济学的
faulty 有缺点的	proportion 比例
acceptable quality level 可接受的质量水平	enthusiasm 热忱
scrap 碎片，边角料	liason 联络
statistical method 统计方法	

Notes

[1] 全句可译为：施工过程中的质量控制一般指保证材料和施工工艺符合最低标准，确保建成设施的功能达到设计要求。

[2] for the purpose of 指"为了"。batches of materials 意为"材料批"。全句可译为：为了确保符合标准，我们通常用随机抽样和数理统计的方法作为接受或拒绝已完工作和材料批的基础。

[3] acceptable quality level 意为"可接受的质量水平"。全句可译为：这些传统的质量控制做法隐含的假设中有这样一个概念，可接受的质量水平，就是有缺陷点的事项所占的允许比例。

[4] 全句可译为：来自供应商的材料或某个组织完成的工作，只有当其缺陷比例在允许的质量水平以内时，才可以被当作合格并检查通过。

[5] zero defects 指"零缺陷"。permanently 意为"永久地"。全句可译为：尽管零缺陷这个目标永远都无法实现，但它是组织的一个目标，使组织在缺陷数目逐年显著降低的情况下，仍不满足于其质量控制计划。

[6] the International Organization for Standardization 指"国际标准化组织"。ISO9000standard 指"由国际标准化组织颁布的9000族质量体系认证标准"。

[7] 全句可译为：其他因素包括广泛的员工培训，把发现缺陷的责任从检查人员身上转移到工人身上，并对设备进行经常性的维护。

[8] quality circles 指"质量环"。in which…为定语从句，修饰 quality circles。全句可译为：在质量环当中有一个正式的有关工人对质量控制改进的环节，在这里工人们定期会面并对质量改进提供建议。

[9] microeconomic 意为"微观经济的，微观经济学的"。optimum 意为"最佳的，最优的"。全句可译为：对于质量控制的传统微观经济观点认为存在着一个缺陷点的最佳比例。

[10] 全句可译为：然而，许多企业发现遵守全面质量控制会带来被传统方法所未认识到的巨大经济利益。

[11] 全句可译为：每一项建筑产品的独特性，劳动力的流动性，分包商的多样性以及教育和程序方面的必要支出，都使得对建筑施工开展全面质量控制计划困难重重。

[12] who…是定语从句，修饰 workers。全句可译为：质量环小组通常由5到15个工人组成，他们定期开会，识别、讨论和解决生产率及质量问题。

[13] 全句可译为：由混凝土工组成的质量环小组经调查后发现，造成这种现象的主要

原因是检查方法不当。

13.3 Quality Control by Statistical Methods

An ideal quality control program might test all materials and work on a particular facility. For example, non-destructive techniques such as x-ray inspection of welds can be used throughout a facility. An on-site inspector can witness the appropriateness and adequacy of construction methods at all times. Even better, individual craftsmen can perform continuing inspection of materials and their own work. Exhaustive or 100% testing of all materials and work by inspectors can be exceedingly expensive, however. In many instances, testing requires the destruction of a material sample, so exhaustive testing is not even possible. As a result, small samples are used to establish the basis of accepting or rejecting a particular work item or shipment of materials. Statistical methods are used to interpret the results of test on a small sample to reach a conclusion concerning the acceptability of an entire *lot* or batch of materials or work products[1].

The use of statistics is essential in interpreting the results of testing on a small sample. Without adequate interpretation, small sample testing results can be quite misleading. As an example, suppose that there are ten defective pieces of material in a lot of one hundred. In taking a sample of five pieces, the inspector might not find *any* defective pieces or might have all sample pieces defective[2]. Drawing a direct inference that none or all pieces in the population are defective on the basis of these samples would be incorrect[3]. Due to this random nature of the sample selection process, testing results can vary substantially It is only with statistical methods that issues such as the chance of different levels of defective items in the full lot can be fully analyzed from a small sample test[4].

There are two types of statistical sampling which are commonly used for the purpose of quality control in batches of work or materials:

1. The acceptance or rejection of a lot is based on the number of defective(bad)or nondefective (good)items in the sample. This is referred to as *sampling* by *attributes*[5].
2. Instead of using defective and nondefective classifications for an item, a quantitative quality measure or the value of a measured variable is used as a quality indicator[6]. This testing procedure is referred to as *sampling* by *variables*[7].

Whatever sampling plan is used in testing, it is always assumed that the samples are representative of the entire population under consideration[8]. Samples are expected to be chosen randomly so that each member of the population is equally likely to be chosen. Convenient sampling plans such as sampling every twentieth piece, choosing a sample every two hours, or picking the top piece on a delivery truck may be adequate to insure a random sample if pieces are randomly mixed in a stack or in use[9]. However, some convenient sampling plans can be inappropriate. For example, checking only easily accessible joints in a building component is inappropriate since joints that are hard to reach may be more likely to have erection or fabrication problems[10].

Another assumption implicit in statistical quality control procedures is that the quality of materials or work is expected to vary from one piece to another. This is certainly true in the field of construction. While a designer may assume that all concrete is exactly the same in a building, the variations in material properties, manufacturing, handling, pouring, and temperature during setting insure that concrete is actually heterogeneous in quality[11]. Reducing such variations to a minimum is one aspect of quality construction. Insuring that the materials actually placed achieve some minimum quality level with respect to average properties or fraction of defectives is the task of quality control[12].

Words

x-ray   x射线
non-destructive   非破坏性的
craftsman   技工
lot   批，总体
attribute   特征
stack   堆
heterogeneous   异种的，由不同成分形成的

weld   焊接
witness   目击，见证
exhaustive   彻底的，完全的
inference   推断
variable   变量
property   性质，用途

Notes

[1]　concering 是介词，意为"关于"。全句可译为：用统计方法根据样本的检验结果推断有关总体、材料批或工作成果是否可接受的结论。

[2]　全句可译为：我们抽取了其中 5 件作为样本，检验人员经检验后发现这 5 件样本可能全部都无缺陷，当然也有可能全部都有缺陷。

[3]　全句可译为：我们在此基础上便推断材料批全部无缺陷或全部有缺陷显然不准确。

[4]　It is…that…在这里是强调句型。全句可译为：只有使用统计方法，才能根据样本检验完整地分析和推断出整批检验对象中有缺陷者不同缺陷水平的机率。

[5]　sampling by attributes 指"特征抽样"。

[6]　全句可译为：与前面的方法有所不同，我们用量化的品质标准或可计量的变量值来判别质量是否可以接受。

[7]　sampling by variables 指"变量抽样"。

[8]　sampling plan 意为"抽样计划"。全句可译为：无论在检验中使用哪种抽样方法，通常都假设样本能够代表总体。

[9]　全句可译为：如每 20 件中抽样 1 次，每 2 个小时抽样 1 次，或者在运输卡车的顶层货物中抽样等便捷的抽样方法，在产品随机成堆放置或使用的条件下是能够保证抽样的随机性的。

[10]　全句可译为：例如，在一栋建筑物当中只检查易于接触到的总部位就不太合适，因为真正可能发生结构问题的都往往是那些难以接触到的部位。

[11]　全句可译为：尽管设计人员对于一幢建筑物的所有混凝土也许是有相同要求的，但由于材料特性、生产、加工、浇筑及养护温度等因素的波动都可能使得混凝土的质量不尽相同。

[12]　insuring that…是现在分词短语作主语。with respect to 是"关于"的意思。全句可译为：确保实际使用的材料在平均性质方面达到最低质量水平或缺陷率就是质量控制的任务。

13.4　Safety

Construction is a relatively hazardous undertaking. As Table 13-1 illustrates, there are significantly more injuries and lost workdays due to injuries or illnesses in construction than in virtually any other industry[1]. These work related injuries and illnesses are exceedingly costly. The *Construction Industry Cost Effectiveness Project* estimated that accidents cost $8.9 billion or nearly seven percent of the $137 billion (in 1979 dollars) spent annually for industrial, utility and commercial construction in the United States. Included in this total are direct costs (medical costs, premiums for workers' compensation benefits, liability and property losses) as well as indirect costs (reduced worker productivity, delays in projects, administrative time, and damage to equipment and the facility)[2]. In contrast to most industrial accidents, innocent bystanders may also be injured by construction accidents. Several crane collapses from high rise buildings under construction have resulted in fatalities to passer-bys. Prudent project managers and owners would like to reduce accidents, injuries and illnesses as much as possible.

Table 13-1　Nonfatal Occupational Injury and Illness Incidence Rates

Industry	1996	1997	1999
Agriculture, forestry, fishing	8.7	8.4	7.3
Mining	5.4	5.9	4.4
Construction	9.9	9.5	8.6
Manufacturing	10.6	10.3	9.2
Transportation/public utilities	8.7	8.2	7.3
Wholesale and retail trade	6.8	6.7	6.1
Finance, insurance, real estate	2.4	2.2	1.8
Services	6.0	5.6	4.9

Note: Data represent total number of cases per 100 full-time employees.
Source: U. S. Bureau of Labor Statistics, *Occupational injuries and Illnesses in the United States by Industry*, annual.

As with all the other costs of construction, it is a mistake for owners to ignore a significant category of costs such as injuries and illnesses. While contractors may pay insurance premiums directly, these costs are reflected in bid prices or contract amounts. Delays caused by injuries and illnesses can present significant opportunity costs to owners. In the long run, the owners of constructed facilities must pay all the costs of construction. For the case of injuries and illnesses, this general principle might be slightly qualified since significant costs are borne by workers themselves or society at large. However, court judgments and insurance payments compensate for individual losses are ultimately borne by the owners[3].

The causes of injuries in construction are numerous. Table 13-2 lists the reported causes of accidents in the US construction industry in 1997. A similar catalogue of causes would exist for other countries. The largest single category for both injuries and fatalities are individual falls. Handling goods and transportation are also a significant cause of injuries. From a management perspective, however, these reported causes do not really provide a useful prescription for safety policies. An individual fall may be caused by a series of coincidences: a railing might not be secure, a worker might be inattentive, the footing may be slippery, etc[4]. Removing any one of these compound causes might serve to prevent any particular accident. However, it is clear that conditions such as unsecured railings will normally increase the risk of accidents. Table 13-3 provides a more detailed list of causes of fatalities for construction sites alone, but again each fatality may have multiple causes.

Table 13-2 Fatal Occupational Injuries in Construction, 1997 and 1999

All accidents	1,107	1,190
Rate per 100,000 workers	14	14
Cause	Percentage	
Transportation incidents	26%	27%
Assaults/violent acts	3	2
Contact with objects	18	21
Falls	34	32
Exposure	17	15

Table 13-3 Fatality Causes in Construction, 1998

Cause	Deaths	Percentage
Fall from/through roof	66	10.6%
Fall from/with structure (other than roof)	64	10.2
Electric shock by equipment contacting power source	58	9.3
Crushed/run over non-operator by operating construction equipment	53	8.5
Electric shock by equipment installation or tool use	45	7.2
Struck by falling object or projectile (including tip-overs)	29	4.6
Lifting operation	27	4.3
Fall from/with ladder (includes collapse/fall of ladder)	27	4.3
Crushed/run over/trapped operator by operating construction equipment	25	4.0
Trench collapse	24	3.8
Crushed/run over by highway vehicle	22	3.5

Source: Construction Resource Analysis.

Various measures are available to improve jobsite safety in construction. Several of the most important occur before construction is undertaken. These include design, choice of technology and education. By altering facility designs, particular structures can be safer or more hazardous to construct. For example, parapets can be designed to appropriate heights for construction worker safety, rather than the minimum height required by building codes[5].

Choice of technology can also be critical in determining the safety of a jobsite. Safeguards built into machinery can notify operators of problems or prevent injuries[6]. For example, simple switches can prevent equipment from being operating when protective shields are not in place. With the availability of on-board electronics (including computer chips) and sensors, the possibilities for sophisticated machine controllers and monitors have greatly expanded for construction equipment and tools[7]. Materials and work process choices also influence the safety of construction. For example, substitution of alternative materials for asbestos can reduce or eliminate the prospects of long term illnesses such as *asbestiosis*[8].

Educating workers and managers in proper procedures and hazards can have a direct impact on jobsite safety. The realization of the large costs involved in construction injuries and illnesses provides a considerable motivation for awareness and education. Regular safety inspections and safety meetings have become standard practices on most job sites.

Pre-qualification of contractors and sub-contractors with regard to safety is another important avenue for safety improvement[9]. If contractors are only invited to bid or enter negotiations if they have an acceptable record of safety (as well as quality performance), then a direct incentive is provided to insure adequate safety on the part of contractors[10].

During the construction process itself, the most important safety related measures are to insure vigilance and cooperation on the part of managers, inspectors and workers. Vigilance involves considering the risks of different working practices. In also involves maintaining temporary physical safeguards such as barricades, braces, guidelines, railings, toeboards and the like. Sets of standard practices are also important, such as:

- requiring hard hats on site.
- requiring eye protection on site.
- requiring hearing protection near loud equipment.
- insuring safety shoes for workers.
- providing first-aid supplies and trained personnel on site.

While eliminating accidents and work related illnesses is a worthwhile goal, it will never be attained. Construction has a number of characteristics making it inherently hazardous. Large forces are involved in many operations. The jobsite is continually changing as construction proceeds. Workers do not have fixed worksites and must move around a structure under construction. The tenure of a worker on a site is short, so the worker's familiarity and the employer-employee relationship are less settled than in manufacturing settings[11]. Despite these peculiarities and as a result of exactly these special problems, improving worksite safety is a very important project management concern.

Example 13-1: Trench collapse
To replace 1,200 feet of a sewer line, a trench of between 12.5 and 18 feet deep was required down the center of a four lane street. The contractor chose to begin excavation of the trench from the shallower end, requiring a 12.5 deep trench. Initially, the contractor used a nine foot high, four foot wide steel trench box for soil support. A trench box is a rigid steel frame consisting of two walls supported by welded struts with open sides and ends. This method had the advantage that traffic could be maintained in at least two lanes during the reconstruction work.

In the shallow parts of the trench, the trench box seemed to adequately support the excavation. However, as the trench got deeper, more soil was unsupported below the trench box. Intermittent soil collapses in the trench began to occur. Eventually, an old parallel six inch water main collapsed, thereby saturating the soil and leading to massive soil collapse at the bottom of the trench. Replacement of the water main was added to the initial contract. At this point, the contractor began sloping the sides of the trench, thereby requiring the closure of the entire street.

The initial use of the trench box was convenient, but it was clearly inadequate and unsafe. Workers in the trench were in continuing danger of accidents stemming from soil collapse. Disruption to surrounding facilities such as the parallel water main was highly likely. Adoption of a tongue and groove vertical sheeting system over the full height of the trench or, alternatively, the sloping excavation eventually adopted are clearly preferable.

Words

hazardous 有害的	principle 原则
exceedingly 非常地	prescription 规定，处方，解决办法
insurance premium 保险费	inattentive 不专注的，不经心的
passerby 路人，行人	fatality 死亡
wholesale 批发	parapet 栏杆，女儿墙

jobsite 工作地点	compensate 补偿
switch 开关	coincidence 巧合，重合
substitution 替换	slippery 易滑的
asbestiosis 硒肺	multiple 多样的
vigilance 警惕	chip 芯片
barricade 路障	notify 通知
railing 扶手	sophisticated 先进的
employer 雇主	asbestos 石棉
undertaking 事业	incentive 激励，积极性
utility 效用	tenure 职位，任期
liability 责任，债务	race 支柱，支撑
crane 起重机	sensor 传感器
retail 零售	employee 雇员

Notes

[1]　全句可译为：从表13-1可以看出，建筑业的伤害和伤害或疾病造成的工时损失远比其他大多数行业高。

[2]　全句可译为：这个总数当中不仅有直接开支（医疗费用、工人权益赔偿金、责任和财产损失），同时还包括间接开支（工人劳动效率的降低、项目工期延误、管理费的增加，以及对设备和设施的损害）。

[3]　court judgments 指"法庭的判决"。全句可译为：然而，法庭的判决以及保险公司给予个人损失的补偿最终要由业主负担。

[4]　a series of coincidences 意为"一系列的巧合"。全句可译为：工作人员的坠落也许由一系列巧合共同引起：扶手不够牢靠、工人精力不集中以及脚下湿滑等。

[5]　全句可译为：例如，为了建筑工人的安全，女儿墙的设计高度要合理，而不应仅仅满足规范所要求的最低高度。

[6]　…built into machinery 是过去分词短语作定语，修饰"Safeguards"，译为"机械中装设的安全防护装置"。

[7]　on-board electronics 指"面板电子器件"。全句可译为：随着面板电子器件（包括计算机芯片）和传感器的应用，先进的机器监督装置被使用到施工设备和工具中的可能性大增。

[8]　全句可译为：用其他材料替换石棉能够减少或消除如硒肺这样的慢性病的发生。

[9]　Pre-qualification of contractors and sub-contractors with regard safety 指"在安全方面对承包商和分包商的资格预审"。

[10]　全句可译为：只有当那些有着良好安全记录的承包商才会被邀请参加投标或谈判时，就会对承包商保证安全生产提供直接的动力。

[11] 全句可译为：工人在工地的工作时间短，所以工人对工地的熟悉程度，以及与雇主的关系都不如制造业那么稳定。

Exercise

Translate the text of lesson 13.3 into Chinese.

Chapter 14   Organization and Use of Project Information

14.1   Types of Project Information

Construction projects inevitably generate enormous and complex sets of information. Effectively managing this bulk of information to insure its availability and accuracy is an important managerial task. Poor or missing information can readily lead to project delays, uneconomical decisions, or even the complete failure of the desired facility. Pity the owner and project manager who suddenly discover on the expected delivery date that important facility components have not yet been fabricated and cannot be delivered for six months! With better information, the problem could have been identified earlier, so that alternative suppliers might have been located or schedules arranged. Both project design and control are crucially dependent upon accurate and timely information, as well as the ability to use this information effectively. At the same time, too much unorganized information presented to managers can result in confusion and paralysis of decision making[1].

As a project proceeds, the types and extent of the information used by the various organizations involved will change. A listing of the most important information sets would include:

- cash flow and procurement accounts for each organization.
- intermediate analysis results during planning and design.
- design documents, including drawings and specifications.
- construction schedules and cost estimates.
- quality control and assurance records.
- chronological files of project correspondence and memorandum.
- construction field activity and inspection logs.
- legal contracts and regulatory documents.

Some of these sets of information evolve as the project proceeds. The financial accounts of payments over the entire course of the project is an example of overall growth. The passage of time results in steady additions in these accounts, whereas the addition of a new actor such as a contractor leads to a sudden jump in the number of accounts[2]. Some information sets are important at one stage of the process but may then be ignored. Common examples include planning or structural analysis databases which are not ordinarily used during construction or operation. However, it may be necessary at later stages in the project to re-do analyses to consider desired changes. In this case, archival information storage and retrieval become important. Even after the completion of construction, an historical record may be important for use during operation, to assess responsibilities in case of facility failures or for planning similar projects elsewhere[3].

The control and flow of information is also important for collaborative work environments, where many professionals are working on different aspects of a project and sharing information. Collaborative work environments provide facilities for sharing data files, tracing decisions, and communication via electronic mail or video conferencing. The data stores in these collaborative work environments may become very large.

Based on several construction projects, Maged Abdelsayed of Tardif, Murray & Assoc (Quebec, Canada) estimated the following average figures for a typical project of US $ 10 million:

- Number of participants (companies): 420 (including all suppliers and sub-sub-contractors).
- Number of participants (individuals): 850.
- Number of different types of documents generated: 50.
- Number of pages of documents: 56,000.
- Number of bankers boxes to hold project documents: 25.
- Number of 4 drawers filing cabinets: 6.
- Number of 20 inches diameter, 20 years old, 50 feets high, trees used to generate this volume of paper: 6.
- Equivalent number of Mega Bytes of electronic data to hold this volume of paper (scanned): 3,000 MB.
- Equivalent number of compact discs (CDs): 6.

While there may be substantial costs due to inaccurate or missing information, there are also significant costs associated with the generation, storage, transfer, retrieval and other manipulation of information. In addition to the costs of clerical work and providing aids such as computers, the organization and review of information command an inordinate amount of the attention of project managers, which may be the scarcest resource on any construction project[4]. It is useful, therefore, to understand the scope and alternatives for organizing project information.

Words

project Information　项目信息
procurement accounts　采购账目
memorandum　备忘录
archival information　档案资料
storage and retrieval　存储和查询
chronological files of project correspondence
按时间顺序的项目信函

cash flow　现金流量
inspection logs　检查日志
structural analysis databases　结构分析数据库
video conferencing　电视会议
tracing decision　跟踪决策

Notes

[1]　presented to managers 过去分词作定语。result in 意为"造成"。confusion and paralysis of decision making 意为"决策的混乱和瘫痪"。

[2]　全句可译为：这些账目随着时间的推移而增加，新参与单位的加入（如承包商），使账目的数目猛增。

[3]　sth…may be important for sth…to do sth 意为"……可能对做……有重要的意义"。in case of 意为"万一，一旦"。全句可译为：甚至在工程结束后，在设施使用期间历史记录也有很大用途，用于评价设施故障的责任，或者用于今后其他类似项目的规划。

[4]　clerical work and providing aids 意为"行政工作和辅助设备"。project managers, which…为非限制性定语从句，先行词在句中作主语。

14.2　Computerized Organization and Use of Information

Numerous formal methods and possible organizations exist for the information required for project management. Before discussing the details of computations and information representation, it will be useful to describe a record keeping implementation, including some of the practical concerns in design and implementation. In this section, we shall describe a computer based system to provide construction yard and warehouse management information from the point of view of the system users. In the process, the usefulness of computerized databases can be illustrated.

A yard or warehouse is used by most construction firms to store equipment and to provide an inventory of materials and parts needed for projects. Large firms may have several warehouses at different locations so as to reduce transit time between project sites and materials supplies. In addition, local "yards" or "equipment sheds" are commonly provided on the job site. Examples of equipment in a yard would be drills, saws, office trailers, graders, back hoes, concrete pumps and cranes[1]. Material items might include nails, plywood, wire mesh, forming, lumber, etc.

In typical construction warehouses, written records are kept by warehouse clerks to record transfer or return of equipment to job sites, dispatch of material to jobs, and maintenance histories of particular pieces of equipment[2]. In turn, these records are used as the basis for billing projects for the use of equipment and materials.

One common mechanism to organize record keeping is to fill out cards recording the transfer of items to or from a job site. Table 14-1 illustrates one possible transfer record. In this case, seven items were requested for the Carnegie-Mellon job site (project number 83-1557). These seven items would be loaded on a delivery truck, along with a copy of the transfer record. Shown in Table 14-1 is a code number identifying each item (0609.02, 0609.03, etc.), the quantity of each item requested, an item description and a unit price. For equipment items, an equipment number identifying the individual piece of equipment used is also recorded, such as grinder No. 4517 in Table 14-1; a unit price is not specified for equipment but a daily rental charge might be imposed.

Table 14-1 Illustration of a Construction Warehouse Transfer Record

TRANSFER SHEET NUMBER 100311					
Deliver To: Carnegie-Mellon				Job. No. 83-1557	
Received From: Pittsburgh Warehouse				Job No. 99-PITT	
ITEM NO.	EQ. NO.	QTY	DESCRIPTION		UNIT PRICE
0609.02		200	Hilti Pins NK27		$ 0.36
0609.03		200	Hilti Pins NK27		0.36
0188.21		1	Kiel, Box of 12		6.53
0996.01		3	Paint, Spray		5.57
0607.03		4	Plywood, 4 x 8 x 1/4"		11.62
0172.00	4517	1	Grinder		
0181.53		1	Grinding Wheel, 6" Cup		14.97
Preparer: Vicki			Date: x/xx/xx		

Transfer sheets are numbered (such as No. 100311 in Table 14-1), dated and the preparer identified to facilitate control of the record keeping process. During the course of a month, numerous transfer records of this type are accumulated. At the end of a month, each of the transfer records is examined to compile the various items or equipment used at a project and the appropriate charges. Constructing these bills would be a tedious manual task. Equipment movements would have to be tracked individually, days at each site counted, and the daily charge accumulated for each project[3]. For example, Table 14-1 records the transfer of grinder No. 4517 to a job site. This project would be charged a daily rental rate until the grinder was returned. Hundreds or thousands of individual item transfers would have to be examined, and the process of preparing bills could easily require a week or two of effort.

In addition to generating billing information, a variety of reports would be useful in the process of managing a company's equipment and individual projects. Records of the history of use of particular pieces of equipment are useful for planning maintenance and deciding on the sale or scrapping of equipment[4]. Reports on the cumulative amount of materials and equipment delivered to a job site would be of obvious benefit to project managers. Composite reports on the amount, location, and use of pieces of equipment of particular types are also useful in making decisions about the purchase of new equipment, inventory control, or for project planning. Unfortunately, producing each of these reports requires manually sifting through a large number of transfer cards. Alternatively, record keeping for these specific projects could have to proceed by keeping multiple records of the same information. For example, equipment transfers might be recorded on (1) a file for a particular piece of equipment and (2) a file for a particular project, in addition to the basic transfer form illustrated in Table 14-1. Even with these redundant records, producing the various desired reports would be time consuming.

Organizing this inventory information in a computer program is a practical and desirable innovation. In addition to speeding up billing (and thereby reducing borrowing costs), application programs can readily provide various reports or *views* of the basic inventory information described above[5]. Information can be entered directly to the computer program as needed. For example, the transfer record shown in Table 14-1 is based upon an input screen to a computer program which, in turn, had been designed to duplicate the manual form used prior to computerization. Use of the computer also allows some interactive aids in preparing the transfer form. This type of aid follows a simple rule: "Don't make the user provide information that the system already knows." In using the form shown in Table 14-1, a clerk need only enter the code and quantity for an item; the verbal description and unit cost of the item then appear automatically. A copy of the transfer form can be printed locally, while the data is stored in the computer for subsequent processing. As a result, preparing transfer forms and record keeping are rapidly and effectively performed.

More dramatically, the computerized information allows warehouse personnel both to ask questions about equipment management and to readily generate the requisite data for answering such questions[6]. The records of transfers can be readily processed by computer programs to develop bills and other reports. For example, proposals to purchase new pieces of equipment can be rapidly and critically reviewed after summarizing the actual usage of existing equipment. Ultimately, good organization of information will typically lead to the desire to store new types of data and to provide new views of this information as standard managerial tools.

Of course, implementing an information system such as the warehouse inventory database requires considerable care to insure that the resulting program is capable of accomplishing the desired task. In the warehouse inventory system, a variety of details are required to make the computerized system an acceptable alternative to a long standing manual record keeping procedure. Coping with these details makes a big difference in the system's usefulness. For example, changes to the status of equipment are generally made by recording transfers as illustrated in Table 14-1. However, a few status changes are not accomplished by physical movement. One example is a charge for air conditioning in field trailers: even though the air conditioners may be left in the field, the construction project should not be charged for the air conditioner after it has been turned off during the cold weather months[7]. A special status change report may be required for such details. Other details of record keeping require similar special controls.

Even with a capable program, simplicity of design for users is a critical factor affecting the successful implementation of a system. In the warehouse inventory system described above, input forms and initial reports were designed to duplicate the existing manual, paper-based records. As a result, warehouse clerks could readily understand what information was required and its ultimate use. A good rule to follow is the Principle of Least Astonishment: make communications with users as consistent and predictable as possible in designing programs[8].

Finally, flexibility of systems for changes is an important design and implementation concern. New reports or views of the data are a common requirement as the system is used. For example, the introduction of a new accounting system would require changes in the communications procedure from the warehouse inventory system to record changes and other cost items.

In sum, computerizing the warehouse inventory system could save considerable labor, speed up billing, and facilitate better management control[9]. Against these advantages must be placed the cost of introducing computer hardware and software in the warehouse.

Words

construction yard   施工场地   warehouse management   仓库管理

equipment sheds	设备棚	plywood	胶合板
wire mesh	钢筋网	concrete pump	混凝土泵
rental charge	租赁费	preparer identified	写上编制者的姓名
time consuming	费耗时间的	warehouse personnel	仓库管理人员
air conditioning	空调	communications procedure	沟通程序
warehouse inventory system	仓库储存管理系统		

Notes

[1] 全句可译为：堆场里的设备可以是钻机、锯子、拖车、平路机、反铲挖土机、混凝土泵、起重机等。

[2] in typical construction warehouses 意为"在典型的施工仓库中"。dispatch of material to jobs 意为"材料的分发"。全句可译为：在典型的施工仓库中，仓库管理员要对材料的分发、设备的转移或归还、具体设备的维护过程等进行书面记录。

[3] individually 这里指"分别地"。at each site 意为"每一个工地"。全句可译为：设备的移动过程，必须分别记录，记录在各个工地上使用的天数，计算用于各个项目上的费用总和。

[4] planning maintenance and deciding on the sale or scrapping of equipment 意为"制订维护计划、决定设备是否出售或报废。"

[5] in addition to 是"除了"的意思。to 是介词，后面跟名词或动名词。speeding up billing 意为"加快账目编制速度"。全句可译为：除了加快账目编制速度外（因此降低了成本），应用程序能够迅速地提供上述各种报告和物资储存的基本信息。

[6] dramatically 意为"值得注意的是"。the computerized information 意为"计算机处理信息"。全句可译为：更值得注意的是，用计算机处理信息不仅使仓库管理人员能够提出有关设备管理的问题，也能方便地得到回答这些问题所需的数据。

[7] field trailers 意为"现场的活动房"。been turned off 意为"被关掉"。全句可译为：现场的活动房空调费就是一例：尽管空调留在工地上，但是在寒冷月份，空调关掉后就不应再向项目收取空调费用。

[8] Principle of Least Astonishment 意为"最小惊讶原则"。as consistent and predictable as possible 意为"尽可能保持一致并使其能够预见"。

[9] in sum 意为"总之"。全句可译为：总之，用计算机进行仓库储存管理不仅节约大量人力，加快做账的速度，而且改善管理控制。

14.3 Relational Model of Databases

As an example of how data can be organized conceptually, we shall describe the *relational data model*. In this conceptual model, the data in the database is viewed as being organized into a series of *relations* or tables of data which are associated in ways defined in the data dictionary[1]. A relation consists of rows of data with columns containing particular attributes. The term "relational" derives from the mathematical theory of relations which provides a theoretical framework for this type of data model. Here, the terms "relation" and data "table" will be used interchangeably. Table 14-2 defines one possible relation to record unit cost data associated with particular activities. Included in the database would be one row (or *tuple*) for each of the various items involved in construction or other project activities. The unit cost information associated with each item is then stored in the form of the relation defined in Table 14-2.

Table 14-2 Illustration of a Relation Description: Unit Price Information Attributes

Attribute Name	Attribute Description	Attribute Type	Key
ITEM_CODE	Item Code Number	Pre-defined Code	Yes
DESCRIPTION	Item Description	Text	No
WORK_UNIT	Standard Unit of Work for the Item	Text (restricted to allowable units)	No
CREW_CODE	Standard Crew Code for Activity	Pre-defined Code	No
OUTPUT	Average Productivity of Crew	Numerical	No
TIME_UNIT	Standard Unit of OUTPUT	Text	No
MATL_UNIT_COST	Material Unit Cost	Numerical	No
DATEMCOS	Date of MATL_UNIT_COST	Date Text	No
INSTCOST	Installation Unit Cost	Numerical	No
DATEICOS	Date of INSTCOST	Date Text	No

Using Table 14-2, a typical unit cost entry for an activity in construction might be:

ITEM-CODE: 04.2-66-025

DESCRIPTION: common brick masonry, 12″ thick wall, 19.0 bricks per S.F.

WORK_UNIT: 1000 bricks

CREW_CODE: 04.2-3

OUTPUT: 1.9

TIME_UNIT: Shift

MATL_UNIT_COST: 124

DATEMCOS: June-09-79

INSTCOST: 257

DATEICOS: August-23-79

This entry summarizes the unit costs associated with construction of 12″ thick brick masonry walls, as indicated by the item DESCRIPTION. The ITEM _ CODE is a numerical code identifying a particular activity. This code might identify general categories as well; in this case, 04.2 refers to general masonry work. ITEM _ CODE might be based on the MASTERFORMAT or other coding scheme. The CREW _ CODE entry identifies the standard crew which would be involved in the activity. The actual composition of the standard crew would be found in a CREW RELATION under the entry 04.2-3, which is the third standard crew involved in masonry work (04.2). This ability to *point* to other relations reduces the *redundancy* or duplication of information in the database. In this case, standard crew number 04.2-3 might be used for numerous masonry construction tasks, but the definition of this crew need only appear once.

WORK-UNIT, OUTPUT and TIME _ UNIT summarize the expected output for this task with a standard crew and define the standard unit of measurement for the item. In this case, costs are given per thousand bricks per shift. Finally, material (MATL _ UNIT _ COST) and installation (INSTCOSTS) costs are recorded along with the date (DATEMCOS and DATEICOS) at which the prices were available and entered in the database. The date of entry is useful to insure that any inflation in costs can be considered during use of the data.

The data recorded in each row could be obtained by survey during bid preparations, from past project experience or from commercial services. For example, the data recorded in the Table 14-2 relation could be obtained as nationwide averages from commercial sources.

An advantage of the relational database model is that the number of attributes and rows in each relation can be expanded as desired[2]. For example, a manager might wish to divide material costs (MATL-UNIT-COST) into attributes for specific materials such as cement, aggregate and other ingredients of concrete in the unit cost relation defined in Table 14-2. As additional items are defined or needed, their associated data can be entered in the database as another row (or tuple) in the unit cost relation. Also, new relations can be defined as the need arises. Hence, the relational model of database organization can be quite flexible in application. In practice, this is a crucial advantage. Application systems can be expected to change radically over time, and a flexible system is highly desirable.

With a relational database, it is straightforward to issue queries for particular data items or to combine data from different relations[3]. For example, a manager might wish to produce a report of the crew composition needed on a site to accomplish a given list of tasks. Assembling this report would require accessing the unit price information to find the standard crew and then combining information about the construction activity or item (eg.

quantity desired) with crew information. However, to effectively accomplish this type of manipulation requires the definition of a "key" in each relation.

In Table 14-2, the ITEMCODE provides a unique identifier or *key* for each row. No other row should have the same ITEMCODE in any one relation. Having a unique key reduces the *redundancy* of data, since only one row is included in the database for each activity. It also avoids error. For example, suppose one queried the database to find the material cost entered on a particular date. This response might be misleading since more than one material cost could have been entered on the same date. Similarly, if there are multiple rows with the same ITEMCODE value, then a query might give erroneous responses if one of the rows was out of date[4]. Finally, each row has only a single entry for each attribute.

The ability to combine or separate relations into new arrangements permits the definition of alternative *views* or external models of the information. Since there are usually a number of different users of databases, this can be very useful. For example, the payroll division of an organization would normally desire a quite different organization of information about employees than would a project manager. By explicitly defining the type and organization of information a particular user group or application requires, a specific view or subset of the entire database can be constructed[5]. This organization is illustrated in Fig. 14-1 with the DATA DICTIONARY serving as a translator between the external data models and the database management system.

Behind the operations associated with querying and manipulating relations is an explicit algebraic theory. This algebra defines the various operations that can be performed on relations, such as union (consisting of all rows belonging to one or the other of two relations), intersection (consisting of all rows belonging to both of two relations), minus (consisting of all rows belonging to one relation and not another), or projection (consisting of a subset of the attributes from a relation)[6]. The algebraic underpinnings of relational databases permit rigorous definitions and confidence that operations will be accomplished in the desired fashion.

Example 14-1: A Subcontractor Relation
As an illustration of the preceding discussion, consider the problem of developing a database of possible subcontractors for construction projects. This database might be desired by the cost estimation department of a general contractor to identify subcontractors to ask to bid on parts of a project. Appropriate subcontractors appearing in the database could be contacted to prepare bids for specific projects. Table 14-3 lists the various attributes which might be required for such a list and an example entry, including the subcontractor's name, contact

person, address, size (large, medium or small), and capabilities.

Table 14-3 Subcontractor Relation Example

Attribute	Example
NAME	XYZ Electrical Co.
CONTACT	Betty XYZ
PHONE	(412) xxx-xxxx
STREET	xxx Mulberry St.
CITY	Pittsburgh
STATE	PA
ZIPCODE	152xx
SIZE	large
CONCRETE	no
ELECTRICAL	yes
MASONRY	no
etc.	

To use this relation, a cost estimator might be interested in identifying large, electrical subcontractors in the database. A query typed into the DBM such as:

SELECT from SUBCONTRACTORS
where SIZE = Large and ELECTRICAL = Yes

would result in the selection of all large subcontractors performing electrical work in the subcontractor's relation. More specifically, the estimator might want to find subcontractors in a particular state:

SELECT from SUBCONTRACTORS
where SIZE = Large and ELECTRICAL = Yes and STATE = VI.

In addition to providing a list of the desired subcontractors' names and addresses, a utility application program could also be written which would print mailing labels for the selected firms.

Other portions of the general contracting firm might also wish to use this list. For example, the accounting department might use this relation to record the addresses of subcontractors for payment of invoices, thereby avoiding the necessity to maintain duplicate files. In this case, the accounting code number associated with each subcontractor might be entered as an additional attribute in the relation, and the accounting department could find addresses directly[7].

Example 14-2: Historical Bridge Work Relation

As another simple example of a data table, consider the relation shown in Table 14-0 which might record historical experience with different types of bridges accumulated by a particular agency. The actual instances or rows of data in Table 14-4 are hypothetical. The attributes of this relation are:

- PROJECT NUMBER-a 6-digit code identifying the particular project.
- TYPE OF BRIDGE-a text field describing the bridge type. (For retrieval purposes, a numerical code might also be used to describe bridge type to avoid any differences in terminology to describe similar bridges).
- LOCATION-The location of the project.
- CROSSING-What the bridge crosses over, eg. a river.
- SITE CONDITIONS-A brief description of the site peculiarities.
- ERECTION TIME-Time required to erect a bridge, in months.
- SPAN-Span of the bridge in feet.
- DATE - Year of bridge completion.
- ACTUAL-ESTIMATED COSTS - Difference of actual from estimated costs.

These attributes could be used to answer a variety of questions concerning construction experience useful during preliminary planning.

Table 14-4 Example of Bridge Work Relation

Project Number	Type of Bridge	Location	Crossing	Site Conditions	Erection Time (Months)	Span (ft.)	Estimated less Actual Cost
169137	Steel Plate Girder	Altoona	Railroad	200' Valley Limestone	5	240	− $ 50,000
170145	Concrete Arch	Pittsburgh	River	250' High Sandy Loam	7	278	− 27,500
197108	Steel Truss	Allentown	Highway	135' Deep Pile Foundation	8	256	35,000

As an example, suppose that a bridge is to be built with a span of 250 feet, located in Pittsburgh PA, and crossing a river with limestone sub-strata[8]. In initial or preliminary planning, a designer might query the database four separate times as follows:

- SELECT from BRIDGEWORK where SPAN>200 and SPAN<300 and where CROSSING= "river".
- SELECT from BRIDGEWORK where SPAN>200 and SPAN<300 and where SITE CONDITIONS= "Limestone".
- SELECT from BRIDGEWORK where TYPE OF BRIDGE = "Steel Plate

Girder" and LOCATION = "PA".
- SELECT from BRIDGEWORK where SPAN < 300 and SPAN > 200 and ESTIMATED LESS ACTUAL COST < 100,000.

Each SELECT operation would yield the bridge examples in the database which corresponds to the desired selection criteria. In practice, an input/output interpreter program should be available to translate these inquiries to and from the DBM and an appropriate problem oriented language[9].

Words

relational data model 关系数据模型
standard crew number 标准班组人数
payroll division 工资分类系统
cost estimation department 成本估算部门
payment of invoices 支付发票面额，根据发票付款

electrical subcontractors 电气工程分包商
brick masonry walls 砌筑墙体
masonry construction 砌筑结构
algebraic theory 代数理论
site conditions 现场条件
preliminary planning 初步设计阶段

Notes

[1] conceptual model 意为"概念模型"。is viewed as 意为"被看作"。being organized into 意为"组织为……"。全句可译为：在这个概念模型中，将数据库中的数据组织视为一系列关系或按数据字典中定义的方式联系起来的数据表。

[2] is that …是表语从句。be expanded as desired 意为"根据需要增添"，其中 as 相当于"which is"，引起一个定语从句。

[3] with a relational database 是"对于关系数据库"的意思。it is straightforward 意为"简单"。全句可译为：对于关系数据库，查询具体数据段或者合并不同关系中的数据简单而省事。

[4] give erroneous responses 意为"收到错误的查询结果"。was out of date 意为"过期"。

[5] 全句可译为：明确地定义用户组或应用程序需要的信息类型和结构，就可以看到整个数据库的某一具体方面或子集。

[6] operations that can be performed on 意为"可以对……进行运算"。union、intersection、minus、projection 分别为"求和、求积、求差、投影"的意思。

[7] the accounting code number 意为"财务编码"。the accounting department 意为"会计部门"。全句可译为：在这一情况下，加入每个分包商的财务编码可视为关系中的附加属性，会计部门可直接查到地址。

[8] crossing a river with limestone sub-strata 在句中作定语，其中 limestone sub-strata 意为"石灰石地层"。

[9] In practice 意为"在实践中"。an input/output interpreter program 意为"输入/输

出解释程序"。全句可译为：在实践中，应当有一个输入输出解释程序将这些查询指令转换成 DMB 和适当的专用语言。

14.4 Information Transfer and Flow

The previous sections outlined the characteristics of a computerized database. In an overabundance of optimism or enthusiasm, it might be tempting to conclude that all information pertaining to a project might be stored in a single database[1]. This has never been achieved and is both unlikely to occur and undesirable in itself. Among the difficulties of such excessive centralization are:

- **Existence of multiple firms or agencies involved in any project.** Each organization must retain its own records of activities, whether or not other information is centralized. Geographic dispersion of work even within the same firm can also be advantageous. With design offices around the globe, fast track projects can have work underway by different offices 24 hours a day.
- **Advantages of distributed processing.** Current computer technology suggests that using a number of computers at the various points that work is performed is more cost effective than using a single, centralized mainframe computer. Personal computers not only have cost and access advantages, they also provide a degree of desired redundancy and increased reliability[2].
- **Dynamic changes in information needs.** As a project evolves, the level of detail and the types of information required will vary greatly.
- **Database diseconomies of scale.** As any database gets larger, it becomes less and less efficient to find desired information.
- **Incompatible user perspectives.** Defining a single data organization involves trade-offs between different groups of users and application systems. A good organization for one group may be poor for another[3].

In addition to these problems, there will always be a set of untidy information which cannot be easily defined or formalized to the extent necessary for storage in a database[4].

While a single database may be undesirable, it is also apparent that it is desirable to structure independent application systems or databases so that measurement information need only be manually recorded once and communication between the database might exist. Consider the following examples illustrating the desirability of communication between independent application systems or databases. While some progress has occurred, the level of integration and existing mechanisms for information flow in project management is fairly primitive. By and large, information flow relies primarily on talking, written texts of reports and specifications and drawings.

Example 14-3: Time Cards

Time card information of labor is used to determine the amount which employees are to be paid and to provide records of work performed by activity[5]. In many firms, the system of payroll accounts and the database of project management accounts (i.e., expenditure by activity) are maintained independently. As a result, the information available from time cards is often recorded twice in mutually incompatible formats. This repetition increases costs and the possibility of transcription errors. The use of a preprocessor system to check for errors and inconsistencies and to format the information from each card for the various systems involved is likely to be a significant improvement (Figure 14-1). Alternatively, a communications facility between two databases of payroll and project management accounts might be developed.

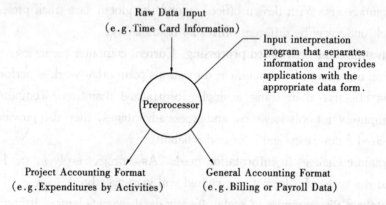

Figure 14-1 Application of an Input Pre-processor

Example 14-4: Final Cost Estimation, Scheduling and Monitoring

Many firms maintain essentially independent systems for final cost estimation and project activity scheduling and monitoring. As a result, the detailed breakdown of the project into specific job related activities must be completely re-done for scheduling and monitoring. By providing a means of *rolling-over* or transferring the final cost estimate, some of this expensive and time-consuming planning effort could be avoided[6].

Example 14-5: Design Representation

In many areas of engineering design, the use of computer analysis tools applied to facility models has become prevalent and remarkably effective. However, these computer-based facility models are often separately developed or encoded by each firm involved in the design process. Thus, the architect, structural engineer, mechanical engineer, steel fabricator, construction manager and others might all have separate computer-based representations of a facility[7]. Communication by means of reproduced facility plans and prose specifications is traditional among these groups. While transfer of this information in a form suitable for direct computer processing is difficult, it offers obvious advantages in avoiding repetition of work, delays and transcription errors. A de facto standard for transfer of geometric information emerged with the dominance of the AUTOCAD design system in the A/E/C industry[8]. Information transfer was accomplished by copying AUTOCAD files from user to user, including uses on construction sites to visualize the design. More flexible and extensive standards for design information transfer also exist, such as the Industry Foundation Classes (IFC) standard developed by the International Alliance for Interoperability (See http://www.iai-international.org/iai_international) and the "Fully Integrated and Automated Project Processes" developed by FIATECH.

Words

design offices 设计事务所
centralized mainframe computer 主机
dynamic changes 动态变化
existing mechanisms 现有机制
specifications and drawings 技术要求说明书和图纸
preprocessor system 预处理系统
project management accounts 项目管理账目
Final Cost Estimation 最终成本估计
Design Representation 设计表示法
distributed processing 分布式处理
access 存取
integration 集成
information flow 信息流
Time Cards 计时卡
databases of payroll 工资数据库
project accounting format 项目核算格式
Scheduling and Monitoring 进度计划和监控
engineering design 工程设计

Notes

[1] in an overabundance of optimism or enthusiasm。意为"过于乐观或积极的情绪"。it might be tempting to do sth 意为"情不自禁地"。

[2] personal computers 意为"个人计算机"。全句可译为：个人计算机不仅在成本和使用便利上有优点，而且还有用户希望的冗余，进而增强了可靠性。

[3] 全句可译为：单一数据组织的确定，需要权衡不同类别用户和应用系统的要求，一类用户认为好的组织，另一类用户可能认为不好。

[4] in addition to 是介词短语，意为"除了"。a set of untidy information 意为"一些杂乱的信息"，在定语从句中作主语。全句可译为：另外的问题是，总有一些杂乱的信息不容易定义或确定格式，以满足数据库存储的要求。

[5] time card information of labor 意为"人工计时卡"。is used to 意为"被用于"，属于被动语态。全句可译为：人工计时卡信息用于确定需要支付工资的雇员数量，并成为活动已完成的工作记录。

[6] by a means of … 意为"通过……手段、方式"。*rolling-over* 意为"传递"。expensive and time-consuming planning 意为"既废钱又费时的计划"。

[7] 全句可译为：因此，建筑师、结构工程师、机械工程师、钢结构制作承包商、施工管理承包商和其他人可能都利用计算机各自表示一个设施。

[8] a de facto standard 意为"实际标准"。全句可译为：传递图形信息的实际标准随着 AUTOCAD 设计系统在 A/E/C 行业中成为主导系统而形成。

Exercise

Translate the text of lesson 14.4 into Chinese.

参考译文

1.2 建设项目的主要类型

由于大多数的业主通常仅对某种特定类型的建筑设施感兴趣，因此他们应当对相关建筑类型共性的行业实务有所了解。同时，建筑业还是一个融多样化构件和产品于一身的关联产业。有些业主在很长一段时间内可能只洽购一次建筑设施并且倾向于关注短期利益。然而，还是有许多业主会定期设法购得新的建筑设施或对已有设施进行翻修重建。正是他们使得建筑业健康且富有生机。总的来说，这些业主有着更多的连他们自己也意识不到的影响建筑业的能力。因为通过其个人行为，他们对建筑产品的创新、效率以及质量施加着积极或消极的影响。业主在建筑业中发挥积极的作用和施加有益的影响是符合所有参与方的利益的。

在对不同建筑类型进行规划时，获取专业服务、授予建设合约以及进行在建项目融资的方法与手段是大不相同的。为了方便讨论，建筑设施的范畴从广义上划分为四类，每一类均有其自身的特点。

住宅类房屋建设

住宅类房屋建筑包括单居户房屋、多居户楼房和高层公寓。在开发和建造这类项目的过程中，对建筑十分通晓的开发商或发起人通常以代理业主的身份出现，负责指定设计和施工必要的合同条款，并负责完工房屋的销售。住宅类房屋的设计通常由建筑师和工程师来完成，建筑施工则由雇用结构、机械、电气和其他专业分包商的建筑承包商来完成。这种类型的一个例外是单居户房屋，它的设计和施工可能由同一家建筑商承包完成。

住宅类房屋市场极易受宏观经济、税收政策、政府货币及金融政策的影响。由于许多住宅项目可以在不同的地点由不同的开发商在同一时间开工，因此往往市场总需求的一些微小的增加就能引起此类建筑童子地点急剧增加。或许因为市场进入相对容易，很多建筑商被吸引到住宅类建筑项目上。这样一来，市场竞争就很激烈，风险也相应增加。

办公和商业用房建设

办公和商业用房建设包括一系列不同规模和类型的建筑，如学校、医院、娱乐场所、体育馆、大型商业中心、仓库、办公摩天大楼以及酒店等，这类房屋的业主本身并不精通房屋建设的实务，但他们可聘请有能力的专业咨询人员为其服务，他们自己只需考虑项目融资上的安排。专业的建筑师和工程师负责具体房屋的工程设计，而专业的建筑承包商或总承包商承担房屋的建造。

同住宅类房屋建设相比，此类房屋建设成本高且功能复杂，所以市场份额由减少的竞争者来瓜分。同时这类房屋建设从开工到完工所经历的时间比较长，故其对市场宏观经济条件的反应不如商业住宅房屋建设那么敏感。这类房屋建设的业主通常会面对在同一市场竞争的寡头垄断式的总承建商。在这种情况下，一个市场只有为数不多的竞争者存在，而服务价格则取决于当地市场的竞争水平。

专业化工业项目建设

专业化工业项目建设涉及范围很广，含有高等级技术复杂性的这样一类项目建设，包括原油提炼厂、钢铁厂、化工厂、火力发电厂或核电厂等，业主通常会参与项目的进展，并倾向于采用设计半字线建造方式，因为这样可以缩短项目的建设周期。业主还会有选择地同一些设计方和施工方保持长久而良好的工作关系。

尽管这些项目的启动受经济状况影响，但由于这类项目属于资金密集型，且需相当长时间的规划和建设，故长期的需求成为最重要的因素。政府出台的行业指南对这类项目的决策也有着深远的影响。

重大基础项目建设

重大基础项目建设包括如高速公路、隧道、桥梁、管网、排水系统和污水处理厂等这种类型的项目。这些项目大多为公用项目，并通过债券或税收来融资建设。这一类项目以自动化程度高为特点，并逐步取代了劳动力密集的操作方式。

参与基础项目建设的设计方和建造方具有相当程度的专业化水平，这是由于这类项目的市场划分比较细。然而，由于有些基础项目的市场已趋饱和，这样一来便有可能加剧其他类型基础项目市场的竞争。比如，高速公路项目的市场在经过快速发展后，已日趋萎缩。因此，有些从事高速公路建设的承包商便会迅速转向矿山开发等其他基础项目市场。

2.1 何为项目管理？

进行项目建设管理不仅需要熟悉有关建筑和设计的过程，同时还应具备现代管理知识。建设项目有特定的一些目标和约束条件，比如说必须在限定的时间内完工。尽管相关的技术、组织机构的设置或步骤有所不同，但建设项目同其他如航天、医药和化工等专业领域的项目，在管理上仍然有共同之处。

总的来讲，项目管理取决于项目以任务（目标）为导向的这个特征，有别于公司的宏观管理。一个项目的组织在其使命完成后一般便随之不复存在。项目管理协会（PMI）对项目管理做出如下定义：

项目管理是在项目的整个周期内，用现代的管理技术指挥和协调人力和物质资源以实现范围、成本、工期、质量和分享成就等预定目标。

与此形成对照，工商企业的宏观管理却着眼于未来更佳的经营连续性。尽管如此，对于宏观管理适用的现代管理技术也应当同样适用于项目管理。

项目管理的框架体系见图2-1。行之有效的宏观管理知识和与项目有关的专业知识对项目而言均为不可或缺。而诸如计算机科学和决策技术这样的支持性学科也非常重要。实际上，现代管理实务和不同专业领域已经吸收了这些支持性学科里的许多工具和技术。比如，对于宏观管理，给予计算机的信息系统和决策支持系统已是常用的工具。同样，许多如线性规划和网络分析等运筹学中的技术也已在其他知识或应用领域广为使用。因此，图 2-1 仅表示项目管理体系框架和其他技术或学科的关系。

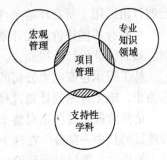

图 2-1　项目管理的知识体系

具体来说，建设项目管理包含一系列通过完成许多服从资源和约束条件的运作才能实现的目标。在有关范围、成本、时间及质量等明确的目标与施加于人力、物力和财力上的约束条件之间存在着一些潜在的冲突。通过做出必要的平衡或找出新的替代方案，在项目的启动阶段就应当解决这些冲突。建设项目管理总的来说包括以下功能：

1. 项目目标说明和包括范围描述、预算、进度、设定绩效目标和选择项目合伙人等在内的各项计划。
2. 根据规定的进度和规划，通过采购使各资源的有效利用最大化。
3. 在项目全过程中，通过适当的协调和控制来执行规划、设计、预算和合同中的各项事务。
4. 在项目各参与方之间建立有效的沟通机制以化解冲突。

项目管理协会制定了项目经理应学习和具备的九个方面的知识领域：

1. 项目整体管理，用以保证项目各要素相互协调。
2. 项目范围管理，用以保证包括所有需要完成的工作。
3. 项目时间管理，它提供了一个有效的进度计划。
4. 项目成本管理，用以识别所需资源和保持预算控制。
5. 项目质量管理，用以确保满足功能需要。
6. 项目人力资源管理，用以合理进行人力的开发和使用。
7. 项目沟通管理，确保项目内、外的有效沟通。
8. 项目风险管理，用以分析和减轻潜在的风险。
9. 项目采购管理，用以从项目外部获得必须的各种资源。

这九个源自 PMI 认证体系的知识领域对于任何行业的项目经理来说都必须掌握。

3.4　施工组织设计

施工计划的制订同好的设计是一样的。计划者必须在考虑技术可行性的同时，权衡不同方案的成本和可靠性。施工计划有时实施起来很困难，这是因为施工过程是一个动态的过程，现场平面布置和临时设施会随着工程进度的推进而有所变化。另一方面，施工作业从一个项目到另一个项目，看上去似乎是标准的，但是这两个项目结构或基础的具体情况会有很大的差别。

要制订好施工计划是一项非常有挑战性的工作。对于任何一个具体的项目，都有许多可能的方案可以选择。虽然过去的经验是制订施工计划的主要依据，但是每个工程项目都有其自身独有的问题或机会，需要相当大的灵活性和创造性去克服或发掘。不过，不太可能制订出适用于所有环境条件的施工计划。

尽管有一些评价施工计划特性的指标，但这并不能使计划者了解如何制订好的施工计划。然而，就设计阶段而言，工作分解方法是较为通用的。

从工程承包商或大公司的专业分包的角度来看，从施工计划开始制订，到完成施工过程为止，施工计划的计划过程包括三个阶段。

估算阶段主要包括对整个项目设施建设做出费用和工期估算，这是承包商提交给业主的建议的其中一部分。在这个阶段中，计划者要对项目设施建设的必要活动做出所需资源投入的假定。通过对项目设计和现场条件不同情况的全面的分析，来确定最适当的估算。估算是承包商成功的关键，因为它不仅要能承揽到业务，还必须在完成建设任务的同时获得最高的利润。计划者必须综合考虑工期和费用的各种组合，以便承包商能成功地完成建设任务。过高的估算往往会使承包商失去业务；而较低的估算虽会使承包商获得业务，但也会使承包商在建设过程中损失利润。当变更发生时，他们应适当提高估算，其中不仅要考虑当前的影响，还要考虑竣工结算。在实际工程中，很少出现竣工结算与最初提供给业主的估算差不多的例子。

在建设过程的监督和控制阶段，项目经理必须对施工作业的工期和费用保持持续的跟踪。那种认为只要建设能按期或提前执行，那么费用也必然不会超出预计费用的想法是不正确的，尤其是在发生许多变更时。在建设完成前，持续地进行估算是必要的。在建设过程中，当某项作业完成时，相关信息要提供给计划者。接着，计划过程的第三阶段就开始了。评估阶段主要是将建设过程的结果与估算做比较。计划者在这个阶段要对不确定性做出分析。只有当了解了建设工程的实际产出后，才能对估算的准确性进行评估。只有到计划流程的最后一个阶段，才能确定初始假定的正确性。如果这些假定不正确，或有新的限制，就必须对未来的计划做出相应的调整。

4.2 材料采购与运输

材料采购中反馈和控制的主要信息来源是需求、出价和报价、采购单和分包、递交和接收文件以及发票。对于大量使用关键资源的项目，业主为了避免材料短缺和延误，在选择施工方之前，可以开始采购的过程。在通常的情况下，施工方将以设计方规定的最优价格/性能特征来处理现场材料的购买。在采购过程中一些搭接和再处理是不可避免的，但它应该被最小化，以保证在良好的条件下及时地运送材料。

从施工现场运进或运出材料主要可以分为：（1）大数量材料；（2）标准的库存材料；（3）制作的构件或单元。运输的过程包括交通、现场储存和安装，对各类材料是不一样的。用来处理和拖拉各类材料所需的设备同样是不一样的。

大数量材料是指在自然状态或半加工状态的材料，例如土方开挖、湿混凝土拌合物等。这些材料通常在工程中数量巨大。一些大数量的材料，例如土方和砂砾可以用堆积（在原位置的固体）的数量来计算。明显地，根据这些材料的特征，用不同的计量方法时，材料运输的数量可以完全不一样。

标准的管道和阀门是化工工业中大量使用的标准的库存材料中的典型例子。因为，储存标准的库存材料是容易的，它的运输过程相对简单。

为了使现场安装过程简单化，制作的构件（例如大楼的钢梁和柱）是在工场预先加工而成的。有部分焊接或螺栓接头附在构件上，这些构件为了很好地吻合起来而切割成精确的大小。相似地，钢罐和压力容器经常在送到现场前部分地或完全地制作完成。一般来说，假如可以在能够更好地控制工作条件的工场进行工作，则提倡在工场做。条件是可以按合理的成本和用一种满意的方法运送所制作的构件到施工现场。

作为进一步使得现场装配简单化的方法是，整个一面墙包括管道和配线，甚至整个房间都可以预制，并且运送到现场。在这些情况下，虽然现场劳动力大大地减少了，但事实上所运送的材料是通过另一类劳动力进行增值后的制成品。借助于建筑材料和制成品的现代化运输方法，假如在施工过程中使用更多的预制品，可以改变一个项目直接劳动成本和材料的百分比。

在建筑业，供特定工艺使用的材料通常由工匠们处理，而不是一般的劳动力。这样，电工处理电器材料、管工处理管材等。这种多样化处理把稀缺的技术工人和承包商的监督变为没有对工程做出直接贡献的作业。因为，承包商通常不做运输生意，他们不能有效率地进行运输工作。对大型项目，所有这些因素使得货物运输问题加剧。

例 4-2： 阿拉斯加管道工程的货物运输

阿拉斯加管道工程的货物运输系统设定处理 600000t 的材料和补给。这个吨位没有包括另 500000t 通过不同的线路系统运输的管道，这个运输系统的复杂性如图 4-2 所示。矩形表示地区，起点表示贯穿美国和其他地方的工厂。部分材料运至西雅图的主要分段运输

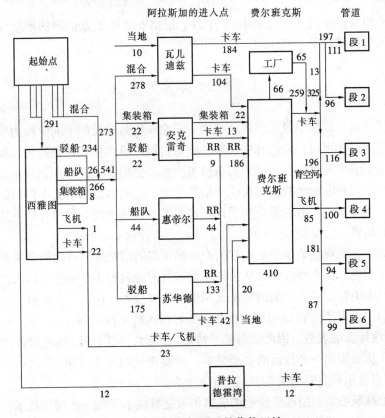

图 4-2 阿拉斯加项目的货物运输

点,部分则直接运往阿拉斯加。有五个港口可进入:瓦儿迪兹、安克雷奇、惠帝尔、苏华德和普拉德霍湾。在费尔班克斯有次分段运输区域,并且管道本身分成六段。除了育空河之外,只有一条肮脏的道路可用于运输。以千吨计的运往各地或来自于各地的货运量用靠近网络流的数字表示(用箭头表示材料流的方向),并且运输的方法标注在线上。在各地,承包商监督和派人认证材料、从运输线路上卸货、确定材料运往什么地方,假如要求分开运输时再打包,随后再装运材料运出。

例 4-3:加工厂设备采购

假如大数量材料(假如管道电气和结构构件)不是标准的和/或有库存,它们的采购和运输包括一系列活动。用于购买这些构件的各种活动所需的时间估算如下所示:

活动	时间/天	累计时间/天
由设计方准备购物申请	0	0
业主同意	5	5
向供货商询价	3	8
收到供货商的报价	15	23
有设计方完成投标评估	7	30
业主批准	5	35
下定单	5	40
收到初步的安装图	10	50
收到最终的设计图	10	60
安装和运输	60~200	120~260

结果这类设备的采购一般要求 4~9 个月。根据安装施工方忙碌的程度等因素,对这个标准的时间安排进行平移或压缩同样是可能的。

5.1 成本估算的方法

成本估算是项目管理中最重要的环节之一。它在项目建设的不同阶段为项目的成本建立了一条基准线。在项目开发过程中的某一特定阶段的成本估算就是造价工程师在现有数据基础上对未来成本的预测。根据美国造价工程师协会的定义,工程估价是运用科学理论和技术,根据工程判断和经验,解决成本估算、成本控制和盈利能力等问题的活动。

实际上,所有的估价活动都是基于以下这些基本方法中的一种或几种方法的中的一种或几种方法的组合:

产出函数 在微观经济学中把过程的产出和资源的消耗这两者之间的关系叫做产出函数。在建筑工程中,产出函数则可认为是建设项目的规模和生产参数(如人工或资金)之间的关系。产出函数建立了产出的总量或规模与各种投入(比如人力、材料、设备)之间的关系。例如,代表产出的 Q 可以用由代表各种投入的不同参数 $x_1, x_2, \ldots, x_n$ 等通过数学和/或统计方法表达。因此,对某一特定的产出,我们可以通过对各个投入参数赋予不同的值,从而找到一个最低的生产成本。房屋建筑的大小(用 ft^2 表示)和消耗的人力(用 h/ft^2 来表示)之间的关系就是产出函数的一个例子。

成本经验推断法 利用基于经验的成本函数估算成本需要一些统计技术,这些技术将建造或运营某设施与系统的一些重要特征或属性联系起来。数理统计推理的目的是为了找到最合适的参数值或者常数,用于在假定的成本函数中进行成本估算。通常情况下,这需要利用回归分析法。

用于工程量清单的单位成本法　由工程量清单表达的各项任务或各个组成部分的单位成本能够明确,总成本就是各项产品的数量与其相应单位成本的乘积之和。单位成本法虽然在理论上非常直接,但是难以应用。第一步是将某工作分解成许多项任务,当然每项任务都是为项目建设服务的。一旦这些任务确定,并有了工作量的估算,用单价与每项任务的量相乘就可以得到每项任务的成本,从而得出每项工作的成本。当然,不同的估算中对每项工作分解的详细程度可能会有很大差别。

混合成本分配法　有时候要从现有的会计账目上去分解,从而确定某项具体操作的成本函数。这种方法的基本思想是,每一项花费都能够对应地分配到操作过程中的某一特定步骤。理想情况是在成本分配过程中,混合成本能够有因果对应关系地被分解,并确定为某种基本成本。可是,在很多情况下,子项目和其分配成本之间难以确定或者根本不存在因果关系。例如,在建设项目中,基本成本可定义为以下5个方面:

(1) 人力;(2) 材料;(3) 建筑设备;(4) 建设管理;(5) 日常办公开销。这几个基本成本有可能会按比例地分配到工程子项的不同任务中去。

6.1　经济评估的基本概念

对一个设施进行系统的经济评估需要做到以下几步:

1. 列出一系列可选项目或采购对象供投资分析。
2. 为经济评估做一组远景规划。
3. 估算每一个备择项目的现金流。
4. 确定可接受的最低收益率。
5. 在投资目标的基础上,建立一个评判标准,用来判断接受一个项目还是拒绝它,或者用来在一组互斥项目中挑选最优的项目。
6. 进行灵敏度分析和不确定性分析。
7. 在已确立的评判标准上决定接受还是拒绝一个方案。

必须注意的是:在经济评价中由决策者提出的设想和方针,无论是显性还是隐性,管理者们的主观判断与客观的系统分析一样会很大程度地影响到决策过程。

一个公司或组织的管理层对未来进行预测的阶段又称规划周期。对于未来的不确定性,规划未来的远近受到对未来预见的精确程度的影响。对资本投资来讲,实体设施的使用期限影响着规划周期的长度,因为一旦有用的资产被变卖,就会在财务上发生一定的损失。

在经济评价中每一种备择项目都用它以后 n 年或者在规划远景期内的现金收益流来一一对应。计息期一般用年表示($t=0, 1, 2, \cdots\cdots, n,$),$t=0$ 时代表当前时刻。我们用 $B_{t,x}$ 来代表一个投资项目 x 在 t 年末的年收益,x 代表备择项目的编号,No.1, No.2, ……",即 $x=1, 2, \cdots\cdots$,再用 $C_{t,x}$ 代表一个投资项目 x 在 t 年末的成本支出。这样一个项目 x 在 t 年末的年净现值就用年收益减去年成本费用得到,用 $A_{t,x}$ 表示。公式为

$$A_{t,x} = B_{t,x} - C_{t,x} \tag{6.1}$$

$A_{t,x}$ 是正值或负值还是零值,都取决于 $B_{t,x}$ 与 $C_{t,x}$ 的取值(它们都取正值)。

如果决策者将一笔资金投到了一个项目中,那他必须考虑到由于没把这笔资金投到其他项目而丧失的获利机会,这就是机会成本,它是所有投资机会中,选择最优投资的回报。一个被放弃的投资机会不但包括资本投资,还包括金融投资或者社会公益项目投资。一个值得投资的项目,它的回报至少要与被放弃的投资项目的回报相同(在可接受的最低收益率 MARR 下)。

一般来讲,MARR 值由私营企业的最高层管理人员制定,它反映这个公司的机会成本和市场的借贷利息,以及投资项目的风险估计。对于政府项目来讲 MARR 值由政府部门(财政部或美国国会)确定。这个 MARR 值反映着社会整体的财富情况,又称社会贴现率。

不管 MARR 值是由哪个组织确定的,投资项目经济评估中的 MARR 值,从企业立场上来看,对于确定此项目是否值得投资具有关键性的作用。由于一个组织确定的可接受的最低收益率 MARR 值不可能定得很精确,所以建议用各种不同的 MARR 值来做灵敏度分析。

7.1 融 资 问 题

建设项目投资的特点是投资期短,回收期长。也就是说投入要早于回报,因此项目的业主必须获得强有力的资金保障以满足项目的资金需求。没有足够的资金保障,一个项目是无法进行的,而融资成本又是相当大的。正因如此,注重项目资金问题是项目管理的重要方面。另外,资金也是项目参与方共同关注的问题,比如施工总承包商和材料供应商。除非业主能够及时向各方支付合同款,否则项目各参与方也要对各自的融资问题。

推广开来说,项目融资只是公司财务活动的一个方面。如果同时有多个工程在建,并且都存在融资问题,那么净现金流量反映的资金需求问题就构成资本投资中的融资问题。不管是从项目层面还是公司层面来考虑项目融资问题面临的最基本的资金问题都是相同的。

从本质上说,项目融资就是获得资金,以满足在获得收益前项目的各项成本、费用支出要求。以项目概念策划、费用估算和施工计划为基础,项目的现金流入和流出情况是可以估计的。一般来说,这种现金流应该包括项目早期的费用支出。如何以最有利或最有效的开支方式来平衡现金结余就是项目融资问题。在策划和设计阶段,业主的费用开支是相对较少的,而相当大部分的开支是发生在施工阶段,只有到项目建设全过程竣工以后才会有收益。相反,在项目建设的过程中,承包商会定期收到业主支付的工程款。然而,承包商也可能会遇到现金负结余的问题,主要原因是业主的延期支付和考虑适当的利润及业主方可能的索赔要求。

业主在考虑项目融资计划时通常都会包括短期和长期两个方面。从长远看,受益的来源包括销售、拨款以及税收返还。借款最终必须由这些收入来偿还。从短期看,存在很多融资方式,包括借贷、拨款、公司投资基金、延期支付等等。这些融资方式都需要第三方的参与,例如银行或债券认购者。对于私营项目(如写字楼)来说,通常在建设阶段和使用阶段的融资策略是完全不一样的。在项目使用阶段,项目自身的价值可以用于抵押或贷款担保。这样，在项目的不同阶段就可能有不同的融资方案和融资参与者，所以融资计划的实际操作通常是很复杂的。

另外，承包商在费用支出和取得收入这段时间，直接用于保证工程建设的贷款选择是相对受到限制的。对于中小规模的项目，从银行账户进行透支是最常见的建设融资方式。通常，银行会以建设工期内的预期支出和收入为依据，设置一个账户透支的限额。而对于规模较大的项目来说，其承包商通常都拥有相当的资产，并且可以运用其他的融资方式，这些方式的利息费用比账户透支更低。

最近几年，DBO（design-build-operate）项目的运用越来越多，这种项目中业主提出功能需求，而承包商进行融资操作。承包商在一定时期内从项目收入或政府支付获得回报。项目所有权最终完全转移给政府。这种类型的项目中的一个代表作就是加拿大通往爱德华王子岛的联邦大桥。

在这一章中，我们会首先从业主的角度来研究项目融资问题，并充分考虑项目融资与项目中其他参与方的相互影响。随后，我们会讨论项目实施阶段的融资问题，这对于建设承包商的盈利性和清偿能力是至关重要的。

8.2 分担风险的合同条款

除了总价合同，合同各方风险分担的条款在合同中到处可见。有代表性的是这些条款分配了出现可能的或不可遇见事件时的费用责任。可以分配给不同合同参与方承担伴随风险责任的部分如下：

- 不可抗力（这项条款免除业主或承包商支付由于"上帝的安排"以及诸如战争或罢工等其他外部事件所产生的费用）。
- 损失赔偿（这一条款免除受损方支付由第三方如相邻物业业主所造成的损失和损害而发生的费用）。
- 留置（保证第三方的主张和要求得到实现，如为保证工人工资而"机械留置"）。
- 劳动法（在工程施工现场违反劳动法律和规定而支付的费用）。
- 场地条件的变化（承担由于未预见的场地条件而支付的费用）。
- 工期延滞和延长。
- 先约赔偿金（事先同意支付的为任何工程缺陷而支付的费用）。
- 后果赔偿金（由工程缺陷引起的经评估的实际损失费用的支付）。
- 职业安全与工人健康。
- 许可、证书、法律和法规。
- 均等就业机会法规。
- 由承包人责任而引起的工程终止。
- 工程中止。
- 保证和担保。

在这些方面，用于详细说明风险分担的语言必须符合随不同权限或实效而变化的法律要求和以往的解释。如果没有使用标准的法律语言，合同条款可能就不能够得到执行。不幸的是，为了这个目的的标准法律语言可能很难理解，结果是项目经理通常难以理解他们的精确责任。这就需要有胜任的法律顾问,为合同各方在各自承担的责任方面达成一致提议建议。

合同的标准格式可以从许多途径获得,例如美国建筑师协会(AIA)或承包商联合会(AGC)。这些标准格式可能包括风险和责任分担,这些风险和责任由合同的某一或几方面单独承担是不能被接受的。应特别注意的是,合同标准格式可能会被用来降低标准格式发起组织或团体的风险和责任。因此,合同中的各方应仔细阅读和评审所有的合同文件。

下面所给出的三个例子,解释说明了合同语言如何导致承包商(CONTRACTOR)和业主(COMPANY)之间不同的风险分担责任。不同的合同条款给承包商带来不同程度的损失赔偿风险。

例 8-1:承包商承担高风险的合同条款示例

除了单纯由于业主的疏忽情况外,承包商应该赔偿业主及其职员、代理人和雇员,并使其不受损害,包括任何所有的损失、损害和责任,任何所有的由于人身伤害不仅只限于承包商、业主和任何分包商在内的雇员的死亡而引起的损失索赔,任何所有的财产损失,包括业主和第三方的、直接及/或间接的财产损失,只要是由于承包商或其代理人、雇员、供货人或分包商的疏忽行为,或是与合同文件实施有关的承包商的雇员或代理人的疏忽行为造成的,无论何时或何部分,或是由此引起的索赔,不管是保险或未保险的;承包商应该以自己的成本和费用应付任何索赔、诉讼、行为和行动,不管其是否具有理由,其可能是有一定的原因或联系而引起的针对业主的,承包商应该支付由这些行为、索赔行为或诉讼而引起的所有裁决,尽管可能是胜诉的,承包商也应该支付所有的费用,包括由这些行为、索赔或诉讼而产生的成本和律师费用。

评论:这是一个对承包商来说难以承担的条款。这项规定使得承包商实际上对所有可能发生的损坏情况以及类型承担责任,除非损失或损害索赔完全是由业主的疏忽造成的。在实践中,工程上的完全责任是很难明确认定的,因为工程实施往往都涉及合同双方。由于承包商的缺陷责任没有费用上的限定,所以很难制定出特定最坏风险的责任规避方法。承包商能够采用的最好办法是购买尽可能完整和广泛的超额责任保险。这种保险的价格非常昂贵,所以承包商应该保证合同价格足以提高到能够覆盖这部分的费用支出。

例 8-2:承包商承担中等风险的合同条款示例

承包商应保护、防止、避免伤害和赔偿业主,包括所有的损失、损害、索赔、诉讼、责任,或任何要求(包括有限定的成本、费用以及律师费,无论诉讼与否或是与之关联的)、造成任何人身伤害(没有限定的包括业主、承包商或任何分包商雇员的伤害),包括由于任何伤害导致的,或由损失或由财产和不动产的破坏导致的死亡,或由以任何方式引起的,或可归于或与整个工程或工程任何部分(无论是承包商或任何分包商实施的)的实施关联人为原因,包括(业主、承包商以及任何分包商的财产,包括承包商、任何分包商或工人使用的工具和设备,无论其是自己拥有的或是租用的)导致的死亡,承包商应以自己的费用应付基于上述事件的任何或所有的诉讼,除非上述人身伤害或财产损失是由业主或业主的雇员的疏忽造成的。由业主引起的与上述事件相关的任何损失、损害、成本支出或律师费用,包括相应的调整,将从承包商的赔偿中扣除,然后受付或其后应付。业主为了承包商的利益应放弃对现有工程的代位清偿,包括后果赔偿金。例如,不作为限定,工期延误造成的利润损失、产品或生产损失,但需扣除存在于该合同工期以内的延误时时间;然而,假设上述代位清偿的放弃,应该扩大到包括所有上述的在业主已接受工程上可以扣除的内容。

评论:这个条款为承包商减轻了不少压力。承包商仍然必须对所有人员和第三方财产负无限责任,但只限于由承包商疏忽导致的范围。惟一疏忽条款并没有出现。而且,承包商对于业主财产损失的责任只是限于扣除业主保险后的意外部分,这是大型化工联合体工程的承包商最为关心的,因有时承包额可达数十亿美元。业主保险的承担机构对承包商没有追索权。承包商涉及业主工程的有限责任在工程完成时终止。

例 8-3: 承包商承担低风险的合同条款示例

承包商据此同意赔偿并使业主和/或其任何母公司、下属公司或联合者,或业主和/或其职员、代理人或他们的雇员不受损害,包括直接产生的任何损失或责任,或是缘由财产的损失或损害、人员的伤害或死亡引起的任何索赔或诉讼而间接产生的任何损失或责任,财产的损失或损害不仅只限于承包商的财产和业主的财产,承包商实施工程引起或导致的人员的伤害或死亡不仅只限于承包商的雇员,还包括其代理人和分包商,承包商应该按照承包商的选择在任何诉讼中以自己的惟一责任保护业主,无论工程是由承包商、其雇员实施的或是由其分包商雇员实施的或是由他们共同或单独实施的。在任何情况下,承包商对业主的赔偿应只限于承包商最大责任保险范围内的收益。

评论:关于对业主的赔偿,在这个条款下的承包商只有最小的额外风险。责任是被限定在能够从承包商的保险公司所获得的数据。

9.2 施工技术与方案的选择

正如建筑设计中面对多方案比选所遇到的问题一样,在项目施工过程中如何选择适当的施工技术和方案也常常让人感到棘手。例如,一项采用泵送混凝土还是采用吊斗浇注混凝土的施工方案的选择,不仅会影响施工成本,同时还会影响到施工进度。而在这两种相互可替代的施工方案中选择其中一种,需要我们综合考虑与其相关的成本、可靠性及设备的可得性。然而不幸的是,诸如劳动者的经验和技能以及现场的具体条件等,我们在比选不同方案时所需要考虑的因素在计划阶段却往往是十分粗略的。

在可相互替代的施工技术和方案之间进行比选时,我们有必要针对这些不同的施工技术和方案制定不同的施工计划。这些不同的施工计划可用来对可相互替代的施工技术和方案之间在成本、进度和可靠性等方面进行评审。这种对可相互替代的方案之间的评审在竞争性招标中表现得十分明显,在设计招标中会有很多设计方案被提交上来,而在施工招标当中,不同备选方案之间的比选则会用到价值工程。

在制定施工计划时,一个非常有用的方法是根据计划者的揣测或以基于仿真技术的计算机为手段对施工过程进行模拟。通过观察和分析模拟,不同计划之间存在的差异或现有计划当中存在的问题就可以被识别出来。例如,当我们决定使用一台特定的机械设备进行施工时,可能会遇到这样一个问题,即是否有足够的工作面容纳这台设备。那么这时使用计算机辅助设计系统中的三维图形模拟对施工中的空间进行模拟,并对干扰因素进行识别就能够帮助我们解决这个问题。与此类似,我们还可以用计算机对施工过程中的资源使用状况进行模拟,并根据模拟状况提前制定资源供应计划。

例 9-1：一条公路的修复

本例引自匹兹堡的一个公路修复项目，PA 提供了一个好的施工计划的重要性及方案选择影响的成功范例。在这个项目当中，我们需要对立交桥的路面和立交桥下方的高速公路的路面进行返修施工。初始的施工计划是立交桥的路面施工从两端向中间进行，而桥下高速公路的路面也与此同时进行。那么，这样一来就会出现立交桥路面施工所需的施工机械和混凝土运输车无法通过立交桥下方的高速公路而到达立交桥上（因为此时立交桥下方的高速公路也在同时施工）这么一个严重的问题。然而，我们可以通过在规定的时间内停止立交桥下高速公路的路面施工，而使得立交桥路面施工所需要的通道得以畅通的方法来解决这个问题。我们可以在立交桥下的高速公路使用泵送混凝土来完成立交桥的路面返修施工。这样一来，不仅成本得以降低而且工期也大幅缩短。

例 9-2：激光水平测距装置的选择

这里关于技术选择的例子源自对用来提高开掘隧洞生产率的激光水平仪的使用。在这套系统中，激光测距设备被竖立在现场的某个位置上，用以测量移动设备的相对精确高度。我们通过在一个水平面上发射穿过施工现场的激光束，然后观察移动设备接收器对于光束反射的准确位置来完成这个高度的测量工作。由于激光束不易发散，我们使用这种方法便可以精确地测量施工现场中任何安装激光接收装置的移动设备的高度。反过来，接收装置所处的相对高度则被用来推算掘进片、料斗和设备等其他装置的相对高度。这样我们就可以精确地和自动地对掘进设备进行施工过程中的控制。完工后测算可知，用这种方法可以在降低成本约 80% 左右的同时，还能够提高生产效率。然而，使用这种自动化程度较高的系统却不仅需要在激光测距装置上进行一次性初始投资，同时为了保证电子反馈控制器的正常运行，还要经常性地对设备进行校正调试。尽管如此，激光水平仪仍在多种施工条件下受到人们的青睐。

10.1 进度计划的概念

工程进度计划除了可以为各项活动安排日期外，还能够将工程全过程中用到的设备、材料和劳动力等各种资源进行合理的配备。一个好的计划可以消除生产瓶颈带来的问题，同时也使各项必需的物资得以及时的采购，因而保证工程尽可能完工。相反，如果工程计划没有做好，则会在工程完成过程中造成窝工，对人工、设备等造成浪费。由于计划编排的不合理造成整个工期拖延，也会使业主对工程设施的正常预期使用造成不良影响。

一般对工程的正式计划看法是比较偏激的。许多业主要求承包商提供详细的工程计划，作为控制工作进程的手段。通常用实际的工作进展与计划进行比较，来确定工程进展是否令人满意。在工程完成之后，通过类似于计划进度和实际进度之间的比较，可以对由于业主提出的变更要求、工人罢工或者其他不可预见的情况导致的工程延期的责任进行分摊。

与那些依赖正规进度表相反的例子是，许多领域的管理人员轻视和不喜欢正规的进度计划。尤其是业主普遍需要的进度计划中的关键路径法，这种方法虽然在大学里面已经讲授了二十几年了，但是在一些领域中，这种方法经常不但被认为与一些实际操作毫不相关，而且是对时间和精力的浪费。结果无论是好的还是导致低效率和低生产率的那些进度计划只能坐在椅子上干喘气。然而，一些日渐进步的建筑公司，每当遇到工作任务繁重复杂和不同的工作之间需要协调合作的情况时，仍使用正规的计划步骤。

随着个人电脑在施工现场的出现以及易上手的软件的问世，正规的计划编制已经变得比较普通了。通过因特网来分享工程计划信息也极大地促进了正式计划方法的使用。聪明的工程管理人员通常携带随身电脑，里面存有工程计划和工程预算资料。事实上，易上手的计算机软件的不断发展和现有计划方法的改进，已经解决了与正规计划手段有关的实际问题。但是，要解决与计划技术使用有关的问题，管理人员需要掌握积理解计划技术合理的使用方法及其局限性。

以资源为导向的计划编制法和以时间为导向的计划编制法之间有着一个明显的区别。对于资源为导向的计划编制法来说，关键是如何运用有效的方式利用那些特殊的资源，并编制资源计划。比如，在一个高层建筑工地上，项目经理主要关心的可能是确保起重机能有效地被用来搬运这建筑材料。如果在这个项目中没有很好的编制计划，在地面上的运输车辆将会排起长队，而在楼层上的建筑工人们却要长时间地等待材料供应。对以时间为导向的计划编制法而言，重点是在给定各个活动之间的必要优先次序的情况下确定项目的完工时间。还有一种混合计划编制法，它是在确定工种优先关系之后进行的资源平衡或有资源限制的计划编制法。大多数用来编制计划的软件都是时间计划编制软件，尽管它们实际上有能力引进资源限制计划编制方法。

本章将介绍安排计划的基本方法。我们的讨论是假设基于计算机的进度计划程序会被广泛应用。因此，各种各样的人工或机器的计划技术均不做详细讨论。人工的方法没有基于计算机程序的方法的那样高效和方便。随着基于计算机计划程序的广泛使用，对于管理者来说，理解这些由计划程序执行的基本运算的概念性框架，就显得尤为重要了。更有甚者，尽管正规的方法不适用于特殊的事件中，正规的计划方法给管理者提供了有价值的参考。因此，本章将提供包括手工计算在内的一些例子，以便读者更好地理解。

11.2 棘手问题的进度计划

在先前的有关工作进度的计划的讨论中，我们是以施工计划的总体框架已知为前提的。在工作、工作之间的逻辑关系以及工作所需的资源已被明确定义出来的情况下，进度计划问题就可以被描述成一个数学的最优化问题。即使当工作持续时间不确定时，我们也可以假设工作持续时间的概率分布是已知的，从而运用相应的数学分析技术来解决进度计划中的问题。

尽管前面已经介绍过的各种进度计划技术都是非常有用的，但它们仍然无法涵盖和解决实际当中所遇到的各种进度计划问题。尤其是当施工现场拥挤而使得工作的持续时间和成本需要依赖其他工作的时候，问题就更加突出了。而在前面的讨论中，各种进度计划技术都是假定各个工作的持续时间是彼此独立的。另外一个问题则源自施工技术的复杂性。在资源的配置过程中，有许多我们无法确切描述的约束条件及其目标。例如，不同的工人可能会在某种类型的工作上有其专长。随着经验的增长，某特定工人班组的工作效率会显著提高。但是，把这种因素考虑到进度计划当中，却是非常困难的一件事。此外，当项目由于没有一个总的计划安排者，而使得工作持续时间和进度计划需要在不同参与方之间谈判确定时，也会出现类似的问题。

对于此类问题，一个切实可行的方法是，富于经验的项目经理在进度计划执行前对其进行检查和调整。这种人为的检查可以使得我们在安排进度计划时，把全部的约束条件或工人及设备的具体特征综合考虑在内。事实上，这种为满足资源的约束条件而进行的互动式的进度计划检查通常比基于计算机的渐进调整方法更为贴近实际。

通常情况下，对于这些更为复杂条件下的进度计划问题的解决，不仅限于在数学方法的使用上。最好的解决方法可能就是我们所说的针对可替代方案或进度计划的"生成和检验"循环。在这种方法中，我们首先假设或生成一个可能的进度计划，然后根据相关的约束条件（如资源或时间）和不同目标下的预期值对该进度计划的可行性进行检验。而往往就在评价一个备选方案的过程中，我们便可以识别出一些具体的问题或得到对于该方案改进的建议，所得到的这些结果则可用于另一个备选方案的检验当中。如此这般继续下去直至令人满意的方案产生。

在应用"生成和检验"方法时应注意两个问题。首先，由于可能的方案和进度计划的数目会很多，因此在生成合理的备选方案时，我们应当对问题有相当的调查。其次，在对备选方案进行评价时也会涉及相当多的工作量。而这样一来则使得能够进行方案检验的实际循环次数受到了限制。解决这个问题的希望寄托在由计算机来承担繁杂的计算工作上，而由计算机来承担进度计划中的计算工作的好处则在于可以节约计划过程所耗费的成本和时间。

例 11-1：人-机交互的进度计划

一个受资源约束的进度计划的交互系统应具备以下特征：
- 在同一屏幕的不同视窗中同时显示横道图形、资源使用状况、工作网络图以及其他一些可以表达出来的图形。
- 根据用户的需要对包括所分配的资源和所选择的技术在内的特定工作进行描述。
- 用以显示建筑设施在任何时间施工进展的三维动画演示。
- 应用便于改变起始时间和所分配资源的方法。
- 在任何时间都可以运行的诸如关键路线法之类的进度计划运算功能。

图 11-1 为该屏幕演示系统的一个示例。在图 11-1 中，横道图出现在一个视窗里，工作描述出现在另一个视窗里，而特定资源的累计消耗量则显示在第三个视窗里。这些显示在计算机同一屏幕中不同"窗口"里的内容代表着不同类型的信息。在这些功能的支持下，项目经理就能够调出施工计划中的不同画面并做出某些变更以满足没有被正式表达出来的目标及约束条件。由于对变更反映及时，变更所带来的影响便能迅速得以评估。

12.1 成本控制问题

在项目执行当中，项目控制和数据处理的程序对项目经理和项目的其他参与方而言，是不可或缺的工具。它起着记录财务交易和向项目经理提供有关项目进展和所遇问题信息的双重作用。项目控制所面临的问题可用一个过去的关于项目的描述来恰如其分地予以总结，即一个虽已完成 90%，但超预算且进度拖延、定义不明确的工作集合。项目控制系统的任务就是致力于有效地解决这些问题。

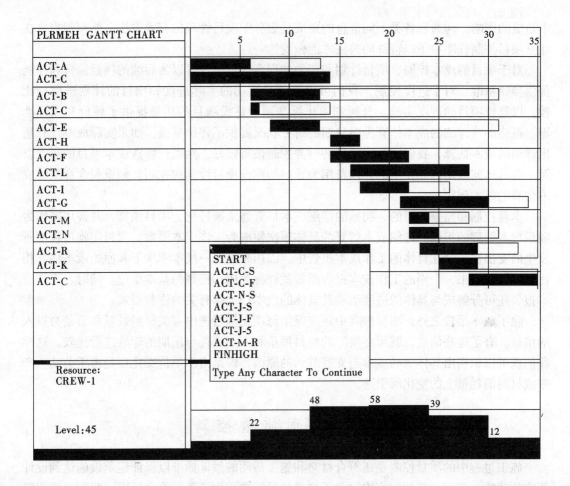

图 11-1　横道图及交互进度计划视窗示例

在本章，我们连同项目过程中的资源利用、会计、监督和控制来考虑这些问题。在本章的讨论中，我们侧重于使用会计信息的项目管理。一般地，项目会计报告直到项目完成后才有明确的解释，而这对于项目管理而言显然是不够及时的。有时，甚至即使项目完成后，会计结果也会令人感到困惑。因此，为了有效地进行项目管理，项目经理应当懂得如何解释利用会计信息。尽管我们的目的不在于详细介绍会计的程序，但从考虑管理问题的角度出发，我们应当讨论一下常用的会计系统和惯例。

项目控制的限定目标值得强调。项目控制程序的首要任务是识别项目偏差，而不是为节约成本提供参考建议，这个特征在项目控制的主要阶段会得以反映。项目的规划和设计是节约成本的主要阶段。在施工阶段，变更可能导致项目拖延和成本的非正常增加。因此，项目控制的重点在于按初始计划执行，找出偏差并予以纠正，而不是在于寻求显著改进和节约成本上。只有当需要一个补救方案时才会在施工计划中出现重大的变更。

最后，我们还需要讨论一下由于信息集成所产生的一些问题。虽然现有技术仍然无法让人对项目活动有综合且完整的认识和考虑，但项目管理活动还是离不开信息的集成。例如，进度信息和成本报告通常是彼此独立的，因此就需要项目经理在亲身观察的基础上，从项目的不同报告中整合出综合的观点。尤其是，项目经理常常不得不推断进度变化对成本造成的影响。沟通和各类不同信息的集成是服务于项目管理的有效方法，然而却需要在建立项目控制程序中予以特殊的关注才能做到这一点。

对于项目的成本控制、项目计划和相关的现金流量估算可以为后续的项目监督和控制提供参照基准。对于进度控制，我们可以将项目活动的实际进度和项目的计划进度相比较，以监督项目的进度实施。合同和工作标准则为建设项目的质量提供了评价和保证准则。最终的或详细的成本估算为项目期的财务状况提供了评价基准。如果实际成本没有超出详细的成本估算，我们便认为项目的财务控制做得较好。然而，特殊成本项目的超支以及一些具体问题是可能发生的。以费用为导向的建设项目计划和控制，侧重包含在最终成本估算的成本项次。

本着控制和监督的目的，初始的详细成本估算通常被转化为项目预算，并被用来作为随后成本管理的指南。详细成本估算的具体项次便成为工作成本要素。项目实施过程中所发生的支出被记录在具体的工作成本报告中，以用来在每一成本项次下和原始成本估算相比较。这样一来，个别的工作成本报告通常就被称为成本控制的基本单位。同时，工作成本报告还可分解成与具体的进度活动及具体的成本报告都有关的作业要素。

除了成本报告之外，项目预算中还应保留每项工作报告中有关材料数量和劳动力投入的信息。有了这些信息，就可将实际的材料用量和人工消耗与预期的标准进行比较。这样我们就可以识别出具体活动成本超支或节约的原因，即是由于单价变化还是由于劳动生产率或材料消耗量上的变化所引起。

13.2　全面质量控制

施工过程中的质量控制是指符合材料和施工活动的最低标准以保证建筑设施达到设计要求的功能，前面一节的内容中包含了这些最低标准。为了确保符合标准，我们通常用随机抽样和数理统计方法作为接受或拒绝已完工作和材料批的基础。所谓拒绝是指不符合或违反了相关的设计标准。有关此类质量控制实际操作的方法及程序将在后续章节中继续介绍。

在这些传统的质量控制实践中有一个隐含的假设——可接受的质量水平，它是指缺陷点的允许比例。来自供应商的材料或某个组织完成的工作只有当其缺陷比例在允许的质量水平以内，才可以被当作合格并检查通过。在这种情况下，材料或产品存在的问题只能在交付后才能得以改正。

而与这个传统的质量控制方法相对照的则是全面质量控制的概念。在这个体系里，施工过程中的任何地方都不允许出现缺陷项目。尽管零缺陷这个目标是永远没有办法达到的，但它却为组织提供了一个目标，使得组织对其质量控制计划从不满足，即使缺陷项目逐年都有显著的降低。这种质量控制的概念和方法首先在日本和欧洲的一些制造企业当中得到发展，然后迅速普及到建筑公司。对于质量改进最为权威的认证是国际标准化组织的ISO9000标准族。ISO9000标准族着重于质量文件、质量目标以及一系列计划、执行和检查的循环程序。

全面质量控制是组织的所有部分对于质量的一个承诺，它通常包括很多要素，用以保证施工过程安全有效的设计评审工作就是一个主要因素。其他一些因素还包括广泛的人员培训,把发现缺陷的责任从检查者转移到操作者身上,以及持续地对设备进行维护等工作。在质量环当中有一个正式的有关工人对质量控制改进的环节,在这里工人们定期会面并对质量改进提出建议。材料供应商在提供产品时,也保证零缺陷。起初,供应商的所有材料都要被抽检,而有缺陷的批次会被退回。有良好记录的供应商可以经核准免去进行全项检验。

关于质量控制在传统的微观经济上的观点认为存在着一个缺陷点的"最佳"比例。试图超过这个最佳比例而达到更高的质量将大大增加检验成本,并且降低工人的劳动生产率。然而,许多企业发现遵守全面质量控制会带来被传统方法所未认识到的巨大经济利益。与库存、返工、次品和维修等有关的成本会有所减少,工人的工作热情和责任心则有很大的提高。顾客也会认同更好的质量工作,并愿意为优异的质量支付额外的价款。而这样一来,持续改进的质量控制就成为一个竞争上的优势。

诚然,全面质量控制的运用也绝非易事,尤其是在建筑施工中。每一项建筑产品都具有独一无二的特征,劳动力的不稳定性、分包商的多样性以及在教育和程序上的必要支出都使得在建筑施工中开展全面质量控制计划显得困难重重。尽管如此,即使没有支持零缺陷目标,对于质量改进的承诺也会使组织受益匪浅。

例 13-1: 质量环经验

质量环小组通常由 5 至 15 个操作工人组成,他们定期开会以识别、讨论和解决生产率及质量问题。质量环小组的领导则在操作工人和上层管理之间起着联络作用。以下是施工中质量环小组的一些成功的例子:

1. 由 Taisei 公司承建的某高速公路项目,人们发现其商品混凝土的不合格率非常高,由混凝土工组成的质量环小组经调查后发现造成这种现象的主要原因是检查方法不当。在采纳了该小组的建议后,不合格率下降了 11.4%。

2. 由 Shimizu 建设公司承建的某住宅项目,经报告混凝土存在不足的事情时有发生。钢筋工质量环小组在详细地检查了他们自己的工作之后,找出了问题的原因,并将劳动生产率提高了 10%。

14.1 工程项目信息的类型

建设工程施工过程中不可避免地生成大量不同种类的信息。有效地管理这些信息,确保其随时提供和准确性是一项重要的管理任务。信息不足或缺陷极易延误工期、做出不合理的决策,甚至造成施工的完全失败。遗憾的是业主和项目经理到了交工日期才发现重要的构件还未装上,6 个月内不可能交工! 如有更好的信息管理,问题就能尽早发现,及时确定其他供货商或重新制定工作计划。准确和及时的信息对工程的设计和目标控制均至关重要,有效地利用信息的能力也同样重要。将大量杂乱无章的信息交给项目经理,其决策将混乱不堪。

在施工过程中,供不同项目参与者使用的信息类型和内容可能不同。最重要的信息应包括:

- 各个项目参与者的现金流及采购账目。
- 前期规划和设计过程中生成的中间分析成果。

- 设计文件，包括图纸和技术要求说明书。
- 施工进度计划和成本估算。
- 质量控制和保险记录。
- 按时间顺序编排的项目文档和备忘录。
- 施工现场活动和检查日志。
- 有效的合同文本和规章文件。

以上的部分信息随着项目的进展不断发生变化。例如，在整个施工过程中，资金支付就是在不断变化信息。资金支付随着时间而逐渐增加，特别是新单位的加入（如承包商），会急剧增加资金支付的数额。有些信息对于工程的某个阶段非常重要，但可能随后就会被忽略。这样的例子在施工或运行过程中一般都不会用到规划文件或结构分析数据库。然而，在项目以后各阶段要考虑变更时，就有可能利用这些信息进行重新分析。在这种情况下，档案资料的储存和检索就非常重要。甚至在施工结束后，历史记录可能用于评估对设施故障的责任。这些信息对于今后在其他地方设计类似的工程也有重要的意义。

信息控制和信息沟通对于建立协同工作环境至关重要。在这种协同工作环境中，许多专家可以进行工程不同方面的工作并分享信息。协同工作环境为数据文件共享、跟踪决策、电子邮件、电视会议等创造了条件。在这样的环境中，数据存储量会非常大。

根据几个建设工程的经验，加拿大魁北克省的 Maged Abdelsayed of Tardif, Mumay & Assoc 公司估计一个 1000 万美元项目产生的信息平均如下：

- 参与者数目（公司）：420 家（包括所有的供货商和分包商）。
- 参与者数目（个人）：850 个。
- 产生的各种文件种类：50 种。
- 文件页数：56000 页。
- 存放工程文件的档案柜数量：25 个。
- 4 抽屉文件橱数量：6 个。
- 如用直径 20 英寸、树龄 20 年、高 50 英尺的树木来制造这些文件纸张的数量：6 棵。
- 用电子数据保存这些文件的大小（扫描后）：3000MB。
- 需要的磁盘数量（CDs）：6 个。

信息的不准确和缺失可能会增加潜在的成本，同时，用于生成、存储、传递、检索或其他信息处理的成本也很巨大。项目经理可能是工程中最为稀缺的资源，但是除了行政工作和提供辅助设备（如计算机等）工作花费时间外，信息的组织和查阅也占用了大量精力。因此，在组织信息时，了解信息的范围和需要选择哪些信息是很重要的。